Jennie Carpenter Rutty

Mothers' counsel to their sons

Jennie Carpenter Rutty

Mothers' counsel to their sons

ISBN/EAN: 9783741180392

Manufactured in Europe, USA, Canada, Australia, Japa

Cover: Foto ©Andreas Hilbeck / pixelio.de

Manufactured and distributed by brebook publishing software (www.brebook.com)

Jennie Carpenter Rutty

Mothers' counsel to their sons

TO THE BOYS.

"God wants the boys, the merry, merry boys,
The noisy boys, the funny boys,
    The thoughtless boys—
God wants the boys, with all their joys.
That he as gold may make them pure,
And teach them trials to endure:
    His heroes brave
    He'll have them be
    Fighting for truth
    And purity.
    God wants the boys."

"Why does society insist that boys must sow their wild oats? There is no legerdemain about life. There is no way to sow vice and reap virtue, any more than there is to sow tares and reap wheat."

—*John B. DeMotte.*

"If you expect virtue and purity from mothers, wives, sisters, and friends, so must they expect the same from you." Page 200.

HAVE YOU WRITTEN TO MOTHER?

Pray may I ask you, worthy lad,
Whose smile no care can smother;
Though busy life throbs round about,
Have you written home to mother?

You are fast forgetting, aren't you, quite,
How fast the weeks went flying;
And that a little, blotted sheet,
Unanswered, still is lying?

Don't you remember how she stood,
With wistful glance at parting?
Don't you remember how the tears
Were in her soft eyes starting?

Have you forgotten how her arm
Stole round you to caress you?
Have you forgotten those low words;
"Good-by, my son, God bless you"?

Oh, do not wrong her patient love;
Save God's, there is no other
So faithful through all mists of sin;
Fear not to write to mother.

Tell her to keep the lamp of prayer
A light, a beacon burning;
Whose beams shall reach you far away,
Shall lure your soul returning.

Tell her you love her dearly still,
For fear some sad to-morrow
Shall bear away the listening soul,
And leave you lost in sorrow.

And then through bitter, falling tears,
And sighs you may not smother,
You will remember when too late
You did not write to mother.

—*Selected.*

CONTENTS.

	PAGE
Mothers and Sons	1
Morality	6
Home Influence	12
Companionship	25
Joys and Sorrows	37
Honor, Nobleness, and Beauty	53
Education	64
Habits	74
The Tobacco Habit	88
Experience in the Use of Tobacco	109
Intemperance	127
Secret Sin	149
As Others See It	179
Social Purity	194
Courtship and Marriage	210
Amusements	232
Business	254
Religion—True and False	273
Salvation in Jesus	293
Conviction	308
Repentance—Conversion	323
Purity	345
Baptism of the Holy Ghost	360
The Life of Faith	373
The Church of God	397
Divine Healing	409
Time and Eternity	425

PUBLISHERS' PREFACE.

A friend and benefactor of boys has said, "Society chaperons her lassies, her lads she pushes out to learn the world alone." Truly it does seem that here is food for much sober thought on the part of parents. And what can cure such a diseased public sentiment more speedily and effectually than the wide dissemination of a literature showing clearly that the responsibility of fathers and mothers on behalf of their sons is in no way less than that which they feel so gravely resting upon them for the protection of their daughters? None too high can the standard of true womanhood be held, and none too carefully can we guard the purity, chastity, and all the fine traits of character and affections of our daughters. But can we claim that our fallen race is being lifted up, much less restored to the high plane on which man was created, if there be not the same attention paid to the development of HONOR, NOBLENESS, and BEAUTY of character in our sons and brothers—the fathers of future generations? Then hand in hand with this enlightenment of parents let there go to every home GOOD BOOKS FOR THE BOYS AND GIRLS, lifting up the single standard PURITY—PURE WOMANHOOD; PURE AND NOBLE MANHOOD.

God's ways are not man's ways. So it was when truth was to be brought forth to mark a new era in the lives of thousands of our sons and daughters. Instead of coming from the pen of the famed, dipped in worldly applause, Heaven's hand of inspiration had been reached down and laid heavily upon the fond mother heart of a humble farmer's wife, Mrs. Jennie C. Rutty, of Meriden, Kansas. With a fair education, a school-teacher's experience, and better than all else, a true and tried Christian mother's trust in God, she began her literary labors; not for fame nor worldly remuneration, but because as a mother she could not withhold counsel from those she loved. Her first published volume, *Letters of Love and Counsel for "Our Girls,"* we gave to the public May 1, 1897. We said then that it was a book for all girls in all places; and then as not before was felt the even greater need of a similar book for the girls' brothers. Almost at once Mrs. Rutty's heart began to be burdened for her boys (not alone her own son, but every other mother's son) that they might not come a whit behind the "dear girls." But with her usual reticence she held back from the work and preferred some brother or some other mother to feel the reponsibility. Yet when the mission was plainly hers to perform, she did not shrink, but looking steadily to Him who had called and promised to supply wisdom liberally, the work was done "in His name;" and how appropriately christened "Mothers' Counsel to Their Sons" those shall know who read its pages, only to find it as their own dear mother speaking so tenderly —so thoughtfully, wisely, and prayerfully. As truly as a boy's best friend is his mother, so surely will boys everywhere, and even those who have grown to manhood, appreciate and be benefited by such a book.

What other guarantee for its contents can this book need than its name? Certainly none to those who have read the "Letters of Love." But to others we might say, This book is designed to give our sons, and sons who have no mothers, the counsel—knowledge and warning—that every boy needs before he can safely go forth to life's battle. Remember, it has been said that where ignorance is bliss it is folly to be wise. In that genial clime Satan's influence over man is supreme. He may steal woman's virtue, decoy innocent girls, and send their souls fast down the road to hell. The State licenses him, society fosters and applauds him; and all because it has not been taught that while our daughters are to be as "corner-stones, polished after the similitude of a palace," it is equally obligatory upon preachers, teachers, and parents to give us sons that shall be as "plants grown up in their youth." A little consideration of what is necessary in the choice of seed and soil, in climatic conditions, and in much laborious and judicious culture to develop a perfect plant, will begin to bring out to the reader's mind the beauty and force of this simile of our sons being "as plants grown up in their youth."

Now with the author's gratitude to many mothers whose prayers have gone up in her behalf while she prayed and wrote, and her thanks to those who have contributed their letters for use in the book, we send it forth, praying Father to bless it to the boys the world over, and to our sons' sons. We wish that every boy who takes up this book might read it through, and give it careful consideration. Finally we ask that each one who feels the words as those of his own dear mother to him and receives a benefit therefrom will loan the book far and wide to many mothers' sons. "God bless the boys."

MOTHERS' COUNSEL TO THEIR SONS.

MOTHERS AND SONS.

ONE of the highest, noblest, and purest emotions of the natural heart is love, and this is most strongly expressed in the mother's devotion to her children. From their earliest existence they have received her care, her most tender and loving solicitude for their welfare, and the great wealth of human affection. Their well-being has employed her thoughts while passing through the greatest physical anguish, and no joy is so great as when she first looks into their faces and sees life, health, perfection of form, and infant beauty. Their care is her delight as she sees them day by day unfolding their God-given powers; and while she dearly loves their infant ways, she is looking fervently to the perfection of manhood and womanhood for her darlings. She dreams of their nobleness of nature, of their moral strength to resist evil, and of their courage and physical strength to face life's battles and lovingly care for her in the declining days of life. She faithfully and uncomplainingly yields herself and all her interests for their good. Her self-denial is proverbial, and many are the instances where her love for them has been stronger than love of life and she has freely suffered death in protecting them from danger. Her affection for her daughters manifests itself in loving solicitude and a shielding from all the hardships of life possible, with the desire to see them quietly anchored in some sweet haven of rest and security. Her love for her sons holds within it a respect for manhood that is beautiful to witness. As she looks into his baby face the words " My baby boy " spring up, and express the tenderness of love mingled with high aspirations and a consciousness that within him should be the possibilities of a greater and a stronger nature than her own.

As the years pass and he dons the dress of boyhood, her affectionate pride expresses itself in the words " My little man." Then as he enters manhood and his height and strength exceed hers, she says in tender respect, " My son;" but all through his youthful years her heart held for him that sacred name that should express more than relationship. All the good mothers give greater honor to the moral and intellectual development of their children than to the physical; and their hearts are made glad by every evidence of intellectual ability and moral integrity, as they know greater will be their influence for what is good and pure.

The religious mothers consecrate their children to God, and use every means to have them enter his service; for they do not seek for them honor, riches, or fame, but that they might sit at the feet of the King of Glory and learn of him. Daily " mother's prayers" are ascending to heaven in their behalf; and how many of their blessings are in answer to these prayers no one can tell. Many are the testimonies of wayward sons who have constantly realized the restraining power of their mother's prayers, the loving and trustful hope for " better things of them;" and who have at last, after many years of willfulness been glad to find " their mother's God " a loving heavenly Father who had made ample provisions for their salvation through Jesus the Redeemer.

Mothers who love their children dearly can give instruction only equal to their own position, and generally have desires and aspirations for them in harmony with their own. If a mother is worldly-wise, her ambition for her sons will be of that nature. If mothers are moral, their greatest desire for their children will be a strong and true morality; but if a mother is deeply and truly spiritual, her desires for her loved ones will be for their spiritual good and to see them honor and serve the true and living God. Because of this variety of instruction and influence it is well for every mother's son to ponder the instruction given, and see if it measures to the highest standard and for good to soul, mind, and body. Many mothers are lacking in natural affection, or in morality, or in wisdom, or in spirituality. So it is wise to pay heed to that which comes from those filled with the spirit of truth, who take the word of God as the man of their counsel, and seek wisdom from above.

Every son should heed his mother's teaching and honor her counsel, so far as they are right, and encourage to godliness and eternal life. Mother love may often desire for her children that which has the appearance of good, which in reality would work for evil to all who sought and obtained it. The problems of life are too full of responsibility to be passed over without due consideration. Therefore we desire to give to all who will read it the loving counsel of saved mothers to their sons, hoping to help many to better things, and some to eternal glory.

When we look out upon this great world of people and observe their different dispositions, conditions, and surroundings, we see there are many who need various kinds of help in order to do justice to themselves and be a blessing to others. How many lives have been turned into different channels of virtue and usefulness by a few words given just at the right time, can never be estimated. With the desire to speak such words of helpfulness to many boys and young men, we Christian mothers want to give you all a few half-hour talks on various subjects of interest to you; and we believe many of you will be glad to know how mothers feel and think on these questions, and will read them with interest and profit. In order to reach many with just the help they need, it will be necessary to use plain language; and so our words will be well chosen to convey strong truths.

As mothers have a great storehouse of affection, all our counsel, reproof, and instruction shall be ballasted with love as though all the readers were our own dear sons. We have no doubt that many of you are longing for and realize the need of mother counsel and love, but have been deprived of it for various reasons. May we not offer ours as a substitute? Will you not carefully ponder over the thoughts given, and receive all the good possible therefrom? We want to write to you as though we were talking face to face in view of the great judgment day that awaits us all.

MORALITY.

Most children have been punished, at different times, by their parents, for evil-doing; so that most of them know they ought to do right and avoid the wrong; but not all are inclined to do the best they know. If every individual would do right as far as he understands, this world would be a much better and happier place; and if all would not only do the best they know but seek for a deeper understanding regarding what is good, and what is evil, then this world would be a moral place, the abode of a moral people. There are few, however, who will truly do this; for nearly all would rather do what they feel like doing than to consider what is right and do it, if it is the opposite of their desires or contrary to their inclinations.

Many love a great many good things, such as truthfulness, honesty, kindness, etc., and are very agreeable acquaintances; and yet may, on some point, be doing just the opposite of what they know to be right. Others will try to convince themselves that whatever they desire to do, is right; but there is a monitor within them that reproves them for doing what they know to be evil, until after being unheeded for a time it ceases to remonstrate with the offender, and he may be at ease regarding that evil. Have you not often heard young men confess how awful they felt when the first evil words were uttered, and how their conscience remonstrated with them, and they felt too impure to "look father or mother in the face"? but that wore away, and the next time they were provoked it was easier to use the evil expressions, and while they felt guilty and mean, their excuses shortened and lessened their condemnation. So after a time their rejected conscience ceased to reprove, and they could "swear as hard as anybody," and never know it; and yet in some other point of behavior be very conscientious.

People may be very moral, do very many good things, and yet not be a particle religious; while others blend their morality with religious observances, until they imagine they are very religious. All our good deeds will never fit and prepare our souls for heaven. It takes the grace of God to do that: but after it is received by faith the believer will walk in obedience to the commandments of God, and his life be much higher and purer than that of the moral man.

The instruction given to most of the young is to induce them to morality. We are always glad to meet a young man having strong convictions of right and wrong and living up to them in daily practice, and we immediately think he "surely has a good mother" who has done all possible to instruct in morality. Then we wish that he could see the need of the religion of Jesus Christ, that could do so much for him;

but we often see that his own goodness prevents him
from seeing the sinfulness of the human heart, that
can be changed only by divine grace, while some poor
immoral creature beholding his bondage to evil and
its exceeding ugliness will turn with joy, to the One
who has promised to break every fetter of sin, and
give new hearts for his service, thus making new
creatures. While we rejoice in all that is good, we
would be very sorry if any one after hearing our instruction should be satisfied with a moral life, which
has reward in this world only and leaves the soul unprepared for the better one.

We need to consider some things from different
standpoints in order to behold the wrong that is hiding within them; for most evils do not appear to the
careless observer as full of evil as they are in reality.
The wrong one may do himself does not look as bad
to him as the wrong some one else is doing; and such
is the weakness of humanity that the argument used
in defense of one's own wrong-doing will often be
used to condemn the misdeeds of others. For instance,
a schoolboy returning home, in the fullness of boyhood life and joy, comes bounding into the house with
a noisy "Hello, everybody!" The mother appears in
a doorway and says, "Softly, my boy." He turns in
anger, muttering, "I think I might do as I want to
with my own tongue." Shortly after, a neighbor's boy
was heard calling him ugly names, and he ran to his
mother, saying, "That boy thinks he can say what he
pleases with his tongue, but I'll show him differently

some time." You see he was, like many others, not very reasonable on the line of personal liberty, nor very consistent in logic. There is an old adage that is forcible and true: "Those who live in glass houses should never throw stones." That is, they should never do what they do not wish others to do to them, but should act upon the golden rule: "Do unto others as ye would that men should do to you." Applying this to our subject, no one who does wrong himself should condemn another for wrong-doing. Oftentimes we have heard men condemning men for drinking liquor, when they were unable to keep from anger, from untruthfulness, and from strife or ill-will. Let him that is without sin cast the first stone. If it is possible to stop drinking liquor, it is possible to stop every other evil. While we do not believe it is natural for men to do so, we know it is possible through grace. Therefore, dear boys, we would encourage you all to seek that grace which will enable you to live godly in Christ Jesus. Where is there one who lives the very best he knows who does not desire to live better? This shows that morality fails to measure to the standard of righteousness, but is simply "making clean the outside of the cup and platter," while the inside is unclean—that is, the life appears fair, while the heart is impure and is conscious of its unclean condition. Salvation makes the heart pure; therefore the thoughts and actions proceeding therefrom are pure also; as far as one has an understanding of what is right, and the one is constantly learning of God.

The word of God is very strong in condemnation of those who are self-righteous; that is, they think they are "good as anybody," "will go to heaven if others do," etc. If this were possible, then there was no need of a Savior dying upon the cross to provide a salvation that would save each one from all sin. As boys are often uncertain about right or wrong, we believe that many will be glad to hear them clearly set forth in different ways upon many subjects, and this is what we want to do first, and then show you that there is an alarming power to save man from his sinful condition.

Sometimes the objection is made to our work that those who most need the help we give will not read nor heed the instruction given. This may be true sometimes, but we do trust and pray that each one who looks upon "Mothers' Counsel" will read it, heed it, and practice it, in his life; because we know it will be good for them in this life as well as in the long eternity. Boys are not as indifferent about good things as they sometimes appear; for the Spirit of God is at work upon their hearts, and did they understand more about such things, they would yield themselves to the service of God. It would be too bad if any should fail to live a life of righteousness because older ones failed to urge them heavenward. There is a backwardness among people when it comes to this subject that needs to be overthrown by the efforts of Christian men and women. Dear boys, as mothers we warn you not to resist what you know is good and true, but yield to the right and be brave Christian heroes; for that is more noble and grand than anything you might find in this world.

A beautiful sight gladdened my heart not long ago. In a meeting were a brother and two sisters. The brother was a Christian; the sisters were not, but were becoming concerned about their spiritual condition. The brother, with an arm around one sister's shoulders, was seeking to win her to the service of God. The act of concern and expression of tenderness and protection so moved my heart that I thought I would give all worldly possessions to see the same among my own dear ones. What can be more beautiful than a young Christian encouraging others to serve the true and living God, because the heart is so filled with the blessed Spirit of Christ?

Be not deceived. Do not "take the hull for the kernel" by taking a moral life for a spiritual, or a mere outward profession for the religion of Jesus. As he is a mighty Savior, his religion is a wonderful and mighty power in the heart of man to change it and make anew and pure.

> Then let us not, in folly, take
> The false, the low, or impure things
> That stand for good, but ever make
> An honest effort for the TRUE.

HOME INFLUENCE.

What a wonderful power in the world is the home! Its influence can never be measured, its responsibility is greater than words can express: and yet the majority of homes never consider their obligation to the world's welfare; for each home is a small kingdom, ruling and reigning for itself, its aim and object its own welfare, and yet greater is its influence upon the common good than upon itself.

The greatest power of the home is through the rearing and training of children; for they are in many respects what the home makes them. No one can clearly discern the powers at work to send out into the world men and women of different character and ability. While it is possible that the strongest power lies in parentage, yet there are influences that extend beyond that into the unknown. Children of the same parents, born under the same circumstances and surroundings, are exact opposites in character, mental ability, and strength, and develop into various types of manhood and womanhood. It is nevertheless true that good homes send forth as a general thing good men and women; for the home training during the tender years of childhood is of great value and turns the current of life into right channels. Much more good would be attained if parents realized the responsibility that rests upon them in regard to the discipline of home.

God gives instruction in the Bible to parents concerning their children, when he says, "Foolishness is bound up in the heart of a child: but the rod of correction shall drive it far from him." If the parents spare the rod, the child is spoiled. Children are commanded to obey their parents in the Lord, and to honor them by being in subjection to them. Many parents seeing no great good arising from a few chastisements of their children, arrive at the conclusion that it does no good, and get along with them the best way they can to avoid trouble, thus permitting them to grow up in their own ways, which are not good. One Bible qualification of a preacher of the gospel is that he be a man "having his children in subjection," showing clearly that God requires it, and therefore it is possible. If it is, then it is necessary, and every one should receive grace from God to attain to it.

We would encourage parents to earnest endeavor to instruct their boys and girls in right ways, because it is profitable for them. The enemy of all good would discourage, with the assurance that it does no good, that young people do not heed your words of counsel and warning: but this is not true; for many precious boys and girls have been saved from entering evil ways by a few words of warning from parents or friends. Should any reject your counsel or seem indifferent thereto, it may come to them in just the time most needed. Anyway, no one should fail to do her duty for fear it would accomplish nothing. How much better that every young person should receive ten times more instruction than he needs rather than that one should fail to receive it once and go into evil from the lack of it.

You may wonder why we speak thus to our sons. Do you not know that some of them are believing that it is childish, yes, even babyish, to honor or obey their parents or to listen to their counsel? Have you not seen some who think every effort made to help them is just trying to keep them from enjoying themselves or to make them old people before their time? Oh, how we wish every one who really thinks thus could understand the loving-kindness of our hearts, that prompts us to try to help them to avoid the rocks upon which many a young person has lost his life, his character, and his soul! It is natural as we look back over the past of our lives to see many things that tended toward evil, or that had a bad influence upon us, or that really hindered us from attaining the strength of character or the blessings of God, that we might now be enjoying. Knowing that each one of us can never live over his life and rectify some of the mistakes made, we would love to save others from like failures, for their good and happiness.

Many sons listen to father's and mother's advice when alone with them, and feel and know that it is wisdom to walk in their counsel; but when they are with young people who disregard their parents' wishes, they weakly submit, and because of it are led to do many things they would not do but for that influence. Arise, young man, in true courage and strength of character, and do what you know to be wisest and best, regardless of the censure of others. Do you not know that if you stand boldly for the right, you may have the pleasure of seeing some of your acquaintances turn from the evil and walk with you in the safe path of right?

It is beautiful to see the young turning to their elders for counsel and help, rather than to those younger. But many dear young people seem to think of nothing but present enjoyment, and turn to whatever seems to offer it to them, no matter how much sorrow it affords in later years. They are not so wise as the little bee who prepares for the future, but like the grasshopper who enjoys the summer and dies when the winter overtakes him; for they enjoy all they can in their youth, and when their folly overtakes them they sink beneath it to perish therein with no future hope as a solace for all the dark hours of misspent lives. What a beautiful picture it makes for life's memory scenes when sons are obedient, kind, and loving, and truly honor their parents! when father or mother speaks, there is quick attention and prompt regard for all that is good.

Let us listen while our mother tells us her dreams as we lay in her arms so helpless and innocent. Here is her first-born son. "O my precious one, I would

have you grow into a strong, handsome man. You
should be wise in all that is good and true, in all that
would make you a power for good wherever you go.
You should be noble in goodness, kind to all, able to
assist the needy and the weak. As you grow up you
will be kind to parents, listening to their counsel and
paying heed thereto in the walks of life. You should
be truly kind to every woman, remembering the
mother who loves you and the sisters who knelt with
you at her knees, and whom you love and care for in
all their times of need. You should be most truly
noble in your service to the Lord, whom the world crucified, and whom it now rejects by not obeying his instruction. Oh, yes, my little one, I shall ever seek
for you what is best for the great eternity, even
though you may have to endure many hardships in
this life; for mother love would seek to carry you into
the blessed haven of eternal rest, as it does now to the
rest of sleep. Sleep now, my precious, and unfold as
a beautiful bud, day by day, your God-given powers,
until you shall be one of the noblest of God's creations
—a Christian man." Would it not be sad if all her
heart's desires for him should never be realized ? if he
should grow up to be just the opposite of her dreams ?
Oh, yes, dear boys, strive to attain true manliness of
character, and comfort and gladden the hearts of
loving parents.

Many homes are unwise in methods and means of
correction and discipline, and many are truly devoid
of the natural affection that should control the home

for the good of all the inmates. Nevertheless the fact remains that children should yield to all that is good therein, and avoid the evil, as they emerge into manhood and womanhood. If all the homes measured to the Bible standard, this world would be an earthly paradise of happiness. If all are not what they ought to be, let each reader see to it that his home receives due care and honor so far as he is able to give it or encourage others to. Often parents have some object before them which they wish to attain, and put forth every effort in that direction, neglecting the present needs of the home to the detriment of all within its sheltering fold.

Day by day and year after year the care of home must go forward; for each day's influence upon the hearts and minds of the young has its portion in the great result. Patience is probably one of the most needed qualifications of parents, coupled with true courage to discharge every obligation toward those entrusted to their care. If they will keep the confidence of their children, and not relax their care as they come to the years when many consider themselves capable of caring for themselves, but give loving counsel on all the secret things of life, they will be able to retain it in the future as the children go out into the world, and find out by careful observation that "father and mother were right." In order for young people to be fortified against sin they must have it revealed to their understanding.

Here is a letter written for the encouragement of

parents, and as a warning to the young. It reads as follows:

Since I have arrived at the years of manhood, in viewing the past I am made to shudder to see the narrow escape I made from some of the pitfalls of sin into which so many dear young people are falling, perhaps never to fully recover from the sad results. Is there no way to check the tide which is increasing so rapidly and taking the young before they come to the years of full understanding? Must we look on this pitiful scene with hearts filled with sorrow for them, and not attempt to lend a helping hand by way of admonition or warning? By no means can we be silent and be blameless; for the "love of Christ constraineth us" to sound out a note of warning. Knowing the terror of the Lord, "we persuade men," and especially appeal to every parent to arise in courage and shake off the false modesty that would prevent confidential conversations with the precious ones our kind and lovingly heavenly Father has entrusted to their care, and said, "Bring them up in the nurture and admonition of the Lord." Are you living so far from your children that you can not draw them to your side and "reveal the hidden things of dishonesty" and darkness to their tender hearts and minds, so they may ponder the path for their feet and "take heed thereto according to thy word"?

Never will the impression made upon my mind and

heart, when first my father ventured to tell me of the sad effects of things done in secret, leave me; for they are indelibly impressed upon my very being. Although I was nearly grown, yet I had not known the awful results of sin and evil company. Now I am made to praise God for this instruction, which I promised my father I would heed; also a few words from a kind and loving mother. But how I wish they had been given years before—how much more good they would have accomplished! though the words were few, and perhaps my dear parents thought they never amounted to much because I seemingly gave little heed to them, they were truly " bread cast upon the waters " and were not in vain; for they followed me, though I was almost two thousand miles from home. Those precious words backed up by a father's and mother's prayers were ever before me, with my promise to cherish them.

When I was thrown among evil companions and they would try to induce me to follow them in the paths of sin, in drinking, playing cards and billiards. or going in the way of all sin and wickedness by following in her path who had gone astray from virtue, I was able to refuse, as I felt I could not break the promise made to my parents. Also, knowing the sad results of such evils, I feared the awful consequences. What a wonderful blessing to me! In after years I often met some of those young men who had taken the path of sin, and oh, how sad were their countenances and condition! On finding out how I was prospering they would confess their sad state, moral, physical, and financial, and wish they had not entered the evil way. How sad to me to look into their once bright eyes and pleasant faces and behold the marks of sin!

So, dear parents, do not neglect to give the so much needed words of admonition and warning to the tender hearts that know not the depths of sin and the awful consequences thereof, remembering that a few words rightly spoken may save that which money can never buy for those who lose it. Ever your friend and brother, Jas. B. Peterman.

You can see, dear boys, the precious results of being warned, and of receiving the counsel of parents. We do hope you may receive such good instruction from some source as to help you to escape from the evil effects of sinful actions or from the great evils themselves, that destroy the soul and body. If you fail to receive the good that surrounds you, and take up with what you know is evil, you will surely be worthy of greater punishment than those who were not influenced for good by their surroundings. Let us listen to the plaintive life story of several boys, and learn a few good wholesome lessons. How it saddens our hearts to hear of those who failed to be rightly influenced by the good, and took their own course, regardless of the tears and sufferings of their dear ones!

Dear boys: ~~I feel confident the Lord would have me write a short story for you.~~ I once knew two dear boys, and I loved them almost as well as my own; for I had the care of them when they were little, and they were loving and good. They had a beautiful home in the country, and everything necessary for their comfort and happiness. Their parents were both Christians and school-teachers, and gave them every advantage they could to obtain an education. After they had attended school a while in the country their parents concluded they could do better in town; so they sold their country home and bought a nice residence in town, where the boys could attend good schools. They always had family worship, sent the boys to Sunday-school, and provided them with plenty of good books and papers; ~~and so did all they knew for their spiritual needs.~~

But these dear boys turned away from all this good, from the tender love and care of parents and friends, and sought such company as led them in evil ways and doings. Many times while their parents ~~supposed~~ they were at school, learning such lessons as would help them forward in life, they were spending the day with other bad boys playing truant; for they deceived the teacher by imitating their father's writing and prepared their own excuses. They learned to smoke, chew, and swear, and then to like strong drink. When they were in their teens their father died, and they ~~broke away from all restraint and instead of going to school they spent their time reading~~ stop going to school

novels and sensational papers. After they were grown
their mother died almost broken-hearted. Her great
desire and aim had been to give them an education
and raise them up to noble manhood. But alas! her
hopes were blasted; for they had chosen evil instead
of good. She left them a small fortune, and one of
them took his portion and went to the Indian Terri-
tory, to live with the Indians, and realize some of the
wonderful stories he had read, and in a short time had
spent his property and had to work by the day for his
living. The other brother continued to run the store
his parents had left him, but his bad habits mastered
him, his property soon disappeared, and now he is a
perfect wreck of his former self, unable to keep himself decently dressed or to associate with former
friends. What a sad—very sad—change!

O dear boys, if you could only realize what you are
doing when you turn from the good influence of your
homes and loved ones (even those who may love you
so well as not to act wisely, in shielding you from
every hardship) to the uncertain and evil influence
outside of those homes and to the companionship of
those who do not love you, surely you would act more
wisely. Dear reader, will you walk more carefully?
will you choose what is wisest and best?

I once knew a bright, beautiful boy who was
brought up in the fear of the Lord, but he too turned
with the evil influence beyond his home and associated
with bad companions and soon learned to use tobacco,
and hid it from his parents for three years; then he

learned to drink and swear. When about thirteen years old he was converted, and his loving mother rejoiced greatly to think her darling boy was going with her in the right way. But alas! her hopes were of short duration; for his old companions followed after him and laughed and teased him out of his religion. He did not take care of the healthy body God had given him, and consumption fastened itself upon him; but he would not believe it, and still said he would get well. He would not allow any one to talk to him about his soul, until he got so low he was conscious only at times. Then his speech left him, and he could not talk, and oh, the agony that showed itself in his face! his eyes would fill with tears and his face work with deep emotion and distress that he could not express. Sometimes he was found praying, and we hope our heavenly Father had mercy upon him in his last hours. He surely would, if he repented and yielded himself to God. He lay three days in that condition before death relieved him.

Oh, dear boys! shun evil company as you would a deadly serpent. It will surely lead you to destruction. The influence of home and loved ones will do you much more good and should give you far greater pleasure than the society of the foolish and gay young folks that are ever ready to entice the innocent. Give your hearts to God in the days of your youth and he will protect, and guide you into right and pleasant paths; and when death shall come you will not need to sorrow over past transgressions or over an uncertain future, but you will be prepared to enter eternal glory. May the Lord bless you all and help you to be wise in seeking first the kingdom of God and his righteousness, and all else needful shall be added.

With much love, and earnest desire and prayer for your welfare, I am your true friend,

"Aunt Fannie."

COMPANIONSHIP.

MAN possesses strong desires for companionship. Few are satisfied to live solitary lives, but seek for some one or more to share their joys and sorrows. The young are especially fond of the society of those of the same age, and the life, frivolity, and gaiety that it encourages. They look not to the future to consider what will be best and wisest, but enter into that which brings present enjoyment. Thus we see the difference between the wisdom of the young and older people; for they seek that companionship that will help them forward in their plans and aspirations for the future. For instance, one who desires to gain prominence as a lawyer will seek the society of those who will assist him in legal education and promotion. If young men and boys could use this wisdom in early years, it would be a great benefit to them all through life.

The old saying that "you can not put old heads on young shoulders," while true to a certain limit, may be much modified by proper instruction. Let each child be firmly impressed with the belief that he has a place to fill in this world that no other can fill, for the God of heaven has given it to him, and he needs to take advantage of every opportunity in order to at-

tain to it for his own good and the good of others: he
becomes careful about all that concerns him, and uses
more real wisdom than one would imagine.

My mind was wonderfully impressed with a few
words from the writings of a religious man, that have
followed me through the greater part of my life, and
have done me much good in various ways. "When I
choose a friend, he shall be the one that is bravest, the
worthiest and most excellent person, capable of doing
me many a kindness that will make me wiser and
better." This has been my heart's desire, to mingle
with those who would be a means of advancement in
every way for my good and the glory of God. How
often do we see dear young people choosing for friends
those far below them in many ways, simply for the
pleasure of being honored by them, and then gradually sinking to their level, and sometimes below it!

Some one will say quickly that the advice to choose
friends who will be a benefit, will not work both ways.
Indeed it will, for you may choose for your friend one
who will do you good, and you will be moving forward
and upward, while some one below you will choose you
for a friend and you will be ready to lend a helping
hand and encourage him to better things, always advancing; for every good deed done moves forward and
upward; so there is no sinking backward. Should
friends prove unworthy of confidence and fail to be a
means of advancement in life, they may be held dear
to the heart because of their many virtues, and other
friendships give the assistance needed. No one is so

strong, however, but the weaker ones may be of great value to him in various ways: if there be a constant and firm moving forward and gaining strength by the lessons learned.

Sometimes the ties of nature and affection prove hindrances to a steady progress in the way of right, but it should not be so; for each obstacle should be surmounted and be a help by the strengthening of decision to move upward. "If one faint in the day of adversity, his strength is small." The greater the opposition, the stronger should be the decision to win; for then the stake is worth something. Before me I see a dear one who from the usual point of view would be obliged to mingle with a very humble class of associates, because of her surroundings; but she had noble aspirations and a decision to conquer difficulties and triumph in right. She went bravely to work doing what her hand found to do, with her might, and fitted herself for a higher sphere; and when the way opened (as it always will for the deserving) to better things, she was prepared for it, and filled well her place until again an open door urged her upward, and still she is pressing forward. How it should encourage our hearts when we have been able to prove a friend to such ones and help them in the battle of life!

There seems to be in most people a part of their nature that seeks for what is good and pure, and then another part that would run downward to what is evil. Here is a boy who loves books, such as histories, biographies of great men, books of travel, etc., that will

store his mind with useful knowledge, and prepare
him for a place of usefulness. He has also a great
love for good eating and drinking, which inclines
him to gluttony and intemperance. Now if he makes
a wise choice of friends, and enjoys the companionship of the learned and studious, he will sacrifice the
lower part of his nature for the better, and find great
gain. If he chooses for friends those who suit the
lower nature, his course will be downward. Some attempt to live a double life, finding pleasure in gratify-
ing both parts of their nature, but it does not last
long; for the lower generally overcomes the better,
sinking him down to the lowest depths. All around
us are examples of this sad state of affairs. Many
orators, statesmen, scholars, and preachers have shone
brightly for a short time and then vanished out of
sight as a falling star. Oh, how sad to see the best
and noblest endowments sacrificed to the lower appetites!

There is one thing that has impressed itself firmly
upon my heart and mind, that would do great service
to you all if you will receive it. If one does right,
he keeps a good conscience and is thus prepared to
seek for good companionship; but if he loses respect
for himself by doing evil, he is ashamed to seek the
society of the good, and so must take up with the evil.
Any one who is awake to passing events has seen this
many times, and perhaps realizes the feeling that
would cause such a course in his own experience. A
criminal who was soon to suffer death for crime was

asked to give the first wrong step that led to his evil course, and after due reflection said he remembered telling a falsehood to cover a slight fault, and then becoming so ashamed of it when his schoolmates taunted him with it, that school became unpleasant and he left it. So after a time he fell into the company of some boys who were too mischievous and bad to go to school, and so he drifted downward to his sad fate.

It may seem a little thing to choose your friends, and some never seem to give it a thought, but just drift along where there is gaiety. Do you know " a boy is known by the company he keeps"? If he associates with bad boys, he is soon called " a bad boy," although he may be far from being as bad as the others. Here are a few words of exhortation from a mother whose heart has been made sad by the course of her sons. Please harken to them and never let your " mother dear " have cause for grief over this fault in you.

" May God bless the boys and help them to receive instruction. I would earnestly and lovingly entreat them never to be in the company of bad boys. We have raised five boys, and our greatest trouble has been on this line. Our two oldest boys grew to the stature of manhood young, and kept company with two older cousins who drank and got into trouble from it; and because our boys were in their company they were mixed up in it. No one can imagine the sorrow it brings to the hearts of parents to see their sons brought into trouble in this way. So we beg of

you to shun bad company, even if it is some of your
relations. 'My son, if sinners entice thee, consent
thou not.'—Prov. 1:10. 'My son, forget not my
law; but let thine heart keep my commandments; for
length of days and long life, and peace, shall they add
to thee.'—Prov. 3:1, 2." There should be a constant
desire in all hearts to befriend and assist any one who
wishes for improvement, but there should be strength
of character to keep firm for the right.

In nearly every city, town, and village are a class
of boys who form a clique for mischief and wrong-
doing, that just escapes the law for punishment.
These boys often have loving mothers who would do
all they could to make pleasant evenings for them at
home with books and music or companions. But this
does not please them, as they want to congregate together and smoke and chew, drink, swear, and tell
filthy and foolish yarns on street corners or in some
low place that keeps open to catch the money that is
freely spent for much that works evil to soul and
body. There might be some excuse for the boys that
have no homes, no fathers or mothers, sisters or
brothers, to make a better place for them to pass their
evenings; but for those who prefer this rough company to the society of loved ones there is certainly no
excuse. Often they know mother weeps while they
are gone, and sits up watching and listening for their
coming; but they call it "babyish in mother," and go
on "making themselves manly" by unkindness to
mother, and bad habits. Here is a nice true story

that a sister sends to you to show you some of the results of bad company.

"When I was a girl, there came to our home to board, in company with several men, a young man of good appearance. He was gentlemanly, neat, reserved, sad, and quiet. Mother said she would like to know what his past life had been, but did not think it proper to ask him. He was slow to enter into conversation, and seldom took part in our games or music, except to sing a song sometimes. Our mother was every boy's mother, and she took care of his clothes and made him feel at home, and so he stayed with us some time. One day she asked him if he had parents living, and he replied, 'A father,' but was so embarrassed that she did not question more. One Sunday my sister had a little conversation with him, and so she finally said, 'Now, Sammy, we have become quite well acquainted, and I believe you are in trouble: tell us all about it, if you wish, and perhaps we can help you. We do not ask out of curiosity, but as friends.' 'Well,' said he, 'I am in trouble. I was not satisfied at home and so wandered away, here and there, until I had no friends except the rough sort. I have kept well dressed, but have not been able to keep good company. I know you would help me if you could, but I am so discouraged. I do not want to do anything bad. If I could get a good situation, I would try to be a man —but that seems impossible to obtain.' My sister told him it would 'pay to be a man anyway, and life was worth living aright.' Soon after we bade him good-by and told him to be true to himself, and he went to work on a new railroad. The next we heard of him was through the county paper. Four men had been arrested for stealing. They were camping in the woods and getting out timber for the railroad. Among the names we read Sammy ——. 'Oh,' we said, 'he is not guilty; it is the result of bad company.' They were sentenced (I think) ten years in the penitentiary. Four years later my sister and I were in a store, when she called my attention to some one standing by the store. She said, 'I am sure that is Sammy.' I said, 'Oh, no; he is a much younger man.' But she would have it so, and walking up to him, said, 'Are you not Sammy ——?' His eyes filled with tears as he recognized us and said, 'Yes, what is left of him.' 'If it had not been for your advice and kindness to me, I might still be in the penitentiary serving out a sentence for something I was never guilty of.' 'Oh, we knew you were not guilty of doing such a thing as stealing.' 'No,' said he; 'we were in the cabin together when they arrested us, and the appearances were against me; but I never stole anything: but it was *bad company again;* so I stood no show at the trial, as they said, "Oh, he's one of them, take him along."' No friends, no money, no home; a stranger and a very discouraged and weak boy—no wonder they thought him guilty when in such company. 'When I was in the cell I had time to think over things, and see where I had made mistakes that had prevented me from doing better: and

I remembered your kindness and advice, and so took courage to do my best, and so they released me much sooner. But, oh! how I have suffered no one can ever know; but perhaps you may have some idea of it from this,' and as he removed his hat we saw that his hair was quite gray. We shed tears together, and begged him to look forward and not backward. He married, and as far as we know has lived an honorable life. Oh, it pays to look after the boys, and take an interest in them. Mothers and sisters, make home so pleasant they will not want to go away to find amusement, and always have a kind word for those who are homeless and throw around them all the good influence possible."

Some might think this too unnatural to be true. But very often do we hear of just such instances where circumstantial evidence and bad company have put men and women behind prison bars to suffer for the crimes of others. Strange things are transpiring, and no boy or man who keeps evil company is sure of the future. How much better to seek such society as will strengthen the good that lies dormant in so many hearts, and make them true and noble men to fill some worthy place in life and assist others to better things. No one can stand still in life; he is becoming either worse or better, either learning or forgetting, becoming either worse or better at heart, either drawing nearer to God or drifting away as the days, months, and years pass. It is true that some after spending a few years in sin make a change for the better and leave off their folly and seek for good. But these will agree with me that it is far better never to know evil ways; for it takes a great fight of faith to become complete overcomers.

Now we want to question every reader. Do you really love what is good and right? Does it look more attractive to you than evil? If so, then you will seek for it and "depart from evil." If you love good, then you should seek after God; for he is the fountain of all good, and you will attain unto good much faster. He also says he is "a friend that sticketh closer than a brother." We pray God to bless every reader of this subject with a strong desire to seek good companionship, that he may seek God, enjoy the society of God's children, and finally when life is over spend the long and blissful eternity with God, all the ransomed, and the holy angels. What high and holy company! Will you not begin to prepare now?

    It seems so strange that any one
      Who thinks upon the things of life
    Should count it foolish, or unwise,
      To choose the best of what is rife
    With virtues great or wealth untold,
      But look upon it with disdain,
    And freely take a thing of naught,
      And hope to find a pleasing gain.

    If one is wise—yes, worldly wise—
      And he may have without a price
    A thing of value rich and rare,
      He takes it quickly--thinks it nice :

COMPANIONSHIP.

He made a bargain such a way,
   That he has value that will keep
The cares of life, some troubles too,
   From reaching him, in waves so deep.

And now, dear boys, will you be wise
   And choose thus well in everything?
Oh, will you choose for friends so dear
   The ones who give no pain or sting:
But prove your friends in deed and truth,
   By helping you to purer life,
To higher views, to deeper thought,
   To life of peace from worldly strife?

Of course you may, you surely can
   Make other choice, but do you think
You'd use the wisdom of a man
   By treading near to danger's brink,
And taking friends who only prove
   No help, no value, and no strength,
But draw you down to depths of sin,
   To folly's height, or to its length?

If we should say in words so plain
   That you were foolish doing thus,
You'd think us far from being kind
   And wonder why we "make a fuss
About such little things of life:"
   And if we'd say, "You are not brave,"
You'd quickly say in accents strong,
   "There's naught I fear this side the grave."

If you are wise, with courage strong,
   You'll choose for life each "better thing,"
And bid adieu to every weight,
   That harms your soul and helps to bring

You into bondage to the one
  Who seeks to lure in different ways
Each one to ruin and to shame,
  That he may darken all his days.

If it were choice but for THIS life,
  'Twould be far best to wisely choose;
But when we think that ev'ry time
  A choice is made we gain or lose
What helps us upward to our God,
  To endless life, to joyous state,
To riches rare and heav'nly place—
  To all within the pearly gate—

Oh, then we'll see that wisdom's way
  Is best in life, and EVER best;
For what is good leads unto good,
  And thus the soul is ever blest.
So now we hope you ever will
  Be strong, and brave, and truly wise,
That you may gain the best of life
  And home so fair above the skies.

JOYS AND SORROWS.

This seems at first thought to be a strange subject for young people: but I am sure you will appreciate its rich lessons, if you will receive them into your lives. Did you ever think that nothing comes by chance—there is an overruling hand in the circumstances of each one of our lives? God loves us, and seeks to do us good from our earliest existence. There are laws that are unchangeable, because they are just. There are also provisions made for certain things because of mercy and love. There is cause and effect all through life that should be reason for every individual's careful consideration of all that pertains to this existence. A wrong step in the commencement of life brings upon the doer certain effects, that may prevent much good from being his portion. There are some actions that bear two kinds of fruit—present pleasure and future sorrow.

If we had our way, life would be one continuous round of joys—some would have them in one way and others in various ways. If some people had their desires gratified, they would not work a day, but rest, rest, all the days of all their years. Victuals would increase upon the table without the use of hands; and eat, drink, sleep, and rest would be the height of joy to them. Others would have money—money to grow in their pockets, and little for anybody else, and they would buy and loan, buy and loan, until the grave swallowed them up. Others would work with good will if everything would *run*—run in their own way. Others would have a good time in any and every way possible, and their cry would be, "Joy, joy; I must have joy."

Now you see all the different classes of people are trying to run their lives to attain just what they desire: and so of course some are going one way, some another; and every little while they are colliding, and crash goes some one's joyful prospects, and here is sorrow instead of joy. Thus people set out for joys, and in their place they gain sorrows; while others start in life enveloped in sorrows, and think, "Thus it will be all my days." All of a sudden the cloud of sorrow parts, and here are precious joys. So we see that the expected generally fails, and the unexpected transpires. In bringing this before you I desire to help you to see the folly of trying to direct your lives in ways that shall bring you only joy. Your ways should be so chosen as to result in most good to yourselves and friends; and you should be firm for the right, let it bring present joy or sorrow.

Here is a young man who starts out to have a good time. He thinks it looks nice to smoke cigars, and he has heard what a comfort they are to those who smoke, and so he expects to find much pleasure therein. He begins to smoke, but the first cigar is not very encouraging, as he feels "oh, so sick:" but he has perseverance, and soon he can smoke quite well, and feels quite manly as he walks the streets puffing away, something similar to a small steam engine. As he turns the corner he meets very unexpectedly a lady friend for whom he has great respect, and, while she greets him pleasantly, he realizes that she is surprised and displeased, which he soon finds is a fact, as she plainly tells him so when she has the opportunity, and urges him to give up the evil before the habit is thoroughly fastened upon him. This serious aspect of a pleasurable indulgence somewhat disturbs his composure, and lessens his enjoyment therein for some days.

Now he returns home after a month's absence, and as his mother greets him and gives the usual greeting of a mother's kiss, she says: "Why, how strong your clothes smell of tobacco! Been riding in the smoker? Oh, no! it is not your clothes, but your breath. Oh, my son! you have not learned to smoke?" He replies, "Oh, I only smoke a little, mother. You know all the boys do nowadays." "*Oh, my boy!* can it be true he is a tobacco-user? I was so thankful you had grown to manhood without using it, and I thought you never would. It hurts me so to hear it; for I know you will be sorry for it when it becomes your master. Better stop now while you can." He replies in comforting tones, "Never mind, mother,

you won't care after you get used to it. I won't
smoke much." But down deep in his heart he knows
she is right, and instead of joy comes sorrow.

But that is not all. Here comes his father's friend
to tell him there is a vacancy in his friend's store, that
he can probably secure if he makes application immediately, as he has just recommended him for the vacancy. The young man is greatly pleased, and prepares to follow the advice of his father's friend. Soon
he is on his way to the store, and lights his cigar as
he passes a friend, and falls to thinking of his mother.
How dear she is! how sad she looked! how she must
love him, to be so concerned about such a little thing!
etc. Before he is aware, he is at the store, and Mr.
B—stands in front watching his approach. He looks
surprised, but says kindly, "Why, Harry, I did not
know you smoked." "Oh, yes, a little now and then,
he replies," carelessly. "When did you take it up?
lately?" "Oh, yes, when I was in C— last month,"
replies Harry, wondering if everybody is thus concerned about his doings. Mr. B— replies slowly, "I
thought it must be recently. Your father's friend
Mr. G—has just recommended you to fill the book-
keeper's vacancy, and I am extremely sorry to disap-
point you. Ever since I gave up the use of tobacco
six months ago because it was the cause of so much
ill health to me, I have taken no one into my employ
who uses the poisonous weed, as I thought my influence would be greater against it. Give it up, my
boy, and be ready for the next place."

As Harry returns home disappointed he muses: "Now this is too much for such a little thing. Just think! a fifty-dollar-a-month place lost for cigars! Well, I'll get along just as well; see if I don't: and I'll not give up my cigars either; for I'm mad to think how foolish people act sometimes."

There is sorrow instead of joy as the weeks pass and he finds no place. His mother is worried, and finally coaxes him to tell her why their friend did not give him the place he wanted so badly. In a moment of thoughtlessness he replied, "Oh, it was because I smoked—he is so good he don't like smokers." "Oh, my son! would you choose the cigar rather than to help your poor old mother? would you see her turn and contrive to keep herself and you fairly decent in dress, and you not give up what has caused all this trouble? Oh, my boy! I never thought you were selfish and cold-hearted, and didn't love me, before! Oh, *oh*, OH!" and sobs shake her feeble frame.

Where is the pleasure from the cigar? In a moment he is by her side, his arms around her as he says, "I'll give it up, mother, if you'll only laugh instead of cry. I can and I will for love of mother. I know you pray for me, and I can give up smoking now better than some other time. See, mother, this is the way I'll smoke the rest of this bunch;" and he tosses them into the stove. His mother smiles, and says in loving tones, "God bless my son. I knew he was better than he seemed." Why, here is joy— deeper, richer, and purer than he had ever dreamed of as a result of smoking. Surely many are wrong about the smoker's joys.

"Well," he muses, "now comes the battle. Shall I go and tell Mr. B— that I am ready for the next vacancy? I don't see any other way out of the trouble I so foolishly got into. Yes, I'll be a man again and do the right, even though it don't feel just as good as it might." The next morning finds him at the store asking for Mr. B—. He is welcomed warmly by the merchant, who says quickly, "Oh, yes, you are ready for the next vacancy. How fortunate for us! One of the men is called away for a week, and you can take his place, and by that time the book-keeper must leave us for a visit to his sick father in the East. How glad I am to have you ready!" Not a word to recall any humiliation, but a ready helpfulness. Again comes a rush of joyous emotions, and he says in disdain, "You old cigar! never shall you darken my life another day, or hour; for there's no joy in you." A few months afterward, when he is established in the store and "happy as a king," a lady enters, and recognizing him quickly, says distinctly, "I am so glad to see *you here*, for I know their principles." Another joy that "fills his cup" and counts a hundred against the cigar.

"Oh," says one, "it don't always work so well." No, not always, but right is right, and gives more lasting joy than wrong does, every time. It may seem sometimes that the wicked are more joyous than the righteous, and that they do not have so many trials, but, if you notice, there is a lightness in their joys that shows it is very superficial. Often people will laugh and joke, and others will think them the happiest people in the world, when at heart they are most miserable.

The righteous may seem to be enveloped in trials and sorrows that would crush the life out of them. For a time they may be heavy and very grievous, but the Christian's trust in God's promises of deliverance gives him abundance of strength to bear them and to learn many precious lessons that bring joys so deep that the soul is stirred to its depth with purest and lasting pleasures. "The joy of the Lord is their strength."

"Well," says one, "you can't make me think there is no pleasure in worldly ways: I know there is; for I have tasted it." No, we are not going to try to do that, but to show you all that what seems to yield joy now has a sorrow also that is deeper. Let me give you an illustration.

Here is a pretty little house of wire that looks very innocent of anything harmful, and on a little wire is a nice piece of cake, meat, or cheese that would make a nice supper for a hungry rat or mouse. So it sits there a few days, and as it does not do anything peculiar or unpleasant, one of them ventures to investigate it, and finally creeps through the door and eats the dainty. While he is so doing he thinks all the rest of the rat tribe very unwise not to know how nice it is to sit there and enjoy such good things.

As he finishes his meal he turns around a few times and concludes to go out as he came in. But, behold, the door is shut in such a way that there is no chance of getting out, and he is a prisoner with nothing more good to feast upon. After trying in vain to make his escape, he settles down to discouragement and awaits results. Here it comes in the form of a man with a stick and a dog. Oh, what will they do? The man takes up the cage and tauntingly says, "Oh, ho, Mr. Rat! we have caught you this time. We were too smart for you. You thought we loved you, and wanted to feast you on goodies, but we'll show you what becomes of such foolish creatures." So he opens the door and out jumps the frightened animal into the "jaws of death;" for the dog springs upon him, and in a moment he is shaken to death by his foe. The other rats take warning and will not venture into the snare. They are far wiser than some men and boys.

Here is a beautiful home. Within its spacious, brightly lighted parlors, the perfumes of many flowers pervade the atmosphere. Strains of music, mirth, and laughter float through them.

Many young people, boys and girls, have gathered, by invitation, to celebrate the birthday of the young hostess. The evening passes with jokes, frivolity, and pleasure. At last refreshment hour comes and with it society's concomitant punch-bowl. Its contents appear harmless, made of eggs, cream, sugar, water, flavoring, and rum, the latter to properly season it.

The beverage seems so harmless, and so delightful to the taste, that the youth and damsel partake more than once, some, many times, until flushed and excited they go to their homes.

This frequent indulgence in homes soon creates a desire to experience the same vivifying effect at other times. These young men begin to frequent places where the mild intoxicants can be obtained. They are just beginning to pass through the door of the wire cage. They go in and out many times without going through the long corridor which leads to the tempting bait. Two years pass, their fears have departed, they go further in, drink deeper, and of stronger and yet stronger beverages. The devil's alluring, shining, enticing bait is at hand, they step on the lever of the cunningly covered trap. It springs. They are caught. The wires of the cage have suddenly become rods of iron. They are fast in the satanic grip of appetite. Still on, and yet deeper they go into all kinds of dissipation and excess, and the bars and bands become stronger. The devil stands without waiting to open the door and let them come out, only to plunge into death's awful doom. Their captor taunts them. All their joys are turned to bitterest sorrow and woe. They cry, "Who can deliver us from the bondage of this death?"

The answer comes, Jesus, Jesus only.

So many have had such experiences that all ought to take warning and seek first the kingdom of heaven; but there are so many who reject instruction, and must prove for themselves that "the way of the transgressor is hard." If all our sons will carefully examine everything that has the appearance of earthly joys, they will find that most always the end thereof is sorrow. All around us are way-marks showing the result of taking different paths in search for earthly joys.

The tobacco-track has its signs in filthiness of the flesh, lost energy, low desires, disease, and poverty.

The track of lust is marked by blighted lives, gray heads brought in sorrow to the grave, as loving fathers and mothers look upon the shame of sons and daughters and with tears, moans, and breaking hearts close their eyes in death. Here are "skeletons in the closet"—separation and divorce, divided families, fatherless or motherless children made so by law or lust, wretched lunatics, ever-dying bodies covered with loathsome disease, and more than all else, lost souls.

Here are the drink-track signs: lost manhood, lost virtue, lost property, lost health, lost friends, lost lifetime, lost peace and joy—and gained eternal sorrow.

Can it be possible our sons or any other mothers' sons should choose these paths for life, thinking to find joy, when all these signs point to sorrow? A brother writes you a loving letter on this subject, which we know should help you much in a strong decision to wisely choose your life pathway that you may not have to taste of such sorrow as his, but have the blissful foretaste of joys eternal all through your manhood days.

Dear boys: I am deeply interested in you, and am sure God enables me to be your true friend. What I shall write you shall be with a prayer and the hope of doing you good. I have passed the days of boyhood and youthful manhood and am entering the middle age of life. I am acquainted with the paths of vice and their attending wretchedness. I have also found the path of peace and its attending joy and happiness. I am aware of the satanic decoys to allure the youthful feet away from the paths of wisdom, truth, and happiness; away from that which is pure, noble, upright, and virtuous, which has its compensation in ease of conscience and rest of soul in this life, and pleasures forevermore in the life which is to come.

I shall relate to you some of the experiences of my youthful days, and beg of you, dear boys, to read with carefulness and prayer and profit by it. I was reared on a large farm in a genial clime, where I had everything beautiful in nature to turn my heart and thoughts to higher things and holier walks; but instead of being influenced by the pure and lovely works of God I inclined my ways toward the iniquitous den of sensuality. I began my life on this low plane of lust by entertaining impure thoughts, acquiring an unchaste conversation, and seeking such company as would awaken and develop the unholy desires of a sinful heart. I early learned the use of tobacco, which very soon enslaved me, which paved the way to the " social cup," these to the ballroom and billiard hall, and finally to lower and hidden vices.

In boyhood I had aspirations for higher things, and educated myself with the hope of ascending, at least to some height, the ladder of fame and doing some good in the world. I now awakened to find aspirations gone, hope fled, and myself encaged within the iron grasp of the monster Vice.

One night on my way home from the ballroom, where inebriacy and sensuality ran high, a pleading came to the better part of my nature endeavoring to move me to a higher, purer life. Strange were the sensations that came upon me. I looked along down through the future and saw misery, wretchedness, and woe in this life, and an eternity with lost souls in the great hereafter if I continued in this course. I also saw a life of usefulness, bright hopes, and pleasures, and a blessed immortality if I would but surrender to the pleadings of the gentle voice within. I consoled and eased my conscience for the time by encouraging the hope that God would hear the prayers of my kind mother, spare my life, and after a few years of sensual indulgence I would turn to a higher, nobler life. But this gentle monitor was not thus to be put aside but came again and again, until my conscience was smitten by his mighty hand and I was made to tremble before the dark, uncertain future. As I would awake in the morning an unseen hand would point out to me my sin, a fear would come over me, and I, startled, would look around as if ready to flee from some hideous monster of the dark. The day would be spent in planning for the evening; for to spend it in the privacy of my chamber was more than I could endure. The place of revelry was sought to drown the voice of conscience. I would throw myself into the festivities with all the force of my being, and appear the gayest of the gay. But when the sound of revelry was hushed, when the cup of sin had been drained, and I on my way home, or within the silence of my chamber with all the world shut out and naught to stand between me and the whisperings of my soul, I would be brought again face to face with eternity. My sins would lie heavy upon my heart and seem to crush me down into the dark abyss of woe. To lie upon my bed was to toss in uneasiness, fearing to close my eyes in slumber, not knowing but the dawning of the morning would find me called to that awful dreaded world beyond, prepared for the wicked.

Thus days came and went and grew to months. Sometimes by force of resolution and fear of awful punishment vice would be overcome to quite a degree, and the surging billows within my soul be calmed accordingly, only soon to be agitated by unrelenting fury of vice swaying the scepter of sin over me, making me groan beneath his grinding power. Thus months grew to years, until I had reached the more sober part of life, when I was persuaded to turn my ways unto Him who has promised to lead us in the paths of peace, and at whose right hand there are pleasures forevermore.

For years the angel of mercy endeavored to win me to a life of peace and virtue, and to turn my thoughts to pure and holy things, and to elevate me above the low degrading walks of sin. But vice had woven his fetters of iron around me until I was not free to obey the nobler qualities and longings of my heart. I stood in the ways of sin, I was pierced by its cruel thorns, and stung by its poisonous sting.

I saw hopes fade and die, and cruel mockings arise. I deeply felt my degradation, and wished I never had received life. I saw far above me the peaceful path of right. I beheld Virtue with all her lovely charms, nobility, true worth, life of integrity and usefulness; and all that was left of manhood blushed for shame. But Hope came with cheering words of encouragement for my fainting heart, and I resolved to gain that plane of moral freedom. Aid was given from above, new strength was gathered, the decision was made stronger; and as I yielded to the sweet embrace of divine love, the dark, fearful night of sin passed away and the light and joy of another world touched my soul, and I was free. In that hour I found perfect deliverance from the power of sin. The appetites that held me captive were destroyed, and I rejoiced in such an atmosphere of freedom and love as was beyond the capability of my mind to imagine of the angels in heaven.

Years have passed since that precious deliverance, and Vice has returned no more. By heaven's grace I am kept in the enjoyable paths of purity, with a conscience at ease, and a heart hopeful in a Redeemer's love. I drank deeply of the pleasures of this world, and found that they contained a sting of great pain and vexation to the inner voice of conscience. I have tried the merits of Christian love, and find therein the true pleasures, a confidence that calms every fear, that quiets every wave, and rolls over us a sweet, tranquil rest unequaled by the joys of the world. The beautiful things in nature, the lovely traits in character, the purity of life and conversation, rejected and unheeded in boyhood, now turn my thoughts and adoration to God.

Dear boy, we exhort you in love to turn away from the coarse, base, impure things of a sinful life and love that which is pure, manly, and right. Seek protection from the vices of this world in the power of Christian love. Court the ways of wisdom and truth, meditate upon things pure and lovely, admire that which is lovely and just, lavish your affection on heavenly things and not upon the coarse things of this world. Every thought and every affection that would have a tendency to lower the standard of your moral being to a level with the world should be instantly rejected. Every thought and every affection that has a tendency to elevate the character and lift up the soul to greater proximity with God should be encouraged. The vulgarisms of to-day in slang phrases, corrupt conversation, impure thoughts, obscene literature and pictures, incline the youth to the beastly course of life. The better qualities are corrupted, the manly principles destroyed, the voice of conscience hushed, the whole moral being paralyzed, until as is given in the last half of the first chapter of Romans the youth has sunk below the brute creation.

I pray, dear boy, that the lovely traits of Christian character, the purity of God's word, the sublime truths of holiness, the admirable paths of virtue, will captivate your heart and fill your soul with an affection that will now and forever incline your heart unto the bountiful Giver of all that is good and pure, in whom are pleasures now and forevermore. Yours in love, A Friend and Brother.

HONOR, NOBLENESS, AND BEAUTY.

NEARLY every person is more strongly and deeply influenced by some words and expressions than others. From childhood three words have conveyed precious meaning to my heart and mind. They have been of great value in my life, and had a restraining and purifying influence. The first word of the title of this chapter made a deep impression upon me while reading a book entitled " Six Steps to Honor." Although much of the contents of the book was quickly forgotten, the impression received was left deeply rooted, and there has since remained a high regard for honor —not the honor and esteem of men, but the true worth that rightfully commands esteem and consideration. An honorable man is one who has qualities of heart and mind that make him worthy of esteem. While it is not right to seek honor from men, it is a worthy ambition to attain an honorable character, and that which has real worth.

Many persons like to appear before people in a way to be counted honorable. They will do almost anything to attain such a position. That which many people would consider worthy of esteem oftentimes would fall far short of the requisites to true honor. The motives of every action must be pure and good, and inspired by a worthy object, and not that which is mean, trifling, or superficial. The plans and purposes are to be in accord with all that is good and great. I know many boys love to think of great things and dream of becoming great men, but they do not seem to think that greatness must have a beginning. They imagine that some time, somehow, and in some way it will come about without effort. A great man is a great boy matured, and an honorable man should be an honorable "boy grown tall. So now, boys, here is a great chance for you. You want to be great and honorable men; begin now by being great and honorable boys. How? Cultivate purity in thoughts, actions, and aspirations. One is only really great, honorable, or wise who has good greatness, honorableness, or wisdom. There have been men who attained to such eminence that the people of the world have called them great, and yet their greatness was a result of wickedness. They may have had great qualifications and much worldly wisdom, but they did not have hearts that throbbed with tenderness and love, and therefore, their natures were dwarfed and sordid.

If these feeble words could only be blessed of God, and inspire you with a real love for true greatness of manhood and honor, and you could all understand their real worth, it would amply repay me for my labor. We will trust and pray for greater things. Christian mothers desire you should not only understand these things but aspire to them with sufficient strength to induce you to put forth an effort to attain them for your own. I say, boys, attain to their glorious height.

Were you to hear some one say, "There is an honorable boy," what would you think was meant? It would mean that he was, as far as could be seen, a boy who measured to that one's standard of honor. He would not swear, drink whisky, fight, tell lies, deceive, or be unkind to any one. That is a great deal to say in favor of a boy. But do you not perceive that this would be just the beginning of an honorable career? If he did any of the things mentioned, he would not yet have begun an honorable life, much less have reached the height of honor. It is not enough not to swear, but he must use pure language at all times. It would not be sufficient not to drink, but he must have his appetites under control. It would not be enough not to fight, but he should be known for his peaceful disposition. Not sufficient not to tell lies, but there ought to be such love for truthfulness that he would be extremely sincere in every word and action. It would not be up to the standard not to "be unkind," but there should be a great abundance of real kindness. Can you see what it means to be honorable? Boys, how many of you want to strive to become honorable men? There are many ways to attain it that you may not think of now. It will be well for you, however, to endeavor to discover the true standard of honor, and to notice how far short of it your life is leading you, then surely you will try to attain it. Before we have finished our talks with you, perhaps you may see more clearly what it is and how to reach it.

Nobleness! Oh, how sweet the sound! Nobleness of mind, of heart, of life, of purposes, of desires, and of actions. Beautiful word because it inspires to greatness of character. Such a man is above a mean action. Should he make mistakes, he is quick to acknowledge them. A noble boy is one who is living up to a good understanding of what is noble. There are many traits of character to which *noble* is applied. If one is courageous or brave, he is called a "noble boy, because he fears nothing;" but while he is noble in that way, he may be far from it from some other point of view. How we wish our sons to be noble, strong, great, and good.

One may be noble yet few recognize it. He who is good and great does not seek to exhibit himself to the world. In the quiet of home are noble characters who are faithfully performing life's duties, bearing burdens, sorrows, denying self, and living day by day to the glory of God, yet known by few outside of their home. How good it is that all have the privilege of being noble and worthy of honor! If it were confined to those who are worldly-wise, or of high standing, or of public prominence, few of those in the humble walks of life would be able to attain to it. It is free to all, because it is nobleness of character and life, without regard to station or position. A noble life is an unselfish one. It is lived to honor God and for the good of others. We may notice noble qualities in our acquaintances, which are very commendable, if put to a just and proper use. But how many use their endowments for selfish purposes which spoil the fruit thereof!

Some want to be considered good by doing a great many creditable deeds without in reality being good and noble at heart. That is very superficial goodness. Another class of persons want to devote all their time and energy upon themselves, in order to obtain a certain standard of blamelessness, and so neglect their duty to others. We need the grace of God to discern the proper standard of just and pure living.

Another one of the words that means so much to me is *beauty*. "Oh," says one, "beauty is nothing." Yes it is, my friend; true beauty is a great thing. The beauty of face and form, which is denied to most people, is not what is referred to, although no one should despise that, as it is a gift that comes from the great Creator's hand. In youthful days beauty meant to me, a pretty face—soft, fair skin, bright eyes, rosy cheeks, and an abundance of nice hair as a soft background. How many times has sadness filled my heart because it was not mine, and when I beheld a beautiful face my eyes would follow it in all its varied changes, as if to absorb every individual feature of its beauty. Often we do not stop to analyze our feelings, and wonder why we have certain desires. It is natural for the human heart to desire what it admires. If one is a lover of the beautiful and appreciates its worth, it is not strange that he should desire to have it as his own. What is the advantage of beauty of face? Does one want it to give pleasure, or is it to attract attention to one's self? The only true beauty of face exists where the possessor is perfectly unconscious of its charm, and the feelings and emotions are expressed with such unconcern and clearness, that the face seems to be an index to the *heart of beauty*. Some have fair complexion, fine eyes, and beautiful hair, and the face, in repose, seems to be perfect; but let worldliness have control, and many an evil shadow falls upon it, that robs it of its fairness. How many times we see a face that would be beautiful but for individual characteristics that spoil it. Whether pride, selfishness, fretfulness, discontent, ambition, hard-heartedness, or any other unholy characteristic, the most beautiful face would be clouded and lined by it.

Many years have passed since I became willing to be considered "very plain-faced;" for beauty produces a charm that requires great wisdom to use aright. How many times it has been the cause of its possessor's ruin can never be told. On every side we hear the cry, "My beauty was a snare that cast me down." Another saying is, "Beware of a pretty face." Surely the work of the Creator's hand is good if properly used, and every one who possesses this gift should see that it glorifies God. Our sons need to consider this subject carefully and thus be so prepared that it does not prove a snare to them. Sometimes a young man thinks his face and appearance is a fortune to him, and he does not need to put forth the effort that others do to attain a position in life, but will trust to it to carry him through. It may do so, but it is at the cost of true manliness.

There is a beauty that belongs to man, that is certainly desirable; not because of its attractiveness to others, but because of its real worth. I refer to that beauty of heart, life, and face that is given by the salvation of Jesus. There may be many beautiful things in this world, but none to be compared to this. The salvation of Jesus removes sin from the heart with all its unlovely fruit, and implants therein love—love to God and to all mankind—which makes one kind, gentle, faithful, meek, submissive, unselfish, long-suffering, temperate, patient, reverential, liberal, courageous, and Godly. These blessed endowments show a heart of purity, and a life of holy living that transforms the plainest face into features of beauty. God himself will "beautify the meek with salvation."

You have seen plain faces good looking and you could not tell why. To a mother surrounded by her dearly beloved children, there is imparted to the face an expression hallowed by mother love, which no artist has yet been able to correctly portray. Should she dwell on life's discouragements and weary of labor and care, the face as an index would quickly show it. Oh, that our privilege to lay all our burdens upon Jesus might encourage our boys to such purity of life during youthful years as to grow into manly looking men, without the blemish of impurity upon their features!

Did you ever notice the honest clearness in the eyes of some? They look into ours with purity and trustfulness. Under such scrutiny we quail and quake. Our hearts are awakened with consciousness of guilt, and then comes to us a longing to be better. Oh, that our eyes should be "windows of the soul" through which those in need may read silent messages of love, helpfulness, and courage. Have we pure hearts? If we have, pray God that the expression of our faces, the intonation of our voices, and that our every action shall show it forth and thereby glorify God in heaven who gives it.

> As sinks the sun behind the hills,
> The earth with brightest tints it fills;
> It lights yon cottage till it seems
> Too fair for aught but childish dreams.

> Canst see that young and noble maid
> Who watches now the tintings fade?
> Canst see the holy light that beams,
> The noble purpose as it gleams
> From every feature of the face?
> 'Tis this that gives her charming grace.

HONOR, NOBLENESS, AND BEAUTY.

> She stands and dreams, but seems to draw
> A lesson from each perfect law.
> "My work! my work! I wish I knew
> What now the Lord calls me to do;
> For I must work for him, who gave
> His precious life, for me, to save."

> "I see it now, how sweet it seems,
> To *shine for him* as holy beams
> Of love, of truth, of peace, and grace
> Shall fill the heart and light the face,
> And help dear souls to home above,
> Where all are blest in God of love."

A love for the beautiful is one of the finest sentiments of human nature. It should be cultivated by allowing the heart and mind to be moved by the beautiful in nature, and receive such lessons therefrom as will glorify the Creator. As we look upon the earth, wrapped in its garments of white, and each little snow crystal glows with rainbow tints under the shining sun, our souls drink in its loveliness, and we spontaneously worship God who makes the heart of man "whiter than snow," and fills it with "the light of life," which causes it to shine for Jesus. As our eyes behold the earth with its carpet of green, and our senses feast upon its beauty such as stately trees, and lovely flowers, we are reminded that "Solomon in all his glory was not arrayed like one of these." The rose and lily speak in sweetest accents: "I am the rose of Sharon and the lily of the valley."

"The heavens declare the glory of God: and the firmament showeth his handiwork. Day unto day uttereth speech, and night unto night showeth knowledge." The waves of the sea say as they roll the surf and wash the sand of the seashore: "Though thou walkest through the waters, they shall not overflow thee;" "He hath set a bound to the sea that it cannot pass over." And when the storm clouds hover over, the sweet voice of comfort murmurs, even amid the mighty roar of the winds: "He that dwelleth in the secret place of the Most High shall abide under the shadow of the Almighty"; "Thou shalt not be afraid for the terror by night."

As we look upon the great and high mountains, whose tops are laden with ice and snow, the voice of the Psalmist in the strength of consolation is: "Beautiful for situation, the joy of the whole earth, is Mount Zion, on the sides of the north, the City of the Great King. God is known in her palaces for a refuge." Then Paul takes up the sweet song and says in love: "Ye are come unto Mount Zion, and unto the city of the living God, the heavenly Jerusalem, and to an innumerable company of angels, to the general assembly and church of the first-born, which are written in heaven, and to God the judge of all, and to the spirits of just men made perfect, and to Jesus."

As the sun sinks from sight beyond the hills, and leaves its glorious light, tinting clouds, sky, and earth with splendor, the soul is filled with joy as it wishes the close of life may be thus beautiful. The words come ringing in our ears as rich and rare music: "The Lord shall be thine everlasting light, and the days of thy mourning shall be ended."

HONOR, NOBLENESS, AND BEAUTY.

Then let us place around these words
A halo bright and glowing,
To say to all in ev'ry place,
You now should stop the sowing
Of all that mars the use of these,
When of your life we're speaking—
That *honor* bright and *nobleness*
With *beauty* true you're seeking.

EDUCATION.

First among the ambitions of every boy should be to obtain a good education. It prepares him for much greater usefulness in life. God has made man a threefold being, consisting of body, mind, and soul. The three are so united that one cannot be neglected without seriously affecting the others. The body should have proper care in order to preserve health and life. The mind must be cared for and developed in order that it may properly minister to soul and body. The soul should receive full consideration as the immortal part of our being. A man, in the true sense of manhood, never fails to properly care for the development of his spiritual nature. In turn, the developed spiritual being, greatly ennobles and perfects the mind and body.

As we study the many problems of life in the concrete, it must be remembered that each individual problem is to be considered, as it bears upon the entire being, body, mind, and soul. Anything that injures one part affects the whole, and hinders the full carrying out of God's designs in relation to man, the noblest of his handiwork. How wonderfully man is formed, and what high and glorious possibilities lie before him. How necessary therefore that he live well the life given him.

As a child begins to reason, a multitude of unknown things appear before him for solution. At first the world to him is chiefly the home circle; mother and father nearest, dearest, and best. His own wants and wishes absolutely rule his actions. As his will and desires are controlled and directed he begins to feel the power that contends against him, and gradually yields to the stronger will and enters a teachable and inquiring state. He now feeds upon what he can see, hear, feel, and learn from questioning. The mind should be encouraged to activity and directed into proper channels. One of the first experiences impressed upon the memory is starting to school. His world begins to enlarge, books open up new fields of thought, and the mind acquires greater strength. Some are so awakened to effort that the mind bids fair to outrun the strength of the body, and must be held in check, that there be no hindrance to equal development. Many parents rejoice to see the mental activity of their children, and push them along as fast as possible, regardless of the physical condition, and are much surprised when dullness of perception occurs. Remarks made in regard to it often produce discouragement in the child and affect its whole future. So the mind should not be forced into greater activity than the health and strength of the child can bear. Other things being equal a healthy, strong body should be accompanied by strength of intellect.

How beautiful it is to notice the craving for instruction that should be manifest in every intelligent child. It is essentially desirable that the instruction be such as will encourage them to the greatest usefulness. The information gained should, as far as possible, be put into daily use. When a child learns to read, he should understand that what he has learned will enable him to gain further knowledge. Books containing useful information should be put into his hands, and daily use made of his ability to read. Many parents seem to think that reading, writing, and arithmetic are accomplishments that are to be laid aside for safe keeping, and work with hands should be the principal object of life. Children sometimes become tired of home, because it is to them only a dreary place for daily labor, when the mind and heart crave something more. We older people with our aims and objects before us as encouragement to our efforts should not forget that the children have need of the same as incentives and encouragement in labor and intellectual development. Many children love sport so well that unless they are restricted, all their time will be spent in that way, to the neglect of the mind.

With all the facilities for education that exist today, there is little excuse for ignorance. Any one who really wants an education and manifests that desire in making use of what opportunities he has will find friends and help to better things. Good education and its proper use will solve many of the problems in life. Ignorance and vice too often go hand in hand.

Many boys would have made their mark in the world if their natural abilities had been properly directed and educated. Not having their time occupied in study, they sought other fields of activity, which generally led them downward to the gratification of fleshly lusts and desires. How it must grieve the Creator to see the work of his hands thus dishonored! Dear boys—whoever read these words—will you not encourage in yourselves, and all you meet in life's pathway, the desires of that better nature that craves useful knowledge?

We often read of men who have accomplished much for the good of nations or individuals, who had to gain their education under many difficulties; but through perseverance and the proper use of every opportunity they succeeded, and were made stronger men and thus prepared for the great works which they accomplished.

Sometimes people seem to be educated above their surroundings, but it ought to elevate the most humble labor to have it done in the best manner that educated and thoughtful minds could conceive. Education unapplied is of small value to its possessor. Every one who has this blessing should endeavor to employ it as a talent entrusted to him for improvement.

Every station of activity and duty is better filled by educated men and women, if their wordly knowledge does not lift them above the teaching of Jesus Christ. An uneducated spiritual mother will fill her place better than one who is educated, but devoid of the salvation of Jesus; and this holds good in regard to fathers, husbands, brothers, and sons, as well as in every position in life. Those places that cannot be filled by those having salvation had better be left unfilled. Education is a great power that may be used for harm as well as for good; therefore it is necessary that the heart's education keep pace with that of the mind.

The tendency of increased knowledge is to lift up into pride, which seeks not heavenly wisdom but often tries to overthrow it by the accumulated knowledge and teachings of men. The Bible says: "Not many wise men after the flesh, not many mighty, not many noble, are called: but God hath chosen the foolish things of the world to confound the wise; and God hath chosen the weak things of the world to confound the things which are mighty."—1 Cor. 1:26, 27. Also, "The wisdom of this world is foolishness with God." A few people understand this to teach that it is not best to seek an education, and permit their children to grow up in ignorance; and point to their lack of education as an evidence of humility. An uneducated person, because of his lack of knowledge, may assume and take responsibilities for which he is altogether unfitted, while one with greater education, is capable of understanding the actual greatness of the responsibilities, and would not feel qualified to assume them. I do not wish to be understood, however, that education always prepares one to fill a position of usefulness.

It is the belief of many, that every minister of the gospel should be well educated in all branches of worldly knowledge, but often some one with very little learning accomplishes more for God and the salvation of souls than those more perfectly educated. A number of the early Christian workers were unlearned men, yet ably filled the place to which God called them. Still one of the greatest " was educated at the feet of Gamaliel."

Education, therefore, is good, and should be sought after by the young, who should improve every opportunity, but withal, be in perfect subjection to the grace of God in the heart. An educated worker in the vineyard of the Lord should realize just as much dependence upon God for help and the anointing of the Holy Spirit for service as one who is not educated. It is not fine language, grammatical sentences, oratory, nor logic that wins souls to Christ; but the Spirit of God using the precious truths of his word and applying them to the heart in such love and power as to convict of sin, of righteousness, and of the judgment to come. Still the anointing of the Spirit may employ fine language, grammatical sentences, oratory, and logic, for the good of souls in carrying them beyond themselves unto the mighty power and truth of God. Some precious souls must have truth so presented to the mind that it is convinced beyond doubt of that truth, before the heart can be touched by the Spirit in applying the truth for individual benefit; while others yield easily to the work of the Spirit upon the heart, and receive the truth in experience without a full comprehension of the mind. In order to meet the different needs of individuals God sends whom he will and where he will, and each worker should have a glad *Yes* in his heart for every call to service; as God cares for the result, as that is his business, if we are careful to do our part in his fear.

Young people should never yield to a " don't-care " spirit in regard to any useful knowledge. Here is a young man who was careless at school and did not learn to spell well. Other branches of common-school education have been faithfully mastered; so he enters business with good prospects of success. He soon has need of correspondence with business men, and his poor spelling is the cause of some trouble and vexation; but he throws it off with the assurance. " I never could spell correctly, even when in school." How much better to provide himself with a pocket dictionary, and when writing refer to it for the doubtful words, and then mark them and in spare moments commit them to memory by repetition orally and in writing. It may be some trouble at first and seem like an endless job; but perseverance works wonders, and before he is aware the bugbear of bad spelling is overcome and he has gained much in several ways.

Some will not write letters because they do not compose as well as others, or do not know how to punctuate or use capitals properly; and thus they lose one of the finest opportunities of happiness and usefulness. How much comfort, gladness, and good a nice letter may give our friends can not be realized by those who have not stopped to consider. Letter-writing, as all else, should be done thoroughly, with the purpose of helping others, receiving good ourselves, and thus for the glory of God. Anything that is worth doing is worth doing well, and God is willing to give us time to do properly whatever he calls us to do. This he taught to me in a very forcible manner a number of years ago. The Lord had filled me with his Spirit and there was a great care for souls resting upon my heart. I did not stop to consider everything carefully, but, as I felt the need of doing all I could to help others to the Lord, I allowed myself to feel in a great hurry to get the housework done, to be ready for other labor. One day I was washing, and had hurried all forenoon to get through but had a few garments to rinse after dinner. As I was hastening in this last effort over the wash, my baby girl came near, and as I put in the last garment to wring, she laid her little hand on the cogs and in an instant I had run her thumb through, cruelly mashing it. I took the child in my arms with the consciousness that I was blamable. Her father was called and everything done to relieve her suffering, without success. Then the thought came, "Take her to the Lord in prayer." I took her in my arms and fled away to a chamber to be alone with God. As I laid her on the bed and knelt by her side, I was conscious there was something for me to learn in it, and so asked the Lord to teach me what he would; and then heal my child. The day's labor came before me, and I saw it was because of my great haste that the accident had happened, and then the Lord spoke to me in this way: "If I want you to do anything, I will give you time to do it." Then I saw that the washing, as my necessary work, was what he had given me to do, and in hurrying it overmuch I had neglected other work he had given me, also the care of my children. The lesson was learned in an instant and then the Lord healed the child, and in a moment she was asleep. I moved and pressed the thumb without her moving or showing the least sign of pain, and she never complained of it again; al- although it received several knocks from herself, and it was several days before it was entirely well.

Many fail to do what God wants them to, because they do not make use of their opportunities to prepare themselves, and feel too hurried to use the necessary carefulness. Often since then I have noted failures on this line, and have seen how it hindered God's work. We should ever "be diligent in business," that is, lose no time unnecessarily; but not to rush things as the world does. Overhaste is sure to produce inferior service.

There are boys and girls who are giving themselves to the service of the Lord, whose hearts are filled with earnest longings to help others into the love of God. Their opportunities of usefulness seem limited, and they wonder what they can do to help in the gospel work. Each one should be careful and observing not to neglect any chance for present usefulness, and then use every opportunity to prepare for the future by earnest study of the word of God, secret devotion, and diligent effort for the acquirement of useful knowledge that shall prepare for a wider sphere of unselfish service. God will greatly bless and help them in strengthening their minds and memories, and in directing into right channels of knowledge.

If every Christian, old and young, were more intent upon obtaining, retaining, and using knowledge and wisdom aright and for God's glory, there would be greater activity and more efficient workers for the good of souls, and heathen lands would soon hear of Jesus the Redeemer.

>
> Then let there be no idle days,
> No moments, and no years,
> To pass in careless joy or ease,
> In sinful doubts or fears,
> To keep us from enchanted ground
> Of knowledge pure and true;
> But live and learn, then learn and live;
> And ever find it new,
> To prove the lessons that we learn
> Are helping others too.

HABITS.

ANYTHING persisted in for a length of time becomes a habit. If one rises for a few weeks at an early hour, it becomes so natural to awaken at that time that he has gained the habit of early rising, which is a very good one and will be a great blessing all through life. If one accustoms himself to retiring late and rising late he is termed a keeper of "late hours," which is many times a great hindrance to his advancement in usefulness, and is therefore a bad habit.

The power of repetition is great. Let one who is not a musician learn to play one tune; as soon as he seats himself at an instrument of music his fingers almost involuntarily take the positions learned, and what seems to have no place in memory is felt in the hands as they move from key to key. The mind also requires habits of rest and of action, according to use. If study occupies certain hours of the day, it turns to that employment at the regular hours, but if light reading is indulged in, it longs for that, and will not take easily to earnest application. So we see th necessity of being careful in our actions, not to form such habits as will be harmful to us in later years.

There are some habits that we want to talk about for a while because they are so full of evil and yet look so innocent to many people, and we hope our sons will not lightly pass over whatever is made clear to them as against these habits.

We will take them up about as they generally appear in boys' lives. You know there comes a time in many of their lives when they begin to think they are " getting most too big to listen to mother's lectures," meaning mother's quiet talks encouraging them in good things. They begin to feel that the world laughs at many good things, and think it better to follow after " some things that are not *too good*." Did you ever realize why that feeling comes? It is because they think that evil things are manly, and good things are womanly, or babyish. Many mothers teach their children to pray, and encourage them in it until they begin to be ashamed to be found praying; and as they are a little rebellious, mothers give up, with the assurance, " Well, I have taught you to pray; and now if you don't do it, the fault will be yours." Unbelief is strong and comes against the children as well as against the older ones and should be driven back by the teaching of God's word, which is the giver of faith; for " faith cometh by hearing, and hearing by the word of God."

One of the first evil habits which appears attractive to boys is " bad words " which they use when parents are not near. These words are sometimes dirty words that are unfit to be spoken by any one, much less the sons of loving mothers.

Sometimes they are slang phrases which mean more than boys comprehend. I remember hearing a child use an evil expression several times after being reproved for it. So I called her to me and asked her why she used those evil words. She said all the children at school used them to one another. Then I told her if she would be sure not to use them again, I would tell her what they meant; and oh, how surprised and disgusted she looked as she said, "I never thought such ugly things could be in such little words"! Never afterwards was she heard to use them.

Now, boys, if the use of "bad words" makes boys appear more manly, why do you not use them when in the society of grown people? Says one, "I only use them when mad at something." Well, if that is manly, why do you not do that before friends? Now do you not see that you do know it is wrong and your conscience reproves you for doing so; and that is what makes you want to be alone when you use them, or with those who encourage to do evil?

While teaching school I had very much trouble with my schoolboys on this line until I adopted a certain kind of punishment. In my desk I kept a cup, a piece of soap, and little cloths; and when any one was heard to use impure language he was called in and given a little talk on how filthiness of language defiled a person, and as the mouth was the offending member, it must be thoroughly washed with good soap-suds. They would think it so strange to punish that way that big and little would take it quietly at my hands, and go away looking much ashamed; and as I have met them in later years they always remembered me as "the teacher who washed our mouths for 'bad words,'" and some acknowledge great benefits therefrom as an impressive object lesson on impure speech. If the mouth is thus defiled by the evil passing from it, how much more impure must be the heart that holds the evil in readiness for some opportunity to emit its poison to defile some innocent mind with evil thoughts! The heart is the fountain of all evil, and if it is washed clean and made pure by the blood of Christ, then there will be no trouble with "bad words" coming forth at everything that would annoy.

As a boy gets accustomed to the use of bad words he is soon ready for something stronger and so takes up "swearing," and tries to feel quite big when he "can swear like a man."

Oh, how many times he has to fight his conscience for hours, and feels so mean he would be glad if mother would not look at him or speak words of love to him. Oh, that mothers were always wise and would know what was the trouble and help the boys to stand against evil habits, by being strong for right and having decision for the boys. Half the trouble comes from parents not commanding the boys and girls with real decision that is felt by them.

You may ask, "Why is swearing wrong?" Because it is irreverence for God when he has told us to love him with all our heart, mind, and strength. If any-one loves another, he is not going to speak lightly of that one or bring his name into contempt of others. All those who have read the Bible or heard of God's love and mercy have no excuse for profaning his holy name, or sacred things of truth and righteousness. One who has been brought up in such an atmosphere of irreverence and ungodliness as never to hear that precious name used but in derision and scorn, should make inquiry into the matter until he knows what he is doing and why he is doing it. Because of careless indifference many are in ignorance of very important things which pertain to life and godliness. With Bibles scattered broadcast over the countries of civili-zation, and millions of professing Christians, is it not strange that there should be so many poor perishing people who never have heard the name of God or the Savior Jesus spoken but in words of cursing? Does *every one* or *any one* try to tell all they can of the power in the name of Jesus to save from all sin and wickedness? Oh, I fear many of us are but unfaith-ful servants who are feasting ourselves instead of feed-ing the hungry. How many of our sons will make the resolve that by the help of God, whenever they hear one using these names in profanity they will ask the ones so doing if they are aware that there is power enough in those names to save and purify from all sin every human being who has ever lived or will live upon this earth, and thus prepare them for a more glorious one? And oh, *our boys,* can it be possible, with this great and glorious truth known unto you, that you will be so unwise, so rebellious, as to pass it by unheeded and lift your voices in scorn of those names that are able to still by a single touch the tongue that speaks so boldly? "Beware—take care."

Many of the sons to whom we are talking have some good person of their acquaintance for whom they have great respect. Perhaps it is father, mother, grandfather or grandmother, uncle or aunt, a preacher or a friend. Now, you who are learning to use " bad words" or to swear, what would you think of that good person if he or she should do as you do, use dirty, bad words or swear? "Oh," says one, "I know father or mother wouldn't do so: but then, John does when he drives the horses and cows." Well, young man, whom do you respect the most—your father and mother, or John, whom you have only known about two months? "Oh, my father and mother, of course; for they are just as good folks as ever lived." "Well, if that is so, why do you not pattern after them instead of after John?" "Oh, I don't know; I never thought very much about it before in that way."

Another boy says, "Why, 'twould be awful to hear our dear old grandpa or grandma swear—why, just think how sweet and good they talk all the time! It makes me think of heaven every time I sit and talk with them, and they always speak so lovingly of Jesus and God. Oh, I'd feel awful bad to hear either of them use swearing words. But then, there was that butcher, who bought our cows; when he came for them he just swore a streak, and snapped his whip and acted as big as anybody could: and I've heard folks say he's a good man—gives lots of meat to poor folks, and saves the best pieces for sick people, and gives lots of money to everything that is good. It seems sometimes that there are two kinds of good people." Yes, dear boy, there are two kinds of people who are thought to be good. The first kind are those who love God and do his will and live humbly before him, like your grandpa and grandma. Then there are those who do many good things, like the butcher, are kind to the poor and sick, and help on good efforts by giving their money liberally. Yet, could you think he loved God and was trying to please him when he would use his name profanely?

There are many people like him, who are good when they want to be and bad when they want to be—good in one way and bad in another. But God's people are *always* good; for he keeps them so; and the other class are no better before God than their very worst actions make them; and for them they must suffer, unless they repent and forsake the wrong.

This boy says earnestly: "Look here! my Aunt Mary is just the nicest little woman in the world, and I'd just as soon think of angels swearing as to think of her doing it. Why! she wouldn't be 'our Aunt Mary' if she'd ever talk the least bit bad. But then, when Uncle Sam and I went fishing the other day you ought to have heard him swear when his foot slipped into the water—he just looked at it, then at the ugly place on the bank, then at the dirt on his pants; and then he just swore like a good fellow. When we went home and grandma saw it, she said, 'Why, Sammie, how did that happen?' and before he could answer she had a cloth and was cleaning the mud from his pants, saying, 'My poor boy; I suspect you got angry again.' He laughed and said, 'I should think I did.' She looked sad, but kissed him and told him to 'be a good boy and please mother.' She loves him very much, so I guess he can't be very bad, if he does swear: and he's so brave, he isn't afraid of anything; and brave men are called noble men, so I'd like to be a man like my Uncle Sam." Did you ever think how boys begin to copy after the bad traits of character rather than the good? Now this boy who wants to be like Uncle Sam will begin by taking up his bad habits of getting angry and swearing and perhaps using tobacco, instead of cultivating his courage into true bravery.

Here is a young man who uses the strongest and vilest language when with his rough companions, but he would not like to have "my little Nellie" know he ever used any but the very best language, which he uses when in company with her. He knows she would be shocked if any one should tell her; so he hopes no one will, and after a while when everything is settled he will move to the next town and make a nice home and give up these boys and rough talk.

So you see boys and young men do have a real regard for what is good and pure, and yet they think it manly to do just the opposite. Do you not think, boys, that it looks a little childish to manifest such a desire for manliness as to take up such things to show it off? Can you not wait a few more years and let height, strength, and wisdom show you have attained manhood? And what shall we do for you to convince you that the good man is the manly one, because he has the courage to do right?

The next bad habit is " doing ugly things for fun." Treading on dresses, looking innocent, begging pardon, and laughing over it with the boys. Filling the girls' rubbers with balls of mud, and then laughing and teasing when the girls get cross and " wish that boy would show his smartness some other way." Pinning mother's apron-strings to her chair, and " laughing fit to kill " when she turns it over as she rises from it. Putting the saddle on wrongside to, when bringing up the horse for father, on a dark night. Thus keeping the entire family on the lookout for pranks and jokes. While some say " boys will be boys," and try to laugh off the annoyance and care, any one can see that such boys bring more sorrow than joy by their childish doings in search for fun, and will be glad when they get too big for such amusement.

Another very bad habit is telling falsehoods just to have people argue, and then finally admit the truth and " wonder why folks must always believe a body when in fun." So it continues until no one believes him under the strongest assurance, and he has formed a habit that will cling to him as long as he lives, unless broken by the power of salvation. Those who play with fire must expect to get burned. This is one of the most disagreeable habits, as it extends to every part of life, entering into the happiness and welfare of friends and acquaintances. It is one of the most dishonorable practices any one can enter into. It may begin in play, continue in carelessness, and become a settled disposition, arising from an evil heart and a sinful practice.

There are more evil habits that we must talk about separately in order to examine into them carefully so our sons will shun them and avoid much trouble and sorrow for the future.

As the power of repetition is great it works for good just as strongly as for evil. Good deeds repeated for some time become easy to perform. It may seem hard to take up a line of duty for a while, but as it is persevered in the nature becomes accustomed to it and it becomes easy and pleasant. Then may we not hope that some of the boys will learn such good ways as will make them a blessing wherever they go? How nice it is to see a good, kind, thoughtful, pleasant, well-mannered boy, who is respectful to his elders and reverential toward sacred things.

"The habit of ill-doing requires less effort than the habit of well-doing. Even without effort we fall naturally into the way of being wrong and doing wrong. Going down hill is always the easiest way going. But well-doing requires effort; for it is uphill work." The reason for this is that we have sinful hearts that naturally incline toward evil-doing, and that is why evil ways are more attractive than good ways. Then, perhaps, some one may think, "Well, we are not responsible for that." Yes, every one is responsible after he knows right from wrong, and should guide his footsteps into right paths, even though it require much effort. The greater the effort needed the greater necessity for the effort, as that shows the strength of the evil nature.

Few individuals expect to spend their lives in evil habits and ways. They think they can do what they want to and stop when they wish. Many a young man will look in contempt upon an older one who will acknowledge his bondage to evil ways, and firmly assure him: "If you *want to, you can stop;* for what one wants to do, he surely can." Some of course have stronger will-power and endurance than others, but there are many habits that bind with fetters of iron the victims of their allurements. As an illustration of this power, take a boy and cast a thread around his arms to pinion them to his side, and with a slight effort he breaks the band and sets himself free. Cast the thread a few times around them, and still he can quickly deliver himself; but let it be cast around him twenty times and he begins to see that there is a possibility of becoming so entangled that he cannot do so. Let the slender thread cover his entire body, and he is as firmly bound as if he were tied with heavy and strong cords. Applying this to evil habits, one who smokes, chews, or drinks a few times a week may for a week feel no bondage to them and may be able to break away from them as the boy tied with a single thread; but let it be repeated each week for a month and he may begin to see danger ahead. Let it continue a year, perhaps two, and one can generally see that there is small desire to be free, as the evils become so pleasurable that the will is captured. Sometimes conscience arises to action and gains the consent of the will that it is wise to stop. Then begins a battle of will against habit strengthened by effects of poison in the system. Generally it is an unequal contest and habit is winner. The boy bound by threads may easily be set free by a friend with knife or scissors. So those bound by habits may be set free by the friend of sinners, Jesus Christ, for his salvation breaks every bond and sets the captive free.

Here is a little letter on this subject that ought to open some one's eyes to see the need of keeping clear from evil habits.

Dear Boys: I feel like writing you a letter to give you the benefit of my experience. When I was about sixteen years old the suggestion came to me, "You should learn to smoke." I listened to the evil voice of temptation, and began to cultivate the habit. At first I only smoked one cigar a week, and that on Saturday evening. In a short time I wanted to smoke more often; so bought a pipe and smoked several times a week. The habit grew on me, and after a while I was a perfect slave to it. Then I began to see the evil and resolved to quit, but it had such a hold upon me that I could not get free. In the meantime I had cultivated the habit of playing cards. It was begun just for pastime, but afterwards I wanted to play for money, and this habit also grew upon me as the tobacco habit; also playing billiards and pool—they are all very evil habits, and it is a very hard matter to get rid of them. I tried several times to get rid of these habits that I had taken up and cultivated, but without success. At last I resolved to get free from these bonds of the Devil by getting free from him. So I gave myself to the Lord, and when I met the conditions of his word he accepted me as his child, giving me grace to set me free. Thus was I delivered from my habit. But it is easier to bend a twig than a tree; so it is easier to come to the Lord before one becomes entangled with these ungodly habits. While praising the Lord for this deliverance, my prayers are ascending for you, that you may be thus blessed with this perfect and free salvation.

Your brother in Christ,
Lewis E. Smith.

HABITS.

Thus these habits one by one
Form a chain around thee, son;
Break it quickly and be free,
Ere it's welded fast to thee.

If you do not, then you may
Be a slave, and rue the day
When you first began to do
"Just like others" that you knew.

Did you ever think, my boy,
While you hope to find a joy
In each one, of habits bad,
That you make your mother sad?

Do you think it good and kind,
Hunting joy, to ever bind
Sadness, pain, and heavy care
On to her whose love you share?

May these habits one by one
All be "let alone," my son,
Proving manhood, strength, and will
Keep thee free, and ever fill

Mother's heart with joy and praise,
That will bless thee all thy days,
Please thy God, and help thee seek
Purer joys among the meek.

Purer joys in higher ways,
Purer hours, and better days,
Purer life, and sweeter breath,
Purer friends, and happy death.

THE TOBACCO HABIT.

An evil habit that often fascinates the boys is the use of tobacco. Why it should appear nice to them is a mystery to me, as the very appearance of chewing and smoking has always been so repulsive to me that I had to exert myself to avoid indifference toward the users of the disagreeable stuff. Nevertheless it is true that many boys do see something manly in chew, chew, and spit, spit, and in smelling strong and unpleasant. They generally have a hard time in learning to use it, as it makes them sick. If they had to work half so hard to please father as they do to become accustomed to the filthy weed, they would think him very unkind. So you see, they will do more to acquire a bad habit than they would to please a good friend.

Surely the Bible is true when it says, "Foolishness is bound up in the heart of a child." And shall we mothers just as firmly believe that "the rod of correction shall drive it far from him"? There is not the decision used against these things that there should be. If some one were to offer a deadly poison to our children, we would raise up in all the strength of parental love and protect them from it: but when some one tempts them to use the poisonous weed, many dear parents assume the attitude of helplessness and say, "Well, I suppose he will learn some time, like the majority of boys do; so there is no use feeling bad about it or making any fuss." If parents will restrain them until they get to years of manhood, they may then be so well instructed in regard to its evil workings as to count it safer and better to "let it alone."

After it is an acquired habit it is almost impossible to break, as its effects are all through the system so that the entire being craves its continuance. There are a few who "leave off tobacco," but they are very few. If we ask those who use it why they do not quit its use, many will say candidly, "*I can't*. I have tried to, but there is such a craving for it, that I am in distress until I use it again." Is that a fine picture of manhood? Is that personal liberty that is valued so highly? Dear boys, is that really where you wish to be all through life? Is that your ambition while you are learning? Is that not bondage; and if bondage, is not tobacco master? And if it is master, who is the slave? Now, if you were my boys and I knew you were learning to use it, I would keep these words in letters large in every available place so your eyes should see them until they rested upon heart and mind in letters of fire—*Tobacco Slave*. Where is the boasted manliness of such a condition? Bound to chew or smoke no matter how offensive it is to father or mother, brothers or sisters, wife or children. Bound to use it and pay out money for it no matter if the dear ones go without sufficient food or raiment.

Must have it, when the children are obliged to stay away from school from lack of shoes and books. Must have it, although what is spent for it in a few years would provide a comfortable home for the dear ones. Must have it, even if it causes all manner of disease and suffering and makes weak hands provide for a fatherless family of little ones. Must have it, though its use causes one to lose his soul because he loves it more than God. Oh, the heathenish god Tobacco! How it stirs our souls with holy indignation to hear people complaining about hard times, having no home, no clothes, no food; and yet using from five to fifty dollars a year for that which does not answer for food or anything else that is good.

"Well," says one, "it is work, work, work, all the time to provide for the family and one ought to have a little pleasure as he goes along. My tobacco is great company to me." How is that? I never heard anyone say that their food and drink were great company to them. If it is the movement of the mouth in chew, chew, and spit, spit, you might use elm bark, or wheat, or corn, or anything else that is good and nourishing. You say, "I can't; for nothing suits me but tobacco." Now, can you not see, dear boys, that it is the effect of chewing that is pleasurable just the same as the effect of drinking liquor is pleasurable to the drunkard?

Yes, many are really tobacco drunkards. As the effect of liquor upon the human system while pleasurable for a short time, is very injurious, so also is tobacco; for its use creates a craving for it that can not be satisfied by anything else, and in a degree impairs the system and prevents the natural working of different parts. We are sorry to be obliged to write so plainly about this pet and idol of many of our sons, and yet facts are facts, and it may do some good to state them plainly.

Come, boys, let us stand Mr. Tobacco up for trial, and see what the evidence is against him, and if there is sufficient to convict him as a fraud, a swindler, and a murderer, then we will all bid him good-by and choose a better friend. We will have volunteer witnesses and lay the case before all the boys of the world as jurymen. It is a great case, greater than if all the wealth of the world were at stake; for there are souls, virtue, loved ones, prosperity, and many lives depending upon the decision of our sons.

Now let the boys talk. Who will be the first witness? That is right, John; we will be glad to hear what you have to say about Mr. Tobacco.

(John)—My father is a great hand to figure up the cost of everything, as he says that is business. One day I asked him how long he had used tobacco. He said, "Just forty years last Christmas. Would you like to know how much it has cost me? I counted it up on New Year's day when figuring up our expenses. Of course I can not be very exact, as I don't just remember what I used at first. I was fifteen years old when Uncle John gave me the first chew on Christmas when mother and I went to her father's for dinner.

Uncle John and I were in the barn looking around when he took out his tobacco and took a chew, saying, 'I guess you're about as big as I was when I learned to chew. How would you like to have a taste?' I said, 'Mother does not want me to learn.' He laughed and broke off a piece and put it in my pocket, saying, 'Now when you want to you can.' We walked around the barn-yard talking, and when he took his next chew I took just a little nibble at mine, and so on until dinner was called. I did not feel just right, but went in to dinner, and just as soon as I entered the warm room and smelled the victuals, I turned dizzy and faint and went back to the barn and oh, how sick I was! No Christmas dinner with grandpa and grandma and no long miserable day—just able to drive home for mother and then go to bed and have her wait on me most all night. But I kept chewing a little every week until I could chew as big as anybody. At first, ten cents a week was all it cost me. Mother had been giving me that much a week for building fires in the morning; so I could have something of my own to give for Sunday-school and mission purposes—as I had done until I learned to chew. Then it went for tobacco; so that was about five dollars a year. Then when I went to school in town I chored for my board and was given fifty cents a week for spending money. I used this for candy and tobacco; but most of it went for tobacco; as I had so learned to love it that I would rather have it than candy. That was when

I was seventeen. So we will count that year $15, and that amount for my eighteenth and nineteenth years. I remember quite well that in my twentieth year I spent just $20 for tobacco, and was quite proud of it. After that it was about $25, until my 30th year, when it was $30, and about that much for a number of years; and now for the last ten years it has been about $40. So I counted it up, and I had spent $1,175."

Now, boys, that was just enough to buy a farm that father wanted to purchase for me, but could not as he did not think it right to mortgage the home to do so. I laughed when father told me how much tobacco had cost him, and told him he " had chewed up my farm." He said, " Yes, it has been a tough job; for I have chewed myself sick several times. That last sickness was caused by the tobacco in my system, the doctor said; and he advised me to stop if possible; but here I am, bound to it by fetters I can't break. That sickness cost me a hundred dollars, beside all your mother's hard work and care; but if all this will only influence you to let it alone, I shall be satisfied." I told my father I had heard some preachers claim that religion could stop the use of tobacco by taking away the appetite. I soon noticed him reading the Bible more than usual, and then when summer came he went to a camp-meeting and came home praising God for freedom from tobacco; because the appetite for it was all gone. Then he wanted me to promise him that I would never learn to use it. He said that

if I would not use it, when I became twenty-five years
old he would give me all I saved thereby, at compound
interest at 10 per cent. I have counted it up and it
will be a little over $300 if used just as he used it.
Now $300 is a good large sum just to spend to look
like others, who might make fun about being a "goody,
goody boy." Don't you think so, boys?

Thank you, John, for your nice little talk and for
the figures you give that are stronger than words.
Now, boys, how many of you think this evidence
counts one against Mr. Tobacco on the line of finance?
Why! we cannot count all your hands; so we are sure
it carries, and a good many of you will think many
times before you will agree to chew up that much
money for nothing, but pain and sorrow. If you
worked for a dollar a day at hard farm labor, you
would have to work just one year to make up the loss
for chewing until you were twenty-five years old. Oh,
how awful; to waste our lives in such ways. Now,
who comes next as a witness in this case? Oh, here
is Dr. Smith's son Henry ready with a testimony.

(Henry)—Yes, boys, I am always ready to give a
word against old Tobacco. As my father is a doctor,
he tells me some things that are real interesting, and
sometimes tries experiments. Tobacco is a plant
that was found growing here when America was discovered. It has been one of its chief articles of agri-
culture and commerce, and is now cultivated in nearly every civilized country. There is a story told of
the early settlers buying their wives of the London

Company for a hundred pounds of tobacco at 50cts. a pound, for each one. Then afterward it was 150 pounds. I often think of this when I see girls taking up with men who chew and smoke, when there are far better ones who do not use tobacco. It seems as if they must like it some way, even though they say they do not. Father says it is agreed among scientific men that tobacco in all its forms contains a very strong poison, and there are from two to seven pounds of this nicotine poison in every hundred pounds of dry leaf tobacco. Father keeps a small bottle of this poison, and one day as we were riding in the country we saw several boys just ready to kill a snake. Father called to them to wait a moment, and we drove up close and he got out and held the snake with sticks and then told one of the boys to spit his tobacco juice into its mouth. What do you think happened to it? It just twitched a little, half uncoiled its body, and never moved again. It was dead in an instant. The boys looked so surprised that father asked them if they had anything they wanted killed real easy, and one boy said, "Yes, there is a stray cat that catches chickens." So father told him to get it quick, and in a few moments he returned with it. Father said it was too bad to kill a cat, but maybe a lesson might be learned that would save some one's life, and therefore he would do it. He took out his bottle of nicotine oil and put two drops on the cat's tongue and it was dead in just three minutes by my watch. Then father told the boys that every pound of tobacco contained 320 grains of nicotine and one grain would kill a large dog just as quick as the cat had been killed. The boys were so interested that father told them to come to our house and he would show them something more. So they came last Saturday and he had a couple of frogs, several mice and rats, a snake, and several birds. We called in our neighbors, and had quite a time observing different things. A small piece of wood covered with nicotine oil and placed in a small wound in a bird's leg made it fall insensible in a few seconds, and another one vomited when a little oil was touched to its muscles. The rats and mice acted very strangely when father pierced them with his penknife that had a little oil on it. Some vomited, others were too sick to stand, and one fell over dead. Then father took a needle and thread that had been dipped in the oil, and ran it through the skin of a frog, and in a few minutes it was dead; but it acted like a drunken person, vomiting, hopping about fast as possible, and then lying down and twitching awfully for a moment, and then became insensible and soon was dead. When father got through, the boys all looked sober, and he asked them what they were going to do about it? Two of the boys said firmly: "I'll never chew again; for if that awful poison is in the body, it cannot help doing us harm some time." Several of my neighbor friends did not speak; for they were wondering if they could give it up. The next day two of them told me they were trying hard, and if they succeeded they were going to make my father a nice present. It is almost a week now and they say they have not taken a single chew. I believe they will come out all right, for I told my mother about them and she talked with their mothers concerning it, and so every morning they pray together for the boys. I never knew before how mothers hate to have their boys use tobacco.

Well, Henry, I'm real glad to hear you speak so plainly and forcibly about this matter. And now, boys, what will you do with this testimony? Shall we count it one against Tobacco? "Yes, yes, yes," I hear you say. Suppose those who doubt these experiments try them for themselves, and then they will be ready to give their voice against Mr. Tobacco. Well, boys, who speaks next?

(Charles)—I am Charles, the dentist's son. My father has been a dentist 25 years. He says people talk nonsense when they say tobacco preserves the teeth; for the worst teeth he has to care for are those whose owners are forever chewing tobacco. He says the reason they do not have toothache is because the poison of tobacco contains creosote that deadens the nerves so they do not feel the pain of their badly diseased and decayed teeth; for they are even *worse* than others, as the tobacco injures the gums, and the linings of the stomach and bowels, and therefore affects the teeth, making them wear out faster. Several physicians of renown have asserted that the use of tobacco, because of its poisonous and relaxing qualities, is positively injurious to the teeth, and most physicians agree with them. The teeth of tobacco-users are a dark-brown color instead of a pretty white; for the tendency of tobacco, either in smoke or juice, is to darken whatever it comes in contact with. My father keeps two boxes for the teeth he pulls, and whenever he takes out a tooth he asks the man if he uses tobacco, and if he does, the tooth is put in the tobacco box, and you ought to see the difference between them and the others. Father says to every boy who comes into the office, "Do you want to see my specimens?" And then he gets out the two boxes. You ought to see them look. Father says it is a "good object lesson."

Well, Charles, we are very glad to know about the teeth, for we often hear people say they use tobacco to keep their teeth sound and white, but we see they are mistaken. What shall we do with this evidence presented against Mr. Tobacco? Shall it count one against him? As most of you say "Yes," we will count it one. Who will be the next witness? Oh, here is our friend and neighbor, little Sam. Now, boys, listen carefully while he speaks, as he is so weak he cannot make you hear unless there is good attention.

(Sammy)—I would like to put all my weight and strength against Mr. Tobacco, for I owe him a good fight for what he has done for me. My father and mother both used tobacco for many years before I was born. When I was a baby my father had a sick spell, and as he was a long time getting well he sat in the house smoking most of the time. My mother was not strong. She did not smoke, but chewed, and she said she felt just awful bad and had fainting spells. I was sick also. So when a new doctor came to see a neighbor mother called him in and told him how poorly we all were. He looked at mother carefully, then at my father, who sat smoking, and said he did not wonder at us all being sick in that close room with the tobacco smoke so thick. Then he went on to explain how the smoke is breathed into the lungs as fine particles of poisonous substance that irritate the delicate membranes of throat and lungs, causing inflammation and preventing the organs from performing their natural office. If the room was full of smoke, there was an overabundance of carbonic acid gas, just the substance the lungs are continually throwing off. This prevents the reception of pure oxygen gas, the life-giving principle. He told her much more about the use of tobacco, and she was so thoroughly alarmed that she stopped chewing, and tried to persuade father to give up his pipe. When he looked at me he said unless there was a great change, in less than a month I would be in the grave. Then my mother kept me in another room and made my father open the window when he smoked. So father seeing her concern tried hard to stop smoking and used less and less every day until he stopped in a long and severe illness. When he recovered, the appetite for it was gone and he could hardly bear the sight or smell of the stuff any more.

The doctors agree that my nervous system, my brain,

and my lungs are all affected by tobacco. My father
and mother often cry when I am sick, and wish they
could take my place, as they consider themselves to
blame for my condition; but I tell them that ignorance of the harmful effects of tobacco is the cause, and
I mean to talk all I can against it. I have heard of
different people being healed by the power of God,
and so I am learning to trust the Lord, and after
a while when my faith is stronger I expect to be
healed of the effects of tobacco, and grow up strong
like the rest of you, who never have been injured
by it.

That is right, little Sam; I believe you will be a
man in more ways than one when the Lord heals you;
for you have the true courage of a man, if the body is
weak and small. Now, boys, shall we count this one
against Mr. Tobacco, since it shows the result of
using it, upon helpless little children? "Oh, yes,
yes," you say so earnestly that I am sure you mean it
from the depth of your hearts.

Well, Lewis, speak out; for you surely have something to tell us worth hearing.

(Lewis)—Well, boys, you often hear it said among
us, that some one is so foolish that he will not learn
to smoke or chew, because his mother thinks it is harmful. You have heard enough testimony to show clearly that it is harmful to the pocketbook and to the body,
and now I would like to help you to see that it is harmful to the mind. You know we boys are generally so
strong in body that we are apt to laugh at folks when

they speak of us becoming sick from the use of tobacco. But I know enough about sickness to know it often comes to those who think they are the healthiest and strongest people living. My Uncle Amos was one of those large, strong men, and often remarked in his droll way that he "s'posed he'd live always unless something happened." He chewed and smoked—would sit in his room and smoke for hours, until the room was full of thick smoke, and then he would sleep in it; as he said he did not want a particle of tobacco smoke lost, for it was too good to lose. Grandma often told him to stop doing it, and would air his room good in the daytime while he was at work. A year ago he began to complain of his head, and so was prevailed upon to stop smoking in his room. His head grew worse; so he went to see a doctor, who said the fine particles in tobacco smoke had affected the membranes of the head, and he must stop smoking or he would suffer much more.

He gave it up for a time and appeared much better, but he had such a craving for it that he began to smoke again. One day he became unconscious, and the doctors said the whole trouble was in his head, and recommended quiet and abstinence from tobacco.

He was able to walk around, but seemed to be simple as a little child; just as if the brain had ceased to work because it was benumbed by poison. He was a great care to his parents, although he was quiet and good and never asked for tobacco or seemed to notice much but his parents. At last they began to pray with him and he seemed to like it and gradually got better, until one day he said aloud, "Mother, it was tobacco that did it. I'll never use it again." He got well real fast after that, and was soon at work. But, oh, how differently he acted! He said to me one day, "Lewis, you ought to praise God that your uncle is not in the insane asylum, and that he has his right mind to serve God and let tobacco alone." I asked mother about it, and she said she had seen it stated that there were 70,000 insane people in this country and over 15,000 of them owed their insanity directly to tobacco. So I have made up my mind to think too much of myself to put something into my mouth to steal away my brains. Some young men have been so affected by its power on the mind as to take their own lives. Now, boys, let us be men, and keep our money, our health, and our minds.

It pleases me very much to hear the boys so strong for the right. Now, how many are willing to give this evidence one in count against Mr. Tobacco? Oh, yes; I see you are willing to do so; for you all want to be *strong-minded.* Who comes next upon our witness stand?

Well, Fred, we are all looking to hear something good from you; for you are "your father's own son" and we know he has told you many good things.

(Fred)—Yes, boys, he has; and besides that, I have kept my ears and eyes open the last year and I know some things by careful observation. Father says he has watched many of his friends who began to chew when they were young, and he finds the larger number of them learned to drink and to gamble. He says he is sure tobacco causes a thirst for strong drink and tends toward other gross evils. The appetite is not satisfied with the tobacco poison, but craves something stronger. I saw this statement in a little book on tobacco. "There were 600 prisoners in the State's Prison at Auburn, N. Y., a few years ago for crime committed when under the influence of strong drink. Of these 500 testified that they began their course of intemperance by the use of tobacco. Prison statistics show with scarcely an exception that forgers, defaulters, and swindlers use tobacco, while 97 per cent. of all male convicts first lost their freedom by bondage to tobacco." Now, boys, I do not want to run any risk of being a drunkard or a prisoner, and so I am going to shun the first steps that lead that way—even tobacco.

I am glad to find that our boys can use their eyes and ears and prove it by what they observe. How many think this is strong for one against Mr. Tobacco? Say *yes* quickly; for we want to get through and shut him up in prison before he does any more mischief. Your answers of "Yes, yes," come so thick and fast that it surely means victory on the side of right.

Well, William, I see you are so full of something good against our foe that you can hardly stand still or keep still; so you may have the floor.

(William)—Oh, yes; I am. I feel like boiling

over, but wanted my testimony to be one of the last. I am glad to say I am a Christian boy and look at things very carefully in view of eternity. A year ago the boys told me I was foolish to listen to mother about tobacco; for she was a Christian, and *they* always make so much fuss about little things that they imagine are bad. So I wondered if it was only Christian people who were fighting the use of tobacco, but I find it is not true. Doctors, authors, scientific men, dentists, business men, farmers; yes, all who do not use it and have studied about it, are uniting in condemning it, for the good of the young men and boys. And now we boys are enlisting in the battle, and whether we are Christians or not we will cry out against tobacco.

But I am sure we Christians ought to be stronger against it, as the Lord has opened our eyes to see how it allures the boys into sin and bondage to evil, and hinders them from loving and serving God. When our friend was speaking about tobacco injuring the mind, I thought how awful it would be to be living without the right use of our minds, and then the thought came: How much worse to have our souls dead in sin, not to be able to see, hear, or feel the things of God that pertain to eternal life and glory. I know, boys, if some great king should set before us life and death and tell us we must give up all to have life, we would gladly lay down all our evil habits, our money, our *all* to gain natural life. The King of glory offers eternal life to all who will give up all sin, and love and serve him. It is a rare opportunity to gain present and eternal joys. In order to gain these we must give up the sinful ones, as they would hinder us in the enjoyment of the good; and when he asks us to do so he provides the way by taking away the desire for them. So if you want to give them up, just look to him and he will give the help needed. It makes me so glad to think that the worst case of tobacco slavery is broken by the Lord Jesus. Now, boys, I believe we have evidence enough to convict Mr. Tobacco as the worst tyrant dwelling among boys. So let's sum up the evidence and see.

Well, William, just wait a moment. How many boys really consider the soul the most important part of our being? Oh, I see most of you do. Now how many counts shall we give this evidence against Mr. Tobacco? Many witnesses testify that no earthly power could break their bondage to tobacco, but Jesus has stepped in and delivered from it, taking away even the least desire for it. If Jesus does this, then it shows how very displeasing to him its use is. Shall this testimony count two against Mr. Tobacco? "Yes, yes." Any more evidence before we close the case?

(George)—Yes, indeed! Medical men are awaking to the fact that tobacco is the cause of many of the diseases that destroy life. It not only affects the users of the poisonous and filthy weed, but it seriously affects all who come in contact with it. It is thus sapping the life from the greater part of humanity.

The children inherit appetite for it, disease from it, and weakened minds and energy, with depraved natures, as the result of parental indulgence. There is not a faculty of our being but what is impaired by the use of tobacco poison. One might just as well take a dose of strychnine daily and expect no serious results as to take into the system in different ways this nicotine poison. Sometimes tobacco is used for a stimulant in hopes of obtaining intellectual strength and victory. The hope is a false one, as its tendency is the opposite, producing dullness and indifference toward mental exertion. Dear boys, if you want to be men, strong, wise, pure, and good, leave tobacco to its natural lovers, for food, the great ugly green worms.

Thank you, George. The boys are getting truly awake on this subject and are crying, " Count one against Mr. Tobacco." " Give him to the worms."

(Tom)—I just want to say that we ought to speak a word against our foe for our mothers and homes. Did you think seriously how anxious they are for our welfare? Well, I heard one mother say she would rather see her little boys laid away in their graves than to see them commence chewing; as it generally led to deeper sins that some of us knew nothing about, at least their most serious effects. Another mother said she would be willing to live on cornbread and water to see her sons grow to manhood without forming the habits of chewing, smoking, and drinking. Then think how some of us have punished our best friends by polluting ourselves, our homes, and the air they breathe. I think the home circle has a right to cry out in thunder tones, " Count one for us." I am sure we could go further by thinking of blighted lives, lost hopes, lost aspirations, betrayed confidence, and selfish and unholy desires; but let us close the case and sentence the offender.

Well, boys, you surely will give a good strong count in behalf of mothers and homes. You may not understand it so well now as when you have homes of your own. Let us sum up the evidence briefly.

One count for Finance.
One count for Scientific experiment.
One count for Dentists.
One count for Children's sickness.
One count for the Mind.
One count for Appetite.
Two counts for Soul.
One count for General good of all.
One count for Mothers and Homes.

Now, there are ten good solid counts against our foe. Who can say a word in his favor? Silence reigns! Now, boys, what shall be the sentence? Stand up, Mr. Tobacco, and answer for yourself why the extreme penalty of the law shall not be passed upon you.

(Tobacco)—" Guilty—The only wonder is why I was not sentenced years ago."

(Boys)—Then hear your sentence. Go back to the dark pit from whence you came, and never show yourself in your deceitfulness to another boy or man while this world shall last; and then receive your final sentence from God Almighty.

EXPERIENCE IN THE USE OF TOBACCO.

It is surely wise and right to warn all we can of the evils arising from the use of anything harmful. A druggist who does not label his poisonous articles with their names or signs of poison is considered responsible for all results arising therefrom. While we are not dealing in poisons, we are in gospel truth, and God requires us to warn the people; to cry aloud, spare not, show the people their sins. This means that we are to label all sins with their right names. If tobacco is a poison so strong as to destroy life, as it is acknowledged and proved to be by learned men, then it is high time that we gospel teachers give the proper name to the use of tobacco. So we will in the grace and strength of God, knowing we shall receive severe censure therefor by those who are addicted to its use. Its name is this: *The sin of tobacco poisoning*.

When men hear of young ladies taking small doses of arsenic daily to beautify their complexion, they are horrified, and exclaim in accents of severe censure, "The idiots; don't they know that is ruin to their bodies?" But here are men who count themselves strong-minded, deliberately taking poison into their system to satisfy the unnatural appetite created by its use; for tobacco creates an appetite for itself that cannot be satisfied by a substitute. Often these same tobacco-users will censure in severest terms those who form the habit of using morphine, when they are "riding in the same boat," as both take into their system that which tears them down instead of building them up in health and strength.

"Well," some one says, "I want to enjoy life as I go, and I'm not particular about living very long." But how about your responsibility before God? Has he not entrusted your body, your mind, your soul, and all your faculties for use and improvement as talents?

What will you say when you stand before him in judgment with a defiled and poisoned body, a neglected mind, and a careless and unholy heart? The Bible says, "Blessed are the pure in heart." Do you not know that a woman who is clean and tidy in her own personal appearance will keep a clean and tidy house? for cleanliness works from the center outward. One who is pure in heart delights in purity, and so it works outward into a pure body, a pure life, and pure surroundings so far as one is capable of obtaining them. No one can have a pure heart long without beholding things in their true condition. Heart-purity soon discovers filthiness of the flesh, let it be in habits or in untidiness of dress.

I heard of a preacher who, after many years of religious service, was one evening walking in his yard smoking his favorite cigar. At the same time his mind was wandering into the future and considering the glories of the better world as the dear old-time

> "I want to be an angel,
> And with the angels stand,
> A crown upon my forehead,
> A harp within my hand,"

was being hummed with religious fervor. Then came the thought, "How would you look with a cigar in your mouth amid that purity and splendor?" His soul was condemned, and he threw away the cigar with the decision nevermore to be guilty of so unholy a practice.

Another preacher who had been extremely earnest in his religious efforts and very decided in regard to different lines of Christian duty, was preparing to use his tobacco as a friend entering the room said kindly, "Is that right, brother?" He thought an instant and replied, "Of course it is not. You may have this; I shall never use it again." And he never did. This shows us the necessity of carefully examining everything we do, to see if there is any evil in it, and of receiving instruction willingly.

In the past there was not so much known about the evil results of tobacco, and there was not so much said in pulpit and by press. Many religious papers are taking a decided stand against this evil, and many fearless ministers and workers are proclaiming freedom from all sinful habits.

Why is tobacco-using a sin? is the question of many. Beside the injury done to the body, there is the waste of money which should be used for better purposes, and the selfishness that demands one's own pleasure regardless of others' needs or wishes; then the example set before others, by which many are influenced to begin its use; and the careless indifference to the instruction "Whatsoever ye do, do all to the glory of God;" and the direct disobedience to the exhortation to "cleanse yourselves from all filthiness of the flesh and spirit, perfecting holiness in the fear of God."

We have several letters of experience from those who once used tobacco, but were set free by the salvation of Jesus, and we wish you to read them carefully and observe every point closely, and make a candid and strong decision for your good and the welfare of friends and acquaintances.

CURED OF THE GREAT TOBACCO SIN.

Dear Boys: I will give you a little of my life experience, as it may help you and thus honor God.

My mother died when I was about five years old, and shortly afterward my father bound me out to a farmer who lived about forty miles from our home. I remained there nearly eight years, during which time I was shamefully abused, even almost unto death. Finally, hoping to better my condition I ran away in company with my two older brothers, who brought me to an uncle, who hired me for a year. Soon after my year was finished at uncle's I saw my father, whom I had not seen since he bound me out about nine years before, nor have I seen him since. This was about forty-five years ago.

After this I went to Cincinnati, Ohio, and became an apprentice in a plow factory. Having neither father nor mother, sister or brother, relative or friend, to advise or encourage me for good, while there were many who influenced me for evil, I naturally chose the evil. I do not remember that any one ever advised me for good while I was young.

Not long after I entered upon my apprenticeship, I was advised by men, who should have known better, to chew tobacco to preserve my teeth, but in reality, as I found out afterward, that they might laugh at my distress resulting from the operation of the poison contained in tobacco upon the physical system. I yielded to their wishes, however, partook of their tobacco, mastered the habit, and then became a slave to it. I was a slave to it for years, and despite all my efforts to free myself I failed. Once for about six months, while in the United States army, during the war of the Rebellion, I abstained from its use; but I was still bound to it, as my system craved the tobacco; and when I finally gave up resisting and began to use it again, its taste was just as agreeable as when I had left off using it six months before, and it did not make me sick. My desire was to be free.

When I returned from the army I was a very wicked man and cared little for anything but self and my dear wife, whom God had given me, and who prayed and watched for me during those long three years of separation.

I was discharged from the army in 1865. During the winter following there was a "revival in our church," for I was a member in good standing of the Methodist Episcopal sect, having joined before the war; but though a "church member," the Lord convicted me of my sins, and during the meeting I sought the Lord for two weeks; and as soon as I submitted my will to his and believed his promises with all my heart, he forgave me all my sins, and I went home justified. Oh, what joy and peace! It was beyond my power to tell it.

In those days we were not taught that using tobacco is sin, and I still continued to use it for about five years after I was adopted into the family of God.

In the summer of 1871, in Chicago, Ill., the Lord showed me that it was wrong to use it. I had a sick wife who needed every dime I could get to buy nourishing food for her poor decaying body. One day I had neither money nor tobacco and felt very miserable indeed, and for the first time I prayed as I walked on Clark street, "Oh, God, take away the desire for it." Then the awful desire left me for a little while, but returned again. Afterwards I received some money and bought a dime's worth, promising myself, "When this is gone, I'll buy no more." Finally, when it was nearly gone I took it out to bite a piece off, but the promise I had made came to my mind and I did not bite it, but said, "No, I won't," and began to pray earnestly, "O, God, take away the desire for it"; and, praise God! it was done. There was not the least desire for it, although about two weeks afterwards the Devil tempted me. My brother came home with a cigar in his vest pocket, and I was tempted to snatch it from him and give it to my brother-in-law near by. I took it and was persuaded to light it, "just to see how it tasted." I did so, and it made me sick. Then I promised the Lord I would never use tobacco as long as I lived. Thank God I have never wanted it since. I praise God for a Savior who answers prayer for both soul and body.

Yours, saved in Jesus,
R. W. Swinburne.

Dear Boys: In the name of Jesus and for the good of souls I will give my testimony.

I cannot remember the time that I did not want tobacco, and when I saw others handling it, it seemed that I could not resist taking it from them. I was about ten years old when I first commenced its use, by chewing, and it tasted the best of anything I ever put in my mouth; I even swallowed the tobacco without it making me sick.

I used it about a year before my parents found out that I was using it. My mother wanted to punish me and make me quit the use of it; but my father said that if I had used it that long, it would not be right to punish me to make me quit its use; but if I could possibly stop using it I had better do so; that it would cause me to pay out a good deal of money throughout my life that would not benefit me in the least, etc. But with all that before me he said he did not think I could quit, for it was a birthmark upon me. I could go without my meals easier than without my tobacco; so I continued to use it, and the longer I used it the more I used, until it cost me about sixty dollars a year for the filthy stuff.

When I grew to manhood and wanted to be in company with young people, my tobacco was in the way more or less; so I made up my mind I would quit its use, and so tried with all my own strength to do so, but had to go back to the miserable habit. Thus I tried several times. Once I did without it for a year, but, oh! dear reader, it was the hardest battle I ever fought; because I was fighting it alone. I had not learned to call upon Jesus to help me. Let me tell you just a little, and you that are in bondage to the weed may know of some of the things I went through. I would dream of it nearly every night, see great piles of it corded up and in every way imaginable, and even be handling it, but never get it into my mouth. Oh, how I wanted it! No one can tell the fight I had against it but those who have had the same or similar experience. I am thankful to say that as long as I used the filthy stuff I was careful to be as clearly with it as possible; for I did despise to see any one use it in a filthy manner, having it spatter over their clothes, running down from their mouths, spitting on the floors and in the wood-box, etc. It is no uncommon sight to see pools of tobacco juice in cars, hotels, depots, streets, and all public places, making them extremely disagreeable to ladies with their dainty garments, and all who abhor filthiness. Yes, dear boys, we say it plainly, it is the extreme of filthiness. Is it any wonder that Christ says for us to cleanse ourselves from all filthiness of the flesh? Dear reader, do you need the cleansing? If so, will you not obey the Lord and be made clean?

I used tobacco twenty-five years, and was condemned for its use before I was converted. Although I was not a Bible-reader and did not know much that was in it, I felt that if I ever became a Christian I would be obliged to stop chewing. In July, 1892, under clear gospel preaching I was convicted of my sins and gave myself to God, and being already condemned for the use of tobacco I went to God with it and told him that as I now belonged to him, if he would help me I would give it up; for I had tried so many times that I knew I could never do so alone. My prayer was: "O Lord, just help me this time, and I know the work will be done; for thou canst take away the appetite, and make me so free that I shall never want it again." Praise the Lord! He granted my request right there and then, and I have never wanted it since; for it has been an offense to me ever since that hour. I carried a small piece with me for a time, to see if I would want it, and would sometimes take it from my pocket and smell of it, but it was very offensive to me.

Now, dear boys, if any of you who read this letter are in bondage to tobacco, take it to Jesus and ask him to help you and give you power to overcome it, and I am sure he will do it, if you ask aright; for he is no respecter of persons. If he has done it for me and many others, he is willing to do it for you when you yield yourself to his service, obey his word, and trust his promises. Let me see if he has promised to answer prayer. "And I say unto you, Ask, and it shall be given you; seek, and ye shall find; knock, and it shall be opened unto you. For every one that asketh receiveth; and he that seeketh findeth; and to him that knocketh it shall be opened."—Luke 11 : 9, 10. "And whatsoever ye shall ask in my name, that will I do, that the Father may be glorified in the Son. If ye shall ask anything in my name, I will do it. If ye love me, keep my commandments."—John 14 : 13-15. "And this is the confidence that we have in him, that, if we ask anything according to his will, he heareth us: and if we know that he hear us, whatsoever we ask, we know that we have the petitions that we desired of him."—1 John 5 : 14, 15. We ought to praise God for these promises and claim them as ours, and receive their fulfillment according to our needs. Ever "the boys'" friend,

T. E. Covey.

Dear Boys: I want to give you a portion of my experience with tobacco. Although you may not think girls know much about it, I believe we know almost as much as boys do concerning it, and as observers are much more competent to deal fairly with it.

My parents were so opposed to tobacco that it seemed all the children would certainly avoid its use. The oldest brothers grew to manhood perfectly free from it, and our parents rejoiced in the precious victory. When we went into company together we sisters were so pleased with our noble and manly brothers that we compared them with our acquaintances in most favorable terms. They were kind, gentlemanly, truthful, upright, studious, energetic, and free from all bad habits; and we looked forward to a bright and happy future for them.

They were sent away from home to attend a high school to better prepare them for usefulness. Here they roomed with other young men of different grades of character, who laughed at their morality and virtue, and tried every way to ensnare them into evil. Away from home influence, associating daily—yes, hourly—with those who honored evil and scorned good, it was not long until our brothers began to partake of their ways. First, it was in smoking a cigar occasionally, then in playing games for treats of cigars or tobacco, then chewing and smoking whenever they had an opportunity, then trying to deceive the dear home folks in regard to the evil habits; and then following their companions into secret evils that destroyed their virtue, their mental ability, their health, and sent them home perfect wrecks of manhood. Think ye there was sorrow in that home? Yes, sorrow deeper and stronger than any of your boyish hearts can comprehend—a mother and father weeping and groaning over the sad desolation of their ruined sons; sisters mourning their loss of companionship and care, their bright hopes forever faded, their high regard turned to pity, their respect and esteem for manhood sorely shattered. Oh! indeed, naught could compensate for all this sadness. How often the weary and aching hearts cried out in bitter anguish, "Oh, give us back our boys!" But they were gone—nevermore would innocency, manliness, and virtue mark their faces and forms. Out into the wide world they go, drinking deeper of carnal pleasure and sinking lower in character as the years roll on.

The sisters, learning from sad experience, resolve never to keep company with any one who shows a weakness for the popular evils of youthful manhood. Alone they stand month after month and year after year, until they are known for many miles as "the old-maid sisters," while still in the bloom of womanhood.

At length there comes into the friendly circle several men of apparently good character and with high regard for feminine virtue and integrity to principle. They finally gain access to confidence and friendly regard, and are in a fair way to be welcomed into the tenderest affections of womanhood. But, alas! they, too, lack moral courage, and when twitted about their "womanish goodness," their "borrowed fanaticism" and their "woman slavery," they begin to relax their appreciation of principle and right and compromise with their scorners by smoking occasionally, and by asserting the "right of each one to do as he may choose," until the barriers of rectitude give way and they are drifting with the multitude into evil habits and vices. Shall the sisters drift with them and compromise the fine sense of right, or still holding fast their resolve, see the gulf of separation widening as time passes? They can in wisdom only do the latter and shield their hearts from the eyes of men who were not worthy of the affections of loyal and true hearts. Yet how sad to think of what "might have been," but for the fatal allurement to evil!

Yes, boys, think of it carefully. How long will it be until the girls must permit the attentions of those addicted to evil practices that affect the welfare of every home circle, or else remain unnoticed and uncared for? Will each of you look over your young friends and see how many are free from the tobacco habit? While your acquaintances may number a hundred, you may count upon your fingers those who do not smoke or chew, and sometimes you may not be able to point out one. Must your sisters and their friends be obliged to marry tobacco-users, no matter how repulsive it may be to them or how sure they may be that the tobacco habit covers even worse ones? All around us are the sad results of so doing; for poor, weakly wives are mourning in their hearts, if not in words, over the sad mistake made in binding their lives to something so repulsive to their very best feelings and desires. A woman may, during the pleasant days of courtship, think she can "put up with" the tobacco habit in the one she loves, because he is so nice and considerate of her in his manner of using it. But, alas! after marriage he ceases to refrain from his indulgence in her presence or to sweeten his breath before kissing her, or to air his clothes after sitting for hours in tobacco smoke; but as the years pass and his indulgence becomes greater, his untidiness becomes more and more annoying. Obliged to receive his embraces and caresses, obliged to live in the impure air when living at the best is one great effort, and obliged to yield into his arms the tiny form of precious life, to be slowly poisoned by contact and impure air and then as it reaches boyhood years see him chew, " 'Cause papa does."

Yes, boys, I shall warn every girl possible not to give her life into the care of those who are so unwisely becoming enslaved to this harmful practice of tobacco-using. Better, far better, is it to take up some occupation that shall enable us to live in purity than to become thus entangled with the offensive and poisonous indulgence.

I have watched carefully and have seen that in the majority of boys' lives the use of tobacco has been followed by a further decline from what is good and right; so that my heart is made sad to see the first step taken in a downward course. Dear boys, may I whisper to you in love and confidence the real cause of so much use of this miserable tobacco? Yes, I will tell you, although I know many of you will not believe it. It is the lack of moral courage. "Oh," you say, "take that back! for we boys have more courage than you think; we are afraid of nothing." Yes, I know you have one kind of courage, and will fight any one who does you a wrong, and make him pay for it; or will venture into dangerous places or rescue one in danger, even to the risk of your lives; but that is not the kind of courage I meant. That in which boys and many men are lacking is moral courage—courage to do right. It is easier for you to face the foe in battle array than it is to bear the taunts of companions for the sake of doing right. Now, boys, just look carefully and see if what you need most is not true moral courage, and then when you see it be sure to use what you have, and you will increase its quantity and quality and make your lives upright, honorable, and spiritual.

Your loving sister,   J——.

Now, boys, I must say a few words more for the girls upon this subject of tobacco. There are, no doubt, some of them who like to have their brothers and friends smoke and chew so as not to be counted odd or old-fashioned, but if the question of using tobacco or not using it were submitted to them there would be a majority against it; for there are many reasons why women should despise the habit, and generally do. Most of the reasons have been expressed in different ways while we have been considering this most important theme.

Look here, boys! would you like to have your sisters learn to chew? Would it please you to have every girl and woman of your acquaintance engaged in the defiling practice? Would you, husbands, or boys who expect to be, be willing to give to your wives as much as you spend for tobacco, to be used in some way equally as foolish and harmful to themselves and children? Suppose a man, who works hard to provide for himself and family, spends twenty-five dollars a year for tobacco for his own pleasure, ought he not to hand that much to his wife for her pleasure, when she labors just as hard for the family comfort and welfare? Does he *"love her as his own body"* if he does not? How many boys want to lay aside, for some one else, a dime every time you spend one for tobacco? "Oh," say a number of them, "it is all we can do to get the dimes for our own use." How much nicer it would be for every man to save his tobacco money for a year, and then spend it in such a way that all the dear ones could enjoy it! How much more generous and noble it would be! Did you ever see a poor farmer's wife take a basket of eggs to town, buy a quarter's worth of tobacco for her husband, ten cents' worth of sugar for a family of eight, and a dime's worth of meat? If so, you saw one of the saddest sights our eyes may look upon—a harmful and selfish habit taking the food from hungry wife and children.

Oh, our sons! cannot we Christian mothers persuade you that it is not wise, kind, just, noble, and good to spend money for that which cannot do you good, while many poor beings are going through life without the common comforts thereof, and souls are perishing, for whom Christ died, without the knowledge of his blessed salvation? Just think what an amount of good could be done with all the money thus wasted for tobacco. In a book on this subject we find that over $350,000,000 is spent each year in our country for tobacco, being about sixty times the amount spent for missionary work. Can it be possible that ours is a Christian nation, when men will spend foolishly upon themselves so much more money than they will use for the salvation of poor, perishing souls in heathen lands? Do figures tell the truth? Then men love tobacco more than they do precious souls. What one man spends in a lifetime for it would sustain a native missionary in some heathen land, and thus save many precious souls.

Will God hold us guiltless if we refuse to cry aloud against this popular evil? If these words could be blessed of God to the good of some boy who would fully decide to forsake this sinful habit and use his money for religious purposes, we Christian mothers would rejoice greatly; and yet by our prayers we expect more than this,

Tobacco is a pois'nous weed,
That blights the life, and sows the seed
Of sickness, death, and sorrows great,
That bring the soul to awful fate;
For misspent life, and wasted means,
For selfish deeds, and lustful dreams,
That lead the boys to greater crime,
To depths of sin in after time.

Tobacco then, our foe must be;
And thus we write, that boys may see
How Christian mothers o'er this land
Do form a large and praying band,
That all our sons (and daughters too)
May hate the weed, and ever do
With "might and main" whate'er they can,
To vanquish him, that ev'ry man
In after years may always be
From tyrant bands and yoke kept free.

INTEMPERANCE.

This is one of the deepest, darkest, most subtle snares for the destruction of humanity that the Devil ever invented, and is accomplishing much in its line of evil. It seems such a little thing to eat and drink whatever is pleasant, that many have been deceived thereby and have been enslaved to the appetite for strong drink before they were hardly aware of danger. Although much has been said and written against this great evil, it seems to fall on dull ears or else many who should hear have not been blessed with the opportunity of gaining instruction; for the ranks seem to fill up as fast as some drop out.

Doubtless many, very many, have been saved from this evil by words given just at the right time and in the right way; and now we Christian mothers would continue to reach the boys with such words of love, counsel, reproof, and wisdom as God may help us to give in his fear and for his glory. "To be forewarned is to be forearmed" is an old expression that means much. If one is warned beforehand of danger that threatens his welfare, then he is armed for his defense against that danger, and not taken unawares.

Supposing an army that was unacquainted with the

Indians' method of warfare were sent to them to restore peace during an Indian rebellion against the " white man's " authority over their reservations, and would undertake to fight them in " white man's" fashion—face to face in open combat—while the Indians, instead of so doing, would lie in ambush behind every bush, tree, stick, and stone, and pick off with unerring aim every one who came within range of their hiding-places; it would be no wonder if they succeeded in defeating the well-disciplined army. From this we may learn that every wrong must be met in the right and wise way in order to be defeated. This evil of intemperance with all its sly and cunning ways of deception and work must be understood in order to know how to meet it in battle. Perhaps some boys would like to know what intemperance is; so we will explain it to you. It is right to eat and drink as much wholesome food as our bodies require for our good. Anything more than this is intemperance; for it is " want of moderation." When men begin to use such drink as is harmful to them, such as hard cider, beer, wine, brandy, whisky, etc., they are becoming intemperate; for "moderation" would stop them from drinking any but good, healthful drink. So the word used as the head of this subject means the habitual use of intoxicating liquors as a drink. Those who use it this way are generally overcome therewith and become drunkards.

One wise way to defeat the evil of intemperance is to instruct the children in regard to the effects of liquor upon the physical system. This is being done quite thoroughly through the public schools in the teaching of physiology.

As there are many children who do not reach that study, it is well to teach the younger ones by object lessons, which is done in many places by efficient teachers. Simple demonstrations of the nature, power, and effects of intoxicants may appeal more forcibly to the mind through the eyes than through the ears. Alcohol is one of the most active stimulants, and is found in nearly all intoxicating liquors. "It is a clear, watery-like, volatile fluid having a hot, pungent taste and penetrating odor." In the object lessons it is shown to be a fluid that burns with a pale blue flame and intense heat. A saucer containing a few spoonfuls of alcohol mixed with several of water may have a cloth laid into it and then lighted and the alcohol will burn leaving the cloth and water; thus showing its inflammable nature though mixed with an opposite element. Another illustration that is forcible, is to put the white of an egg into alcohol and watch the change made in it. The white or albumen coagulates, or hardens, as if cooked. When we see that this fiery liquid must enter every portion of the body with this influence or effect, we can imagine the harm done thereby; especially upon those parts that have the substance of the egg. The brain is albumen, and would coagulate or harden the same as in the illustration. It is a fact also that a greater amount of the liquid is found in the head than elsewhere, so the expression "the liquor has gone to his head" is very true and forcible.

To help the boys more fully, we will give a few lessons from the school physiology, showing that learned men agree as to the harmful effects upon the physical system.

Alcohol is a stimulant and narcotic. "As a stimulant it excites the brain and nerves, increases the circulation of the blood, and *intoxicates* (makes drunk); while as a narcotic it blunts the powers of the brain and nerves and produces stupor and death. Since alcohol contains no nitrogen, it lacks one of the elements of food, and consequently will not sustain life. 'Alcohol has no iron nor salts for the blood; no gluten, phosphorus, nor lime for the bones; and no albumen, or substance which is the basis of every living organism.'—*Dr. Lees.* Hence it cannot be termed a food. Tests in the army, navy, and Arctic explorations have definitely proved the above position. Neither will alcohol allay thirst, and for the following reason: Alcohol has a great attraction for water, and when swallowed draws the water to itself, thus depriving the tissues of the body of that most necessary inorganic food. Again, alcohol causes a rush of blood to the skin, when a sensation of warmth is felt upon the surface of the body. However, the sensation of heat is, like beauty, 'only skin deep,' as the heat of the system has really been diminished rather than increased; because when the blood is upon the surface, it parts with its heat more readily."

"The effects of alcohol upon the heart may be summed up in the following statements:

(*a*) It causes a softening of the muscles of the heart, and a fatty degeneration, thus clogging the workings of this vital organ.

(*b*) It overworks the heart.

(*c*) Oftentimes it renders the heart weak and flabby.

(*d*) It causes an enlargement or dilation of its parts.

(*e*) There is a consequent effect of drowsiness and lassitude.

(*f*) Its general effect upon the heart is to destroy its strength and usefulness."

"Alcohol has the following effects upon the lungs:

(*a*) It makes the blood impure, thus increasing the work of the lungs.

(*b*) It paralyzes the blood vessels.

(*c*) It weakens the various lung tissues.

(*d*) It vitiates the breath."

"Alcohol's effects upon the stomach:

(*a*) Produces chronic inflammation of the stomach.

(*b*) Injures the mucous lining by hardening the tissues.

(*c*) It destroys some of the small glands and impairs others.

(*d*) It precipitates the pepsin of the gastric juice, thus retarding digestion.

(e) It thickens the mucus of the stomach.
(f) The action of the stomach is at first quickened by the presence of alcohol, and then retarded."

"The effects of alcohol upon the liver may be:
(a) It produces a hardened condition of its tissues.
(b) Enlarges the organ.
(c) Compresses and lessens the cells for producing bile.
(d) Stimulates the liver to overaction, thus reducing the bile supply.
(c) It weakens and destroys the usefulness of this organ of digestion."

"Effect of alcohol upon the blood and blood vessels:
(a) It thins and coagulates the blood according to the amount of alcohol.
(b) It hastens the circulation, thus weakening it.
(c) It prevents combustion.
(d) It impairs and destroys the corpuscles, thus affecting their powers of transporting oxygen and carbonic acid gas.
(e) It weakens the arterial muscles by affecting the nerves governing them."

"Effects of alcohol upon the brain and nerves are:
(a) It causes apoplexy and epilepsy by confusing the brain.
(b) It weakens the will and deadens the feelings.
(c) It hardens the brain tissues, producing dullness, insensibility, and insanity.

(*d*) It destroys the nerve fiber of the brain.

(*e*) It temporarily stimulates and finally depresses this organ.

(*f*) *It will at last destroy man, body and soul."*

"Alcohol leads every other drug in its far-reaching influence for mischief and evil. Were the thousands of ruined homes, the untold numbers of blasted lives, the sorrows, the sins, numberless crimes, murders, and deaths brought in panoramic review before us, what a hell-born picture it would be."

"The effect of alcohol upon the morals is awful. All delicacy, courtesy, and self-respect are gone; the sense of justice and right is faint or quite extinct; there is no vice into which the victim of drunkenness does not easily slide; and no crime from which he can be expected to refrain. Between this condition and insanity there is but a single step."—*Extracts from Hotze's Physiology.*

The more thorough the teaching of the young and the better the influences surrounding them the less likely are they to fall into this snare laid for their entanglement and destruction. No home should count its work done that does not warn in love and wisdom the little ones therein, in regard to this awful sin that destroys soul and body. Often parents take it for granted that since they are temperate and have decided and strong convictions against this evil, their children will take the same bold stand, even without any special teaching from them. This is a great mistake, and should be corrected at once. Short temperance pieces should be read to them, the word of God on the subject committed to memory, and every effort made to encourage self-control of appetite and desire. Often children are allowed to harbor the feeling that the height of pleasure is to do just as they want to do, regardless of all consequences. They should be trained early to see for themselves that true pleasure is found in ways of right and wisdom, and every wrong brings sad results to themselves and friends in some manner.

Gospel workers should teach and preach the word on this subject just as faithfully as on any other, as there are many precious souls willing to be delivered from the bondage of the drink habit, if they only knew where to go for help. Most of the religions of the present day are powerless to deliver from evil ways, because most of what is called faith is simply intellectual belief that does not bring deliverance from sin to the heart of man; but the simple religion of Jesus Christ gives victory over all sin and uncleanness, because the soul regenerated by divine grace is sustained by a true and living faith in the promises of God.

Nations may prohibit the manufacture and sale of all intoxicating liquors, when such a law can be enacted by the majority vote of the people. It takes strong effort to procure that law and stronger effort to enforce it. Many are laboring on that line in earnest endeavor and faithfulness to conviction of duty, and are doing much for the betterment of the people. As long as sin rules in the hearts of men, so long will it bring them into bondage to evils of different kinds. Make the heart pure and the life will be pure. So, boys, we would entreat you to give yourselves to the service of God and thus escape all the deceptions and allurements of Satan.

No words of ours can portray the sad results of intemperance, and yet we must try to bring some points before you. If this habit of drinking liquor was confined to the lowest grade of society, as the result of careless living and lack of education, it would not seem so hard to reach: for in its enlightenment and elevation through better surroundings, with education and culture, would be victory; but as we look around we see the drunkard ranks are increased with the brightest and best from all classes of society. Here are those reared in homes of culture and refinement, those who were striving for different stations of prominence and responsibility, and those occupying places of usefulness in the quiet walks of life, going down to the depths of shame and degradation, companions of thieves, murderers, and whoremongers. The social glass drained at feasts, parties, balls, suppers, at clubs and lodges, is responsible for much of this evil. Men of wealth, education, and refinement hold to the belief that "it is a curtailment of personal liberty to banish the wine cup" from their richly furnished tables of princely splendor. Others carefully instructed in temperance and principle lay down their fortifications when coming in contact with those "broader views," and are soon enjoying the personal liberty of making beast of themselves, as well as idiots, for a time at least, as the effect of drinking is to "steal away the brains." Many are the instances of those thus seduced by fashionable folly and unrighteous judgment, and awful will be the punishment of those who "give their neighbor drink." Often the cup is given by the hands of feminine beauty in order to prove more attractive and harder to be resisted by those who are entering into temptation.

The word of God says "he that is deceived thereby is not wise." In what way can boys be deceived by liquor? "Look not thou upon the wine when it is red, when it giveth his color in the cup, when it moveth itself aright. At the last it biteth like a serpent, and stingeth like an adder."—Prov. 23, 30. This Bible instruction every one should receive for his good, for if he is careful not to look upon wine in its attractive state, then he will not be tempted to partake of it or to decide that, "It surely will do no harm to taste it once." Many think they are so manly, have such a strong will, that they "can drink when they want to and let it alone when they want to." Very few of those who have thus thought have been able to do so. The effort to be moderate in their drinking has been greater than the effort to let it alone entirely would have been, and then the risk run was very great. No one is wise to take upon himself such a great responsibility. The nature of drink is like that of tobacco; for it creates an appetite for itself that nothing else can satisfy, and the more one drinks the more he wants, until he has no control over his desire.

There is hardly a sadder sight than a man endowed with gifts and graces from the great Creator's han , so abusing himself by the use of intoxicants as to sink himself below the brute beast. What animals are there that will not choose the best conditions, circumstances, and associations in preference to the worst? The way man chooses these is to choose to drink instead of choosing to let liquor alone. The fact is, he prefers to drink because the effect of drink upon him is at first pleasant, and the rest comes as a result. Therefore it is wise to look further than the first appearance, as "at last it biteth like a serpent and stingeth like an adder."

It may seem to boys a beautiful picture of manliness to see a young man in his strength and youthful vigor calmly holding in his hand and to his ruby lips the sparkling wine-cup and drinking its contents, with the confidence, "It shall never make a slave of me," depicted in face and motion; but to us mothers it is a picture of foolhardiness scarcely equaled by any other sight. A lion asleep in a cage is a far prettier sight than one fastening his jaws upon a man's throat; but as a lion, in a cage, is ready to spring upon the one who shall enter his cage, so is the demon of drink ready to fasten upon the one who lightly tampers with it in an occasional glass. We can but pity those who will not take warning from the sad scenes around them or from the sad experience of millions, but must try the awful experiment for themselves, only to be destroyed therein.

Now, boys, let us take an illustration. There are a number of snakes whose bite has proved to be very poisonous, killing or sadly afflicting all those who receive their bite. Suppose two of these snakes are in a cage, with just the tip of their tails sticking out, and two boys think they will prove that men are mistaken in believing them poisonous. So they seek this cage twice a day, and grasping the tails with their fingers they pinch and pull them gently, and as the snakes do not bite them they go away laughing at the absurdity of those harmless snakes hurting any one. This they do day after day, until the snakes are more out of the cage than in. After a time the day comes when the snakes are liberated. Then with a slight effort they turn upon their victims and thrust them through with their poisonous fangs; and unless they have help from some source they are bound to suffer and to die. "The serpent of the still" is a terrible monster, not to be played with. He lies in the saloon, with just his tail visible at the wine supper, the ball, the lodge feast, and the political jubilee, and thousands of the youth of the land are pulling his tail by partaking of an occasional glass of beer, wine, brandy, or whisky, and laughing at "those teetotalers who think a man is on the road to ruin when he drinks now and then." But alas! the awful monster is pulled forth at last, and his head is seen to have terrible fangs to poison and destroy soul and body: but then it is too late—the sad result must follow the folly; a ruined life, a death of shame, and an eternity of woe.

Few who begin the habit of drink awake to their true condition until beyond their power to stop. But, dear boys and men, there is a power that can break even the bonds of drink and can cure even this serpent's bite. It is the salvation of Jesus; for when one is beyond the help of men and will look to Jesus for it, he is sure to come to that one's assistance. "Come unto me, all ye that labor and are heavy laden, and I will give you rest." Oh, that poor, burdened men, women, and children would awake to the fact that we have a "wonderful Redeemer," one who is "mighty to save" all who will call upon him! Oh, that the burdened ones would cast their burdens upon that Mighty One and find blessed rest and victory! How many aching hearts are tracing their sorrows to this great evil of intemperance!

Mothers and fathers are weeping over the estrangement, degradation, destruction, and future punishment of their children; and parents are meeting the same sad doom regardless of the entreaty, sorrow, and suffering of their children.

Oh, the awful, awful burden that rests upon the frail shoulders of humanity because of this great sin of drink! Dear ones, it is too heavy to be borne by you, and there is One who wishes to bear it for you if you will carry it to him. Then take it to him in simple, earnest, believing prayer, and find how precious it is to cast all your care upon Jesus, who "careth for you." So many look upon God as an indifferent, unconcerned, unloving being who is just waiting to punish the wicked for all their wrong-doing. O dear souls, do not harbor that belief another moment. He has "so loved" you that in infinite mercy and pity he has made provision to do for you exceeding abundantly more than you can ask or think. He will do for each of us all we ask him to in faith and in the name of Jesus. He will bear our burdens, give grace for every trial, send conviction upon the erring ones; and if they will yield to the wooing of the Holy Spirit, he will save them and deliver from the bonds and snares of the evil one. Could we ask for more? Yes; he will quiet the restless heart with his "Peace, be still," and make a way where there is no way—even through a wilderness of woe, until the "Bright and Morning Star" shall eclipse the sun in the brightness of his shining, and night shall be turned to day.

Oh, dear boys, can any one have enough pleasure in this evil habit to compensate for the sadness and trouble brought upon those near and dear? If one could be perfectly isolated from every one, without attachment to or influence over any, then the choosing of the drink track for personal pleasure might not be so fraught with distress and sorrow, as it would be the disposal of life according to the owner's value thereof. But when many are interested therein, and every day brings heartaches and ceaseless longings, and every night dreams and cries of woe, to loving hearts, then it ceases to be a matter of personal liberty, and becomes a question of right to distress others in whose hearts we are held dear. If our influence extended to no one, then it might appear well to dispose of our lives according to our own desires, but when every act, every thought and appearance affects others with wonderful force, then surely no one has the right to choose such a course as will influence others for evil. There is, however, a point that the majority fail to observe. Life is a gift from God and should be used for his glory; for while many think they are " boss of themselves," he has far more right to control, for without his permission no one could live or move. He holds the thread of life, and when his mercy, love, and grace cease to appeal to an individual in sin, then comes death and eternal punishment.

Besides the injury done to the victim of strong drink there is the great evil of transmitting the appetite for it to the children, even to the " third and fourth generation," besides the enfeebled constitutions that come as a legacy from those who have nothing better to give to those they so cruelly have wronged by lives of self-indulgence.

Surely it is right for each individual to examine thoroughly every step he takes, considering his own welfare and the influence upon those dear to him. As I look back over the past, I remember an acquaintance who was a man of influence when I entered the ranks as public-school teacher, and was one to grant my first certificate. His family stood high in social life, and was known for miles around for religious zeal and devotion. The home was a happy one, with influence for education and intellectual development. As years passed rumors came that this young man, while making his mark in his chosen profession, was beginning to drink occasionally to help him in his work, by stimulating his mind to logic, and his tongue to eloquence. Afterward tidings reached us that he had occasional sprees, in which he lost completely all control of himself and was ruining his business. Then again, we heard that as the times of intoxication approached he would hide himself from his family and be a source of deep concern and sorrow. At such times his mother would leave her village home, enter the city, and go from place to place among the dens of vice until she found her son; then take him to some quiet place to recover himself, and then restore him to his wife and children. But the frail body could not long endure such a strain, and he passed away in the prime of life, mourned over by a throng of acquaintances who had expected much of him, in early life. Sad, sad! that any one should be so deceived by the wine-glass, when the word of wisdom says, "He that is deceived thereby is not wise."

Sometimes an inherited appetite for strong drink lies dormant until the first glass arouses it to intense strength, and overcomes every reason and conscience scruple, and gains control of mind, will, and body, and casts down to destruction those whose every prospect for life was bright and glowing with hope and desire. It takes from them the bright prospects, the joyous hopes, the ambitious desire, and makes them beings groveling for the most sensual pleasures, and yet gaining more of sorrow as the years go by.

While the first effect of liquor may be a pleasureable exhilaration of spirits that is very enjoyable, and the insensible condition following a release from activity of thought and motion that may be able to "drown trouble" for a time, the after effect is as full of sorrow as the first was of joy, and the depression greater than the exhilaration, and the "sobering up" the darkest time of life to the inebriate.

This is the reason that drunkards keep drinking to prolong their sprees. Many a man drinks himself dead rather than to sober up and come back to the realities of a life of shame and battle with conscience. Most drinking men will acknowledge in their sober moments that it would be better not to touch liquor, but it has so gained the mastery that they are not free to make the choice that they would like to. Sometimes they think they can, and will make what they and their friends consider such strong resolutions that they will never break them, and they rejoice in the prospect of victory. Then begins a battle that is fought to the depths of despair more often than to the heights of victory for right.

There is a way in which every battle may be victorious for the oppressed, and that is by obtaining the help of God. Many have taken the temperance pledge and tried hard to keep it, but failed because greater is the foe than human strength; but let the failing one look to the Lord and receive his strength and grace through the salvation of his soul, and he will obtain the most glorious victory that tongue ever voiced in praise to God. The victim of strong drink is made just as free from its bondage and appetite as though he had never tasted it, and the effects upon the body are just as fully removed as though they had never existed. Oh, how merciful and loving our God is to poor, weak man! He takes the drunkard from the gutter, all forsaken of friends, destitute of manhood, filthy within and without, devoid of strength of will and courage, and makes him a man, gives him friends of Christian brothers and sisters, makes him clean within and without, gives him strength and grace according to his need, and encourages his heart with the joys of salvation, and gives him power to will and to do his good pleasure; thus giving victory over all the power of the Devil and his works, and thus making him triumph in Christ Jesus. Wonderful, wonderful! Yes, wonderful is the religion of Jesus. "Let the brother of low degree rejoice in that he is exalted: but the rich, in that he is made low." He maketh us "kings and priests unto God," and gives us the privilege of serving him "without fear, in holiness and righteousness before him, all the days of our life."

Some of those who are in the ranks of drunkards were brought there by the lack of wisdom in parents and physicians. Oftentimes when sickness enters the family circle, the most convenient doctor is called, regardless of his principles; and as many of them are somewhat intemperate, it is no wonder they prescribe wines, brandies, beer, whisky, etc., as stimulants, thus bringing the youthful patient under the deceptive influence of alcohol. Far better would it be to allow the dear one to pass away from earth without the use of the remedies than to have him live and finally go down to a drunkard's grave and punishment. Years ago from sad experience, before I knew the healing power of God, I determined that none of my family should be permitted to use stimulants that would encourage toward the drink habit.

Here is a young man who in ignorance of the effects of secret evil habits has brought upon himself severe afflictions, and so he resorts to physicians for help. They examine, and advise first one medicine and then another, until the patient is discouraged; and then they express the opinion that beer or wine might help him considerably. He tries it, and under its influence thinks he is much improved; and so continues its use for some time, vainly imagining he is receiving much benefit, but never getting where he can leave it off. Thus the habit is formed, and soon stronger drink takes its place and the poor boy is on the downward track, and is soon lost to friends and dear ones. Oh, the heartaches, the unspeakable sorrow, and the vain regrets. "Would that we had used more wisdom and suffered not the wine-cup to tear our boy from the hearts of love and home." If the knowledge of this great wrong should keep some one's precious boys from the same sad way, our hearts would rejoice and praise God for the blessed opportunity of sowing good seed.

Drunkards are to be pitied, and should receive our kindest treatment, and be instructed in the ways of truth and salvation. Many times Christian people look upon them as too hard to reach with the Gospel, and so do nothing for them to win them away from the great evil. "Do unto others as ye would that men should do unto you" would make all very earnest for their salvation from sin, and help all to pray for them and to warn them in love to their souls. My heart was wonderfully touched and impressed with the words of a poor homeless orphan boy: "I do not remember that any one ever advised me for my good during my youthful days." Oh, how thankful we mothers are for the privilege of warning, advising, and instructing so many with these little talks with our sons! If these words should reach any one who is beginning to walk in the way of strong drink, oh! let us advise you, as mothers with tears and prayers, to abandon it at once, and flee to God for deliverance, comfort, and peace, that your immortal soul is hungering for.

A sober and virtuous life has more of joy and pleasure than one of sin and folly, even in this world. The Christian life far exceeds our imagination in what is good and desirable.

Let us see what the Bible says about this subject:

"Woe unto them that rise up early in the morning, that they may follow strong drink; that continue until night, till wine inflame them!"—Isa. 5:11. "*Who hath woe? Who hath sorrow?* Who hath contentions? Who hath babblings? Who hath wounds without cause? Who hath redness of eyes? They that tarry long at the wine; they that go to seek mixed wine."—Prov. 23 : 29, 30. "Woe unto him that giveth his neighbor drink."—Hab. 2:15. If any one is thinking about taking up the habit of drinking intoxicating beverages, he ought to consult the word of God first, as it has much to say upon that important subject. Here is an extract from a religious paper, that seems quite suitable for boys to read:

"THE BIBLE AND WINE."

"The Bible is a total abstinence book. Five times it totally prohibits wine-drinking; twelve times it refers to wine as a poison—poison of asps and dragons. There are 131 warnings and reproofs against wine. There is no word of approval of wines that intoxicate, and which at last ' bite like a serpent and sting like an adder.' The wine which is an emblem of salvation is not the kind of wine which is the emblem of damnation. There is as clear a line of distinction between them as there is between good and bad men, or black and white horses, and ' the wayfaring though a fool shall not err therein.' "

Now, boys, here is a little poem that is right to the point, which was selected by a schoolboy in

Pennsylvania. If every one will commit it to memory, it may prove a great benefit all through life, in strengthening decision for right.

SAY NO.

Dare to say "No," when you're tempted to drink,
Pause for a moment, my brave boy, and think;
Think of the wrecks upon life's ocean tossed,
For answering "Yes" without counting the cost.

Think of the mother who bore you in pain,
Think of the tears that will soon fall like rain,
Think of the heart and how cruel the blow,
Think of her love, and at once answer "No."

Think of the hopes that are drowned in the bowl,
Think of the danger to body and soul,
Think of sad lives, once as pure as the snow;
Look at them now, and at once answer "No."

Think, too, of manhood with rum-tainted breath,
Think of its end and the terrible death;
Think of the homes that now shadowed with woe
Might have been heaven had the answer been "No."

Think of lone graves both unwept and unknown,
Hiding fond hopes that were fair as your own;
Think of proud forms, now forever laid low,
That still might be here, had they learned to say "No."

Think of the demon that lurks in the bowl,
Driving to ruin both body and soul;
Think of all this as life's journey you go,
And when you're assailed by the tempter, say "*No.*"

SECRET SIN.

There is in every individual an inclination to a certain course of action, because of inherited tendency, or surrounding influence upon the natural disposition. We see quite small children manifesting different traits of character. A boy may be very energetic, like his grandfather; sharp in trade, like his father; or very kind-hearted and patient with the sick and troubled, like his mother. Another one may show a very proud, rebellious nature, with great love for the good and noble in life and character that he fails to engraft into his own because of the love of approval, that is stronger than any other consideration.

Now, boys, do you not see that it is unwise to do as we please, because our inclinations run in certain directions, just walk in those ways for our own pleasure? That would be making ourselves mere machines controlled by influence and surroundings, instead of conquering inclination and circumstances by a loyalty to judgment and reason. Would it be a noble life to follow our inclinations because it is easier and more pleasant? Would that be seeking the best of life? Oh, no; we have greater battles to fight with ourselves than with circumstances or individuals. To make our lives sublime we need to have every evil inclination removed and every right one strengthened. While many are just drifting along in life, choosing their own course and pleasures as seem most attractive because of their natural disposition, they often do so from lack of consideration, or instruction that should have been given quite early in life. While we are sure some would take their own way regardless of warning or instruction, there are very many who err more from lack of wisdom than from real opposition to what is good, especially in the early years of life, before habits and opinions are firmly formed.

As we have before mentioned we want to talk of those things that will be for the welfare of the entire being—soul, mind, and body. The body, as the house of clay in which the mind and soul abide, needs a portion of care and honor. It is a wonderful mechanism. Every organ has a good use, and one cannot boast itself above another. We Christian mothers think very much of our children's bodies, and look after their interests with unwearied care. Here is the baby, with its delicate little members, who must be kept warm, clean, and properly fed, and rested with change of position, and comfortable place. Then the next little toddler must be kept from harm from scissors, knives, open doors, fire, unwholesome food, and bathed and put to rest at suitable hours.

And now comes "papa's boy," who follows his father from place to place all day long; surely he must have suitable clothes to keep him warm and dry while he trudges through damp and frosty places, "doin' chores" for everybody. As mother clothes and dresses the little manly form in fresh, clean garments, she tells him he is growing into a nice strong boy and he must take good care of himself and never do anything naughty to his little body, and be sure never to let any one see him naked; for that is shame, and if any other boys do so to run away from them. Mother's little talks and watchful care impress the mind, and he is free to tell her of the "bad boys who do naughty things" when they are by themselves; and so the mother increases her instruction, and tells him how very wickedly some boys use their bodies, which were made for a wise and good purpose. So little by little as the mind expands and inquires into deeper things, she unfolds to him what every child must know in some way sooner or later, and in such love and concern that the lessons are not soon forgotten. He is told to keep his mind from dwelling upon secret things, but to learn his lessons at school and take an interest in everything that is good and will make him a useful man. Occasionally she gives him something to read that will help him to see the bad effects of secret evils, and reminds him of her concern for his welfare and honor.

There has been a time in the recent past when all such instruction was counted useless and unwise, as well as immodest, by many of the worldly-wise people; but the sad results of such a course are seen on every side in the wrecks of manhood and the dreadful diseases that are afflicting the young as a consequence of secret evils. Some have been afraid that the instruction given would only cause some who were before ignorant of evil to take advantage of their knowledge, and enter into evil. Surely it would be a very depraved being who would thus abuse the instruction that was intended for such great good. My respect for our youth is too great to harbor that thought for an instant. Of all the testimonies and experiences that have been read, heard, or seen, not one came from *too much* instruction, but all from the *lack* of it. Boys, girls, women, and men are regretting that through ignorance they became enslaved to the habit of self-abuse of the sexual organs.

While perhaps most of our boys know what that means, there may be some who do not; therefore it is best to make it clear to them. It would be well if every father and mother in the land had given their children such teaching as would have made it unnecessary to write it to them, but as many parents are themselves ignorant of the great sexual evils that are taking our children to untimely graves or sinking them into deepest sin and degradation, it becomes very necessary to do so. By the help of God it shall be so worded that it need not offend the modesty of any one; and although the depths of the evil may be deeper and greater than imagined, it is true, and words cannot really depict the awful state that exists because of it. Just the same as words fail to describe the sorrows arising from intemperance.

Self-abuse is the self-use of the sexual organs in order to obtain certain pleasurable feelings.

Most individuals come into possession of a natural power during the early years of life, termed sexuality. The age of its development varies according to circumstantial influence and inherited tendencey. It sometimes appears at the early age of four years, although the average is between eight and fifteen years. The earlier it is developed the more likely it is to be abused through ignorance in innocency. Parents have been awakened to the danger of their children by a little child freely performing the sinful act, without shame, before them; although the tendency is to secrecy and shame, so much so that mothers may watch with vigilance day and night without obtaining evidence, except in the symptoms upon the children. One mother knew nothing of the evil habit until five of her children confessed to it in mature years, and wondered why she had withheld such instruction as would have saved them from years of sorrow and shame.

Another mother being warned by her husband, who was a physician, to "watch carefully her children in every way possible for secret sin" was much surprised in later years by the assurance of another physician that her children were dying of quick consumption caused by the practice of this secret evil. She was not convinced till the suffering ones admitted the fact and wondered why nothing was written or said about the evil and its awful effects upon the physical system, that children might beware of it and avoid an early death through severe diseases.

Why parents should have such an aversion to confidential conversation with their children seems strange, when they are most generally quite free to speak of secret things among themselves. If boys or girls could come into possession of property at an early age, the parents would not hesitate to inform them upon business principles and make suggestions as to its improvement and care. Sexuality is property that is very essential to life and happiness, and nothing needs greater care all through life, in order to perfectly fulfill its mission in this world. How kind and wise therefore are those parents who will inform their children of this God-created power entrusted to them, and instruct them as to its use and care, that it may not be abused or misused for its degeneration and that of its owner.

It is no wonder when an uninstructed child begins to realize strange feelings and impulses, that he should try to investigate matters and that he should conclude that it was given to afford pleasure. But let him be told that sexuality is the gift of manhood and womanhood to be properly used in married life, and in order to have it arrive at a perfect state it must not be abused during the years of boyhood and girlhood, the child at once grasps the situation and proves himself a man by keeping his purity.

If any faculty of the body is misused or overused, it becomes weakened and affects the entire body, according to the Scripture: "Whether one member suffer, all the members suffer with it." If the eye is overused by too steady application to fine work or misused by compelling it to service in insufficient light or too strong light, the sight becomes affected, and the entire body suffers with it and is disabled from perfect labor. Now the sexual organs of both sexes are more susceptive to injury from improper use or overuse than the eye, and when they are used in childhood in improper ways, the evil effect upon the entire being cannot be conceived. The body is weakened; does not properly develop in stature and in strength of different organs. The mind ceases to mature, and the physical being is a mere wreck. The effect upon the morals is even more marked and deeply to be deplored; the being becomes controlled by the lowest desires and impulses, his thoughts dwell upon impurity and the boy-man has fallen from his high estate—to the plane of the beast.

Now, boys, we know you are not ashamed for us to talk thus plainly with you; for those who were not taught concerning these things by parents, know that what we have said is true, from their own or other's experience. Many of you have wondered how others lived, and those you have spoken to about it have laughed and joked and persuaded that "boys are boys, and men are men, and all do about alike—just as they please." It is sad to think how far degeneracy on this line has extended. The majority of men and boys think the stronger their sexuality is the more "manly" they are, when the truth is the *less* manly they are, if it controls them instead of them controlling it.

When sexuality is abused, either in or out of the marriage relation, it is lust and is numbered as one of the sins for which man must suffer punishment; as it is unlawful, carnal desire when beyond the law of righteousness. Then how necessary that every one should know where the line of righteousness lies, and measure to it in the fear of God. Many think they have such strongly developed sexuality that they must be humored and made exception of, when the trouble lies in their not resisting the lustful spirit that is fast taking possession of them. Those who are troubled on the line of sexual desire need to resist that evil with steadfastness and look to God for deliverance, just the same as the tobacco-user or the drunkard. God has a blessed and wonderful deliverance for those bound by the habit of self-abuse or any other secret evil. They can be made just as free from it as though they had never misused their God-given powers. Most of the sad results of that evil upon the individuals may be removed by fervent, effectual prayer. How good to think when we have ruined ourselves in unrighteous ways, that God will stoop to touch us with his healing and restoring power, and make us anew! Oh, dear boys, will you not stop grieving such a loving, heavenly Father, and receive his help, that you may be strong, pure, upright men that can honor him by holy lives?

When boys ignorantly enter upon bad habits they

are not aware of what is to follow their course of action. A sister told me of the sad life of a boy acquaintance. He was a very bright boy, was well raised, and inclined to intellectual pursuits, with strong desire for a classical education. His parents were very loving and wished to gratify their only child's aspirations, and so put forth great efforts to send him to college. Away from home influence, he became companion of those who had formed bad habits and were anxious to initiate others into secret self-indulgence. He learned these evil lessons quite as readily as others do, and having a highly nervous organization the evil effects followed rapidly. He lost his interest in study, and indulged in all the follies of his companions, until his physical constitution was a wreck and his mental faculties impaired. It was not long until it became necessary to inform the parents of his inability to continue in school. His parents were grief-stricken and lamented sending him there, considering it the severe mental application that had wrought the evil.

Returning home he continued to weaken in mind and body, until the physician recommended him to the insane asylum, in order to have the best medical skill for mental trouble. Oh! sad indeed was the day when the poor parents bade him farewell to enter upon a life of mental darkness and wretchedness among strangers.

Months passed, and the parents visited him, hoping and praying that some sign of improvement might encourage their hearts; but instead of that they were well nigh crushed by the sight that met their astonished gaze. The boy—their precious boy, their only son—was bound hand and foot, " in order to prevent him from abusing himself," as the caretakers expressed it. The parents were indignant, as they were sure " he was not guilty of such a debasing practice." The physicians were called, and they informed the weeping parents of the truth of the statement, and explained the circumstances and the need of confinement. They said that it was only one of many such cases. That having a nervous temperament he was not able to endure the strain of the secret evils learned at school and had been so prostrated that the mind was entirely overpowered, and that the only hope of improvement was in confining him so as to restrain him from further abuse, until his body and mind had received strength, when he could be so instructed as to avoid the cause of all the trouble. The parents were amazed, and could not be reconciled to the situation. The physicians said they were willing they should be convinced, and would unbind him and leave him in their care for an hour, unless they should call for help from the caretakers in the next room. The parents agreed to this, and he was set free and received the caresses of parental love and watchful care. They had not been alone long before he began to act very strangely: walked the room in great excitement, looking around nervously, wringing and working his hands; then seemingly perfectly unconscious of others' presence, he knelt in the corner furthest away in the dark shadows and was soon making every effort toward the evil that was destroying him. The cry for help rang out in accents of horror, and he was soon bound by the help of the parents, who were now fully convinced of its need.

Do you think those parents regretted their ignorance, and the lack of instruction given to their child on such an important matter? Do you think they would have been sorry if Christian mothers had given him a few confidential talks through a book? Oh, no; they would now rejoice if it were possible to turn back the wheels of time two years, and give them or some one else an hour for quiet forcible counsel on secret things. But that could not be; for "lost opportunities never return," and their sad hearts must feel as long as life shall last the sad effect of neglected duty.

The boy seemed to improve for a time, but the close confinement and restriction of the body, united with its already weak condition, made it a quick prey for a prevailing fever, and soon the summons came to the parents, "Come quickly." They hastened and reached the sick-bed in time to behold returning reason and to hear the sad laments of a ruined life, and to point him to the Lamb of God who forgiveth all manner of sin, and to have a hope that his soul was anchored within the haven of eternal rest; then to carry the poor, abused and wasted body to the home cemetery to fill an untimely grave, for broken-hearted parents to weep over during their lonely, childless years of life.

Do you know, boys, that this great sin of masturbation is not hidden from human eyes? Do you know that as physicians and many others look into your faces and upon your forms they behold the secret of your life? They pity you, and would love to reach you with words of warning, but the false modesty of worldly pride holds them back. Speak them, brother and sister, regardless of "what the world says," and clear yourselves of the blood of all men. Speak them gently in the Spirit, in love, in mercy, in entreaty, and in faith, and trust the rest in God's hands.

While not all may suffer alike severely, there is not a greater drain upon the physical and mental systems than that of self-abuse. First, it is unnatural; second, it is done prematurely; third, its influence is to extreme excess, until there is no control over the life fluid, and lost manhood with all its terrible ills is the result. Hardly a paper reaches us from worldly circles but has several advertisements of wonderful cures for those who through youthful excesses have lost their manly vigor and strength. For all this, many are those who have "spent all upon many physicians and are rather the worse." Hope fled, strength gone, a manless man, a misery to himself and friends; no wonder he gives way to the sly voice of temptation, and "makes an end of all by his own suicidal hands"—just what the evil one wanted to accomplish when the first impure and sensual thought was given to the boy, and the first act of self-destruction performed in secret.

Oh, my boys! be sure "your sin will find you out" sooner or later. By this self-debasing and sinful habit you unfit yourself for a happy married life, and are unfit to take to yourself a pure-minded and chaste wife, and unfit to have the care and love of dear little children. Would you think it fair to ask a pure, chaste, virtuous woman, strong in her womanhood, and pure in love and respect for manhood, to link her life to a poor abused man, impure in thought and in action, a mere wreck of manhood? Do you want to be united for life to one on the same level as yourself? If not, then do not force yourself upon some one who in ignorance dreams you are all that is good and manly, only to be made sorrowful as she beholds the true state of her husband? Sad indeed must be that union that is unequal, virtue with impurity, or equal impurity with impurity. Then, boys, keep yourselves as pure as you wish your loved ones to be. You have no right to think that women should live pure while you can do as you please. Fairness demands, and God expects, virtue and sexual purity from one, just as much as from the other. And we Christian mothers are holding our boys and girls to the same plane of virtuous living.

The way of escape from this evil is so blessed, so pure and holy, that we wish every sin-bound soul could see it and become willing to take it for his present and eternal welfare. Stop, dear reader, and ponder. Are you free to do what you know is right? Or are you bound by some fetter or band of sin? If so, there is One who can make you a servant of righteousness, free from sin and sinful ways. We have several letters we wish you to read from those whom God has made free from secret sin. When these dear ones saw their evil and hated it so badly as to turn from it, the Savior met them with forgiveness and made them whole again, and they in love and sympathy desire to show you that he is just as able and willing to help you, if you come forsaking and confessing your sin.

Dear Boys:

As I think of you as some mother's dear boys, and remember that the "enemy of all good" is ever on the watch to destroy every pure boy and his open confidence with his mother, I feel quite anxious to write you a letter.

It is so commonly thought that boys can have and take more liberties than girls and do no harm, that I want to warn you. There is just as much harm to your present life and the life hereafter; for God is no respecter of persons. He created the man just as holy as the woman, and according to the law of nature he must live holy and pure, or the effects of sin will be the same upon himself and those who follow after. The cry must go forth for pure brothers, fathers, and sons; or else the effort to better the world by pure sisters, mothers, and daughters will amount to little.

Do not think you can swear, chew, smoke, drink, gamble, or use your body or its members in any way that would not be becoming in your sisters. Dear boys, God loves you. He gave his only begotten Son that you might be saved. You will find this world is no friend to grace to help you on to God. So give it up, and love to be the Lord's boys.

I wish to warn you of the strongest hold the Devil will try to get upon you; and it is one on which you must help yourself, as no earthly friend can aid you. It is in your secret hours, by yourself, or in company with wicked men or boys, that your enemy will try to entrap you into the practice of secret vice. I know the world cries, "It is according to nature;" and men plead, "It is no harm or God would not have made us so." It is harm, as the ruined minds and bodies of millions prove. God did not make men in their present sinful inclinations. He made them pure, and with pure thoughts; but sin has passed from father to son until they are thus defiled. Ezekiel tells us that the son shall not answer for the sin of his father, in the day that he turneth from his sin.

Jesus not only saves from sin, but he will remove the effects of sin, from all who call upon him out of a pure heart. May God save the boys is the prayer of
"Aunt Mary."

My Dear Boys;

I am so glad you are to have a book for yourselves of motherly counsel and love; for we all love the bright, noisy boys and would be pleased to do anything to help them in any way possible. Being a mother of boys, I do praise God that he has given me light upon the great evils that are practiced in these "last days," and enabled me to instruct them concerning the great disaster which always follows in the train of evil habits.

There are many dear boys who for lack of teaching are destroying their bodies by practicing secret vice and bringing themselves to early graves; which is not the worst side of the dark picture, for they cannot spend eternity with the pure in heaven when their hands and bodies have been polluted by destroying their own lives. Therefore, I feel led to write you this letter.

When last visiting my sister in the country, I was very much grieved to hear of the death of a dear boy in that neighborhood at the age of sixteen. The doctors said he was dying of quick consumption, but on his death-bed he confessed that the cause of his death was self-abuse. He could not die until he had made this confession to his mother, telling how a woman who had the care of him had taught him, the habit and how he would often go alone and practice the evil until he would not have life enough to walk back up the garden walk, but would have to wait until a little strength returned to him. At the age of sixteen he died an awful death, and has left his record for you to read.

Oh, my dear boys! do take warning, and if

you have commenced to smoke, which almost always leads to other bad habits, after reading this true story of a poor boy in England, do go right on your knees and pray God to help you, and we will pray for you too, that God will save you from every evil and cleanse your hearts by the precious blood of Jesus, who is so grieved as he looks down upon the dear boys, for whom he gave his life, thus destroying their bodies and unfitting their souls to live with him in heaven. You will then grow up healthy, strong, and manly, with happiness in this world and a bright eternity in the life which is to come.

My sister told me of another boy whom I have known from a baby. She told me how bright and innocent he had always been when he would come to visit her, until this last year, when she was so grieved to find all his frank boyhood had left him and he would not wish to kiss her good night, although he was still very young, but appeared shy and retiring. She noticed, too, how thin and old-looking his face was getting. Soon afterward she received a letter from his mother full of concern for her boy; for while all thought he was going into quick consumption, she found that he was practicing secret vice, but said she felt ashamed to speak to him or to mention it to his father. Oh, dear mothers, as you read this warning, lay aside all such modesty and talk plainly with your children, and in gentle loving words show them the great harm they will do their bodies if they practice this evil. You can begin to teach them while they are very young.

God will give you language, if you seek his wisdom, which will not shock them or put impure thoughts into their minds. Show them how sacred their little bodies are and how careful God wants them to be to keep them pure for him. The children will love you for it, and you will gain their confidence.

I know a little boy very well who has been saved from this evil habit, and he is doing all he can to save other boys by giving out tracts to them, and whenever he has the opportunity he talks of the great evil. He has told me that when at school the boys had a place where they went to practice this evil, and the big boys taught the little boys, and thus hundreds are getting initiated into this sinful habit.

Now, boys, there is a great field for you to work in if you get saved like this little boy. I know you can begin at once, and be home missionaries in rescuing others, and God says in his Word that "they that turn many to righteousness shall shine as the stars forever and ever." I pray God to bless you all and make you boys after his own heart, that you may be pillars in his church to go no more out forever.

Yours in Jesus' love,
"Aunt Kate."

Dear Boys: With a heart full of love for souls that are bound in sin, I feel led to write you a short letter, with a prayer to God that it may instruct some boy into the wonderful gospel light of salvation in Jesus.

I was born in a country home in Kentucky and was my parents' joy and pride, as many little children are; but little did they dream of the demon that was seeking to destroy their boy, both soul and body. At last I grew out of baby years into boyhood, and not receiving any warning from my parents in regard to secret things, the enemy saw his chance and ensnared his victim. There was a schoolmate much older than myself, and through him the temptation was presented. Well do I remember the place and time, but being ignorant and innocent I did not resist the temptation, and the enemy of my soul had begun his binding with the awful sin of secret vice, which led me into many other wicked things, that ruined my health; my parents not dreaming what was the matter with their boy.

As I grew older conviction rested upon my soul, but I tried to fight it away; yet it grew deeper and deeper, until I realized fully my shame in that great evil and I yielded to God for his mercy, and he forgave all my sins. Not having proper teaching, I lost the victory out of my soul, and back into old paths I went, until I heard the pure gospel of salvation from all sin preached, which I received into my heart so I can testify to the truth that Jesus Christ saves and heals soul and body from the awful habit of self-abuse, the use of tobacco, and many other sins.

All praise be to Jesus' name for the victory I have over sin, the flesh, and the Devil. How it fills my soul with sorrow as I meet promising young men, yet behind the curtain we can see this awful sin lingering upon the soul and body.

Dear reader, we trust you will take warning and flee to Jesus with your troubles and sins, whatever they may be. He is patiently waiting, and will pardon all who will come with broken and contrite hearts.

Your affectionate brother, J——.

Dear Boys: My heart is pained as I think of the awful curse of secret sins; of how many precious ones are caught in this delusive snare of the Devil, and almost before they are aware they find themselves bound hand and foot, their bodies dragged to early graves, and their souls hastened to an awful eternity—without God and without hope; for Paul tells us plainly that "they which do such things shall not inherit the kingdom of God."—Gal. 5 : 19-21. See also 1 Cor. 6 : 9, 11. Yet how ignorant the great mass of boys are of its sad and awful results.

Oh, boys! God has laid it upon me to write, and with tears I do so, praying that some precious one may take warning from my bitter experience, and not fall into the same snare. My father was a drunkard, and (as such are licentious) so I inherited " perverted amativeness," and falling into company of bad children at an early age I naturally fell into ways of lust.

As soon as it was possible, I began to indulge in habits which I practiced excessively for several years. I heard my parents talk about things that filled my mind with lustful imaginations, and longed for the time to come when I could indulge my depraved desires in marriage. I loved to read love stories and novels, and to get with other boys to talk about sensual things. While at my work I would allow my mind to be carried away in "day-dreams" of lust and pleasure or building air-castles of sensuality, which were but for the moment, only to awake to the awful reality that I was ruining myself and making my way to the grave of a suicide.

Oh, the deceptiveness of Satan! How bitter is sin! Though for a season we may relish it and "roll it as a sweet morsel under our tongues," yet the end is sure to be "bitter remorse and woe." I wanted to be free, and tried to quit. I prayed that God would help me, I tried, but, alas! in vain. I found myself bound, hand and foot (so to speak), in the iron chains of lust, helpless as an infant.

Then began the battle, I wanted to be free. Again and again I vowed, "This will be the last time," but my vows were as often broken. The Devil and my desire would whisper, "Just this once more, the very last time," but it only proved to be an unbroken chain of failures. I would make strong resolutions, but so completely was I in the control of the destroyer of soul and body that when temptation came I could not resist. My will-power was gone. Oh, wretched one that I was; most miserable! Who would deliver me? Who would help me? There were plenty of evil influences to urge me on in evil, but were there none to help me get the victory? Oh, how I longed for human sympathy—but found none! Even God seemed to have forsaken me, and would not hear my cry, would not regard my tears. Of all the wretched, I felt myself most miserable. What should I do? Where should I go? Was there no help for me?

In the meantime I had fallen still lower, even to the depth of lustful degradation, disobeying the Word of God (Lev. 18:23) and bringing myself into the most miserable condition. Trembling, fevered, physically exhausted, with aching head to toss upon my bed in awful anguish of conscience. Oh, my God! My God! How was it possible? Now as I look at it from a standpoint of salvation, I am compelled to cry, "How is it possible for man to fall so low?" Yet such is the case many times. O, God, deliver our boys! Oh, that parents would throw off the cloak of false modesty, awake to a sense of their duty and responsibility before God, and would instruct their children in these important matters, as they would in others, and thus save them from many pitfalls with which their pathway is beset on every side.

Finally my parents found out my sin. My mother's heart was almost broken; yet they were unable to give me proper advice and help. My unsaved stepfather turned against me more and more, and in despair I left home, to get where no one knew me. I wished myself dead, was only comforted by the thought that this evil was my thorn in the flesh. (How far mistaken!) By this time I had become so weak that I had no control over myself, and from "seminal weakness" my life was quietly passing away. Was there any hope for me? Yes, praise God! there was; for he had, after all, not forsaken me. I met (Was it by *chance?*) a dear young brother in whom I could confide, who proved a sympathizing friend to me and had himself had a bitter experience with this vice. He placed in my hands a book that gave me very much light on self-restoration, by way of temporal aid. I at once began to lead a life of regularity and temperance, denying myself many articles of food (which after all are not food) which were stimulating, took much exercise in the open air, kept my person clean by frequent cold-water hand baths, quit at once all reading of fiction, and applied myself to that which was elevating, ennobling—especially God's Word. I made desperate efforts to banish all evil thoughts from my mind as soon as they would come.

With all this God showed me that I had not a real experience of salvation. I then presented myself, soul and body, for a real deliverance, and my cry was heard, and God, for Jesus' sake, pardoned all my sins, broke the chains that bound, and set me free. Oh, praise his dear name! "Who hath delivered us from the power of darkness, and hath translated us into the kingdom of his dear Son."—Col. 1:13.

I then took the Lord as my Healer, and, "praise his name!" I have been growing stronger and healthier ever since. My eyes were almost blind, but God has wonderfully healed them. When an evil thought or temptation comes to me now, I at once rebuke the Devil and instantly banish it from me. Eph. 4:27. Thus God gives me real victory at all times and sweet peace.

Dear reader, God will do the same for you.

Yours in the love of God, E——

Dear Boys: Through the mercy, long-suffering and loving-kindness of God my Father I am permitted to add my experience in sin, and also of the saving grace of God through Jesus Christ our Lord. I am not glad that my life in sin was so wretched, for it is a shame to live so sinful. My heart is moved in gratitude to my Savior for his merciful deliverance. May God bless this testimony and make it a benefit to some dear readers.

When I was a little over eleven years old, my parents being dead, I was put in care of a guardian who placed me in the home of a school teacher. There I made new acquaintances and friends. Among these was a boy who indulged in the very sinful habit called "self-abuse." It was not enough for him to do wrong on his own body, and to sin against God, but he must also teach it to others. I became one of his victims, and not knowing the awful results that it would have I practiced it more and more, and like my master I taught it to others.

After I reached the age of fourteen I had to make another change, and left my foster-father's, to go to a city to learn a trade as an apprentice. The influence there was not for my good, as it is written: "Evil communications corrupt good manners." Filthy conversation between the workers had its full course, and my young mind drew the poison in until my conversation partook of the same nature. Those filthy talks added fuel to the fire of lust, and fastened the terrible habit closer to me.

Time rolled on—my apprenticeship was over. The thought came that it would be better to still the awful lust of the flesh in the house of the harlot. Although I went there a short time, it gave me no relief from my controlling habit; for when the temptation came, I yielded again and again. I spent a great deal of money for the satisfying of my lustful nature, but all in vain. Not only my hard-earned money went, but also health, manhood, and character. I became diseased with a most shameful disease, although only twenty years old. O beloved reader, if you will escape the awful misery of a sinful life, "flee youthful lusts." It is hard for me to describe the shame, guilt, and remorse of conscience I felt. After reaching the age of twenty-one I left my native country and sailed for South America. New country, climate, language, and people were my surroundings; but my "besetting sin" followed me. Like a serpent fastened to its victim, so this shameful habit clung to me and bound me stronger than ever before.

During this time I often tried to quit the secret evil, but made failure after failure. Sometimes I could abstain from it for a week, and at other times only for a few days; but often I yielded to it every day. Only one time, until my conversion, I abstained three months through a little better influence from my surroundings and a strong desire to live better. This was my happiest time from my first indulgence in that habit until the year 1892. I thought I was delivered from it, but did not know that the old serpent was only at rest for a little time to break forth in double fury. As my surroundings changed I again yielded to its allurements and power. My life became a burden to me. I traveled from city to city, from country to country, earning money, spending money —not only what I earned, but some of that which through the kindness of my dear parents was left to me. Yet in all that I was not satisfied—yea, wretched was my life. My conscience once so tender that I could not tell the slightest untruth without the blood rushing to my face and my heart beating as if it would burst, became "seared as with a hot iron." Where once was a tender heart there seemed to be a stone. Yes, wretched has been my life on many lines. I could tell of many sad experiences with good friends (?), of losses, sickness, and sins of many kinds; but it may not be in place now.

In the year 1890 I went back to California, where I had been once before. My health was not good; although I was more careful on some lines than before, still my secret evil was master. While at San Pedro keeping restaurant, a little mission sprang into existence. For some time the meetings were held there, and about Christmas I went there for the first time; not to seek God or deliverance from my slavish habits, but for the sake of a girl who was working there. I made fun for some time in the singing—where beautiful words were I placed filthy words, and so on. But soon I saw myself as never before. The Lord sent conviction to my heart, and my sins mounted up before me as great mountains. My heart seemed to be darker than the darkest night; I felt I was the chief of sinners. Going to another town on business, I tried in various usual ways to find enjoyment, but most miserable I was with "bitter remorse and woe" upon me. My soul cried, "*I am most miserable.*" I resolved not to drink any more, and only one more drink I took the next day as it seemed most necessary to do so under my severe suffering. I went back home. I tried to stop swearing, to leave off bad and filthy words; but only succeeded in part. I tried to quit that bad habit, but only made a sad failure. Through the testimonies of those who claimed to be saved, there entered a desire to find the peace and satisfaction of which they spoke. I began to pray, but my misery only seemed to get the greater, and I became very sin-sick.

God took my case in his hands, his goodness led me to repentance; he gave me that godly sorrow which worketh repentance unto salvation. I became willing to forsake all sin, my business if need be; for I wanted that heavy burden removed, as it seemed I could bear it no longer. I thought if I could only weep it would be a relief to me, but there were no tears. I began to pray and to plead for mercy, but only felt worse. I stood five nights on the street, hat in hand, to pray, but it seemed God would not hear me. On the 20th of March after meeting I went again to pray, without finding relief; so I went back to the meeting-house, where a dear brother invited me in, which I gladly accepted. After a little talk and a few Bible verses, I knelt down with him (the first time in my life) to pray. He prayed, and then I prayed, confessing my sins and calling on God for mercy. At once the long-sought tears began to stream down my face, the burden of my soul rolled away, and the peace of God entered in. Praise God forever and ever! The dear Lord fulfilled his word: "And ye shall seek me, and find me, when ye shall search for me with all your heart." Jesus became my Savior. I was "born again." Praise his name!

Old things are past; all things are become new. After a life of sin until I was twenty-nine years of age, I found deliverance in the Lord Jesus Christ, freedom from the bondage of sin and bad habits.

Great and wonderful is the change God has wrought in me. Swearing, filthy and foolish talking, jesting, and all bad habits are gone. "If any man be in Christ, he is a new creature." Almost six years are past since God for Jesus' sake gave me salvation. During that time the Devil overcame me once—shortly after my conversion—on that habit of sexual abuse. Again God in mercy granted me true repentance and forgave me. Since that time I made a full surrender of myself and all to him, and he did cleanse me, through the precious blood of Jesus, from all sin, and sanctified my soul and filled me with the Holy Spirit. Since then I am no more troubled in any way by the old sinful habit, for which I do praise our dear Savior.

After my conversion I had to learn to "walk in the light." I had so little knowledge of the Word of God and his desires that I had to learn it little by little, and walk in the light of his Word as it shone upon me in its study. God has promised that his Spirit shall "lead us into all truth." This promise was fulfilled to me, and I saw different things I must do to please God and be obedient. Some old wrongs came up to be made right, and God's grace enabled me to do it. Other things I did not know, I had to do as the knowledge came. I love now to obey and serve Jesus. "His yoke is easy and his burden is light."

Dear reader, if you should be in bondage to sin or evil habits, come to him who is mighty to save. He is no respecter of persons. He will save one and all.

Seek him while he may be found. He will give you life. May God bless you, and deliver you from the awfulness of sin, for Jesus' sake, Amen.

   Your saved brother,
     kept in Jesus' love,
       W————.

"Clap your hands, all ye people; shout unto God with the voice of triumph."—Ps. 47:1.

AS OTHERS SEE IT.

Often the readers of religious books feel great inclination to take exception to unpleasant truths as presented therein, under the pretext that "Christian people are apt to make much out of little." It is a fact that those who are acquainted with the teachings of God's Word and the privileges and benefits of salvation are more apt to see the exceeding sinfulness of wrong-doing than those who are not looking at it from that standpoint. The subject of secret sin may be looked upon in this way by some of our readers; therefore we want to give you some extracts from those who view it from the point of "sexual science," and "for the best good of man."

"Personal Fornication. The Worst of Sexual Vices."

"Masturbation outrages nature's sexual ordinances more than any or all forms of sexual sin man can perpetrate, and inflicts consequences the most terrible. Would that its presentation 'might pass' but 'sexual science' and the best good of man demand its fearless exposition.

"It is man's sin of sins, and vice of vices; and has

caused incomparably more sexual dilapidation, paralysis, and disease, as well as demoralization, than all the other sexual depravities combined. Neither Christendom, nor heathendom, suffers any evil at all to compare with this; because of its universality and its terribly fatal ravages on body and mind; and because it attacks the young idols of our hearts, and hopes of future years. Pile all other evils together—drunkenness upon all cheateries, swindlings, robberies, and murders, and tobacco upon both; for it is the greatest scourge; and all sickness, disease, and pestilence upon all; and war as the cap-sheaf of them all—and all combined cause not a tithe as much human deterioration and misery as does this secret sin.

"Ho! darling youth! Please listen to a little plain talk from one who loves you with a father's affection. If you were walking thoughtlessly along a pathway across which was a deep, miry, miasmatic slough, so covered that you would not notice it till you had fallen in and defiled yourself all over with the filthiest, most nauseating slime possible, so that you could never cleanse yourself from this stench, and so that all who ever saw you would know what you had done; beside it being so poisonous as to destroy forever a large part of all your future life, enjoyment, and capacities; and far more corrupting to your morals than blighting to health and happiness, would you not heartily thank any friend to kindly tell you plainly of your danger?

"SUCH A DANGER, O splendid boy, awaits you; only that it is a thousandfold worse than any description.

It not only poisons your body, destroys your rosy cheeks, breaks down your nerves, impairs your digestion, and paralyzes your whole system; but it also corrupts your morals, creates thoughts and feelings the vilest and the worst possible, and endangers your very soul's salvation. No words can describe the miseries it inflicts throughout your whole life, down to death. But its ravages do not stop there; they follow and prey on you forever! You can never fully rid yourself of the terrible evils it inflicts. You might almost as well die outright as thus to pollute yourself.

"THE PATHWAY OF LIFE you are now traveling is thus beset. This danger is the secret sin of self-pollution. It is by far the worst of all the sins and vices to which you are exposed. It blights nearly all. If it does not spoil you also, it will be because you heed this warning, and abstain wholly from it. Children, I pity you from the lowest depths of my soul, in view of the terrible ordeal before you; and rendered the more appalling by your ignorance of its evils.

"It is called masturbation, and consists in indulging immodest feelings and actions, and imagining sexual pleasures with one of the opposite sex while handling your own private parts.

"ITS PRACTICE ALMOST UNIVERSAL IN CIVIC LIFE."

"Most boys perpetrate it, and many females. * * * The most carefully educated and religious youths are not safe. Apply any numerical test you please;

catechize promiscuously every boy you meet; and nine in ten over nine years old practice it. Many who deny it in words, own up in deed, by manifesting shame—a sure sign of guilt. Of those still older the proportion is even greater. Question the keepers of our hospitals for bad boys and poor children. A friend took a boy about ten years old from an asylum, chastised him often and severely for this vice, but to no purpose; and finally kept his hands tied behind him, but found him incorrigible. He died soon after. Boys not yet four years old sometimes practice it; and millions are ruined by it before they enter their teens. None are safe, not even our own dear children, though watched however closely. The following dialogue during a professional examination represents similar ones by thousands:

"'Consumption, madam, is rapidly fastening on your son.' 'I know it, and expect to lose him within a year, as I lately lost his brother.' 'He can be saved by giving up its only cause, masturbation.' 'You are mistaken! My husband had many patients with that disease; he charged me to watch our boys closely —sheets, linen, etc.—which I have done with a mother's vigilance from boyhood. You are positively wrong.' 'How is this, young man? You know and dare not falsify.' 'I have polluted myself all the way up from boyhood, as did my brother. I knew, then, that this practice caused his death. And our sister, too, does the same thing.'

"Dr. Woodward, who so long and ably presided

over the Worcester Lunatic Asylum, higher authority than whom could hardly be quoted, a discreet man, who means all he says, writes thus touching it: 'Those who think that information on this subject is either unnecessary or injurious are hardly aware how extensively known this habit is with the young, or how early in life it is sometimes practiced. I have never conversed with a lad twelve years of age who did not know all about the practice, and understand the language used to describe it.'

"This is a topic in physiology which artificial modesty has covered up, until a solitary but fatal vice is spreading desolation throughout our schools and families, unnoticed and unknown. 'Thousand of pure minded and amiable boys and young men are undermining their physical constitution, and prospectively corrupting their souls by a pleasurable, and, to many of them, innocent gratification.'—*Wm. G. Woodbridge.*

" 'Self-pollution is undoubtedly one of the most common causes of ill health among the young men of this country. This practice is almost universal. Boys commence it at an early age, and the habit once formed, like intemperance, becomes almost unconquerable. In boarding-schools and colleges it obtains, oftentimes, without exception. Hence the many sickly students, and the many young men of the most brilliant and promising talents, who have broken their constitutions, ruined their health, and must leave college, as it is said " by hard study." '—*Dr. Snow.*

"Its Terrible Effects on Body and Mind."

" ' No other tree bears fruit as bitter or poisonous. We will mention a few only, for their tithe would fill the earth with volumes, as they have with woes. Its drain upon the vital forces is indeed terrible. Semen contains forty times more vital force than an equal amount of red blood right from the heart. Think what wonders it accomplishes. Many of the ills which come upon the young at and after puberty arise from this habit, persisted in so as to waste their vital energies and enervate their physical and mental powers. Nature designs that this drain should be reserved to mature age, and even then be made but sparingly. Sturdy manhood, in all its vigor, loses its energy and bends under the too frequent expenditure of this important secretion; and no age or condition will protect a man from the danger of unlimited indulgence, though legally and naturally exercised. In the young, however, its influence is much more seriously felt; and even those who have indulged so cautiously as not to break down their health or mind cannot know how much their physical energy, mental vigor, and moral purity have been weakened by this indulgence. No cause produces as much insanity. The records of the institutions give an appalling catalogue of cases attributed to it. Consumption, spinal distortions, weak and painful eyes, weak stomachs, nervous headaches, and a host of other diseases mark its influence upon the body; loss of memory and the power of application, insanity, idiotism show its devastating effects upon the mind.'—*Dr. Woodward.*

" 'The empire which this odious practice gains over the senses is beyond expression. No sooner does this uncleanness get possession of the heart than it pursues its votaries everywhere, and governs them at all times and in all places. Upon the most serious occasions, and in the solemn acts of religion they find themselves transported with lustful conceptions and desires which take up all their thoughts.'—*Tissot.*

" ' The sin of self-pollution is one of the most destructive evils ever practiced by fallen man. In many respects it is several degrees worse than common whoredom, and has in its train more awful consequences. It excites the powers of nature to *undue action* and produces *violent secretions* which necessarily and speedily *exhaust the vital principles and energy;* hence the muscles become flacid and feeble; the true and natural action of the nerves, relaxed and impeded; the understanding, confused; the memory, oblivious; the judgment, perverted; and the will, wholly without energy to resist. The eyes appear languishing and without expression, and the countenance vacant. Appetite ceases, for the stomach is incapable of performing its proper office; nutrition fails; tremors, fears, and terrors are generated, and thus the wretched victim drags out a miserable existence, till, *superannuated,* even before he had time to arrive at *man's estate,* with a mind often debilitated even to a state of idiotism, his worthless body tumbles into the grave, and his guilty soul (guilty of self-murder) is hurried into the awful presence of the Judge!

"'Reader, this is no caricature, nor are the colorings overcharged in this shocking picture. Worse woes than my pen can relate I have witnessed in those addicted to this fascinating, unnatural, and most destructive of crimes. If thou hast entered into the snare, flee from destruction, both of body and mind, that awaits thee! God alone can save thee; advice, warnings, threatenings, increasing debility of body, mental decay, checks of conscience, expostulations of judgment, and medical assistance will all be lost on thee. God and God *alone* can save thee from an evil which has in its issue the destruction of thy body, and the final perdition of thy sould.'—*Adam Clarke.*

"All sexual sins are condemned by the entire Bible. Look at its denunciation of fornication, adultery, etc. God grant that you may be kept from both; but if you indulge in masturbation as the lesser sin and evil, you certainly err. Private fornication causes twenty times more misery than any other sexual sin; and this is substantially the opinion of all who have examined this subject. * * * Abstain totally and forever. Every indulgence weakens hope, and is like rowing down the Niagara rapids, instead of toward the banks. Gradual emancipation like leaving off drinking by degrees, will certainly increase both indulgence and suffering. This is true of all bad habits and doubly of this. Now is the accepted time; behold, now is the day of salvation.

Indulgence is triple ruin. Abstinence or death is your only alternative. Stop now and forever or abandon all hope. Will you long debate which of the two to choose—'slavery and death,' and *such a death;* or abstinence and life? Do you 'return to your wallowing' and give up to die? * * *

"PREVENTIONS OF SELF-ABUSE BY KNOWLEDGE."

"Knowledge is its sure preventive. What salvation remains for those yet guiltless. To forestall is infinitely better than to cure. Must all our noble, all our pure, lovely girls be defiled by this moral leprosy, and lost if not redeemed? Is there no preventive? Can they not be kept *from* this fell destroyer? Must all fall over this moral precipice, only to rise maimed for life? What a pity this offering up of human life on this vile altar! We cannot spare our sons, we must not lose our daughters thus. They are infinitely precious. Think what a darling youth is worth! Its entire future, and that of all its descendants, are at stake. The risk is too awful; no parents should sleep until they have first so hedged their darlings around that they cannot sin. In the name of agonized myriads how can this plague be stayed? * * * *Not by ignorance.* That means has been tried, only to fail, quite too long already. All who fall, sin for want of knowledge; nothing can be clearer. Say ye who have sinned, did you not err through ignorance? Would not one seasonable warning have prevented all the suffering it has caused you? Let universal experience decide.

"Parental warning and counseling are its great forestallers and preventers. Parents are bound to feed, clothe, and educate their children, and guard them against lying, stealing, etc.; then why not also against this secret sin as well—as much the worst, as it is the most ruinous to soul and body? *God* in *nature* puts on parents the sacred duty of guarding their darlings against all sinful and self-ruining practices; and their *first* is to preserve them against this vice. * * * Oh, if my parents had only seasonably warned me against this vice, I should have escaped all this impairment of body, and demoralization of mind! How could they let me thus sin ignorantly and thoughtlessly?"—*Extracts from Prof. O. S. Fowler's Works.*

As boys and young men are often disposed to carelessness in searching out for themselves that instruction that they most need, it becomes necessary for those who are interested in their welfare to place the knowledge within the reach of all. There is generally a high regard paid to the testimony and experience of medical men; therefore we desire to give you some of their teaching on this subject of "Masturbation."

"Our object in preparing and publishing this article is to impart correct information upon a subject which is of greatest importance to mankind, but which, from false modesty and a mistaken sense of duty, has been quite generally ignored both by parents and by the medical profession. To this prudery or false modesty, is due an immeasurable amount of suffering, and great injury to the human race. We have only to look about us with a practiced eye, to see abundant evidence of the truth of this assertion. We cannot enter a church or a theater or walk the streets, without being painfully conscious of the terrible consequences of this ruinous habit, which is largely the result of ignorance on the part of the victims. The statements which we have received both by letter and in person, from many thousands of these unfortunates, prove conclusively that this habit is often formed in ignorance of the terrible evils which follow the abuse of the generative organs. * * *

"That such a terrible state of things should, from feelings of false delicacy, be permitted at this period of the world's history is simply monstrous; that medical men should be averse to affording instructive and sound information upon this important subject is equally discreditable. Every one should know that in the marvelous and most perfect work of God, no one set of organs is more sacred, private, or worthy than others of the system, and that there is nothing improper or indelicate in the naked truth concerning their functions, whether in health or in disease.

"From the period of puberty or maturity to old age, the generative organs exercise a more potent influence over the health of both men and women than any other organs, and they are more abused. This is due to the fact that the youth of the land are kept in total ignorance concerning the ruinous effects of self-abuse, or masturbation. They fall easily into this pernicious practice, which saps the vigor, undermines and ruins the constitution, and, if the victim marries and has not by such indulgences rendered himself entirely impotent, he becomes the father of puny offspring; or, more frequently, being entirely impotent, it renders both his own life and that of his companion most wretched. * * *

"Some boys seem to regard the practice of this vice, like the vile habit of smoking and chewing tobacco, as a manly accomplishment. A boy may inherit a predisposition to this practice, or his sexual feelings may be awakened at an early age and his bad example be imitated by many others. In this way, the habit is early acquired, and, when the sexual propensities are habitually indulged to the exclusion of the cultivation of higher and nobler pleasures, if not rendered impotent by these abuses, such a person may transmit the same propensity to his offspring, so that it becomes irresistible.

"The indications of this vice in boys are irritability, impatience, and restlessness, loss of flesh, pallor, and a timid, downcast look. There is loss of memory and the intellect becomes enfeebled. They are melancholy, easily discouraged, and prefer solitude. They do not remember what they learn, the nervous system shows serious impairment, and the general health fails. The symptoms are too significant to deceive the experienced eye. The short, irritable replies of the boy, and his general sensitiveness and nervousness are indicative of the loss of nerve-power, occasioned by this habit.

"This evil can only be prevented by knowing the habits of children and regulating them in early life. * * * Parents hesitate to talk to their boys, because they fear putting impure ideas into innocent minds. Their hopes are strong that *their* sons will never indulge in so degrading a practice. It is a false modesty which restrains them from fulfilling this duty. If they do not attend to their children's interest, who will? The child's confidence should be gained through the manifestation of a tender personal concern. Diffidence and suspicion on the part of the parent destroys confidence in the child. Parents should divest themselves of all false modesty, and by their frankness establish an understanding which will result in mutual confidence. The physician compassionately meets his patient, is pitiful, tender, and kind. When parents are actuated by the same feelings, they can win the confidence, guard the health, and preserve the morals of their children.

"We cannot too earnestly urge upon parents the necessity of forewarning their children against yielding to this pernicious desire. Boys ought to know that they may be thrown into the company of older lads who practice masturbation, and who may solicit them to acquire the same vile habits. They should be taught to resist these solicitations and exercise self-control, or they will be carried by the swift current of licentiousness to utter moral and physical ruin.

"If the lad be instructed that this unnatural sexual enjoyment is a degrading pollution, a low practice, in which no right-minded boy will indulge, the gratification will be followed by an instinctive sense of disgust and self-condemnation. He will then realize that restraint is far more manly, and that *self-control* is a higher test of maturity than the degrading indulgence of his passions. Nature requires her own time to nourish the body, complete the physical framework, and bring every member and organ to perfect maturity. * * * Excitement of the reproductive organs with the hand or other unnatural means is called masturbation, or self-abuse, even when no semen is lost. The practice inflicts injury on the nervous system, causing great loss of nervous power. The habit being once formed, the desire for such indulgence increases, until he becomes * * * a monomaniac on this subject.

"Passion may aptly be termed the voice of the body, by which, if we listen, we are enchanted and led astray. Conscience is the voice of the soul, which remonstrates, and, if we obey it, we shall be guided aright. We cannot reconcile these two conflicting voices, and, if we indulge the passions when conscience forbids gratification, the remembrance of the wrong remains forever, and constant fear is an everlasting punishment. Man possesses few powers which are more highly prized than those of virility, which is the very essence of manhood. He is but the counterfeit of a man, who hath not the life of a man.

"Montaigne says: 'We must see and get acquainted with our sins if we expect to correct them.' Virtue predisposes trials just as much as victory implies warfare. The triumph of virtue consists in overcoming morbid or excessive passion. As men in all ages have been influenced by passions, so temptation has ever found its victims. It is an obligation on every one to overcome every evil passion or weakness to which he is subject, and the discharge of his personal duty requires *moral courage*."—*Extracts from the works of R. V. Pierce, M. D.*

SOCIAL PURITY.

In the previous chapters we have seen some of the evils arising from unrestrained sexual desire, and as they are so much greater than many of us have imagined, some may think the picture overdrawn or think it needless to dwell longer upon it. There are, however, several great needs on this line that have not received the attention necessary among young men; therefore we entreat your careful attention to this subject.

When we see how widely spread is the evil of secret sin among the young, and how its every tendency is to impure thought and action, we may wonder how much further into evil they would go if unrestrained. Surely the depth of sin is without a limit.

When one allows himself to be governed by impurity in imagination, in thought, in desire, and in action he soon loses his love for what is good and pure. Impurity has greater attraction to him than virtue and purity. He becomes a sensualist; a groveling human being, seeking out that which is offensive, low, vulgar, debasing, degrading and vicious, until manhood is lost, and he becomes an object of disgust as well as of pity to those who have retained their moral integrity to principle.

If boys would choose that which is best as they journey along the path of life, they would find themselves gradually aspiring to that which is good and true. Let us follow two boys in their different courses of life. They are two bright, healthy, romping lads, going to the same school, equally capable of receiving a good education and fitting themselves for a useful life. They have good homes, kind parents, and friends. Their teacher is a young man of principle, encouraging his pupils in right and good ways, beside inspiring them with strong desires for improvement and intellectual progress.

James, with clear mind and heart, receives this influence, and his appreciation for the good and true in life is increased, and he moves forward with earnest effort. Each victory over his lower inclinations gives him greater love for all that is admirable, and thus he climbs upward into a purer and better life. He disdains selfishness, anger, impurity, and every mean and low action, and aspires to a clean life in secret and in public. Every impure thought is banished by its opposite, and every unholy action is scorned and supplanted by honorable ones. Thus he avoids impure language, all bad habits, has respect for parents, sisters, schoolmates, and friends, and accords to each all that is due, and as his love for the good develops we find him searching for truth and finding it in the word of God, until he realizes its fulfillment in his life of devotion and service to God.

His schoolmate Harry seems to drift with the influence for good, but fails to appreciate its true worth or to accept it with his mind and heart, and as the opposite influence bears upon him he gradually yields thereto until the influence for good is looked upon with lightness, then with aversion, and finally with scorn. He takes up every impulse that has the prospect of pleasure, ease, comfort, or advancement in worldly ways, until principle, right, and wisdom are rejected and his life path leads downward to all that is degrading. He loses respect for himself by secret evil doings, for his parents by disobedience, for his sisters by impure thoughts, and for mankind in his selfish purpose to make every one subserve his interests and desires. Thus it becomes a little matter to take step after step in evil until the bottom is reached. When he has drained the cup of sensual pleasure and swallowed the dregs of shame, ill health, and despair, he looks back upon his youth and up to his friend James and wonders why there was such a difference in their life pathways. It seems to him that "fate" has been unkind to him and has favored the one more than the other. How little he comprehends the cause, and how far from self-blame he is as he abuses " his luck " and wishes life was as it should be—a "joyous season of existence."

Boys, can you see why these two lives drifted so far apart? Can you see where the turning-point was? Have you, dear reader, made your choice for life? or are you drifting upon the treacherous sea of influence and letting the various winds thereof beat your frail life-boat upon rocks, into gulfs and bays of sin and folly, and into the dark abyss of eternal woe? Ah, dear boys! life is what you make it; a power for good, or a miserable failure. You must either be a conquering hero, battling for right, or a slave to wrong, conquered by evil influence. Which is it with you? The right use of life makes it yield all its attractions, all its beauty, sweetness, pureness, richness, and glory; while the wrong use brings out of it all that could be harmful, sorrowful, debasing, degrading, and loathsome. Sure as the one yields good fruit, so sure the other yields evil fruit. Is it not sad to see so many made miserable for life by a failure to be wise?

As the thoughts of impurity, of unrighteous living and unholy desires, find lodgment in the heart, then begins the life of sensuality that ends in the punishment of the wicked, in banishment from God. To think that God-given powers should be so wrongfully used as to deserve the censure of God in eternal punishment is sad indeed. Man is responsible for his thoughts, and is able to control them by rejecting instantly everything that has a tendency to evil. We learn this from the Bible when it says: "But I say unto you that whosoever looketh on a woman to lust after her hath committed adultery with her already in his heart." Not only the overt act of adultery is blamable, but the desire for it within the heart. Not only is the taking of life murder, but the feeling of hatred within the heart is also. "Blessed are the pure in heart." If the heart is pure, no impurity can come forth in the life, in thought or action. Therefore we ought to be able to see the need of the saving grace of God.

When one has yielded to impure thoughts and secret evil practices, it is not such a great step to other sexual evils, such as adultery, betrayal of the innocent, whoredom, etc. Would to God every boy could have such a respect for womanhood as never to stain his heart with impure thoughts concerning it. Think of women as mothers, sisters, wives, with love and holy reverence for their many lovable traits and qualities. It is possible; and all of our readers should strive to do so. To think of her in a sensual way lowers both manhood and womanhood.

Wonderful in the wisdom of God is the right relation of the sexes—man to stand in his greater strength as provider, guide, and lover; and woman by his side as helpmeet, giving reverence and love in sweet submission. The thought of women as a source of sexual indulgence or as a means of selfish abuse is repugnant to the emotion of true love. Nothing is more the opposite of pure love than uncontrolled sexuality. If any one should think to provide himself with a wife in order to avoid all self-control of sexuality, he misses his mark widely; for in no other station is there greater need of self-control in moderation and wisdom. The health, happiness, wisdom, and spirituality of the family demand it. Much of the illness of both sexes is from the abuse of the marriage relation in over-indulgence, and much of the unnatural strength of sexuality in the young is due to inherited tendency created by lack of control of themselves in the parents.

There is a sentiment among young men of which they should be heartily ashamed, as it is below the dignity of manhood. It is this: Girls should be so strong for virtue that no man could overthrow them by his importunities, deceits, or allurements; therefore it is his right to test his acquaintances on that line, and if he finds one weak enough to yield to him her virtue in the moment of temptation, he may take it, as she is not *worthy* of it, and thus rob her of her most precious possession, and start her on a road of shame. Oh, ye young men, what are you better than she? Do you not also yield your virtue when you take hers? Do you not know that when she respects you and you suggest the evil, she must in a moment cast aside that respect for you or else she must deem the action less sinful because you seem to approve it? And do you not *appear* to do so when you encourage her in it? And is it fair for you to invite her and count her guilty and you innocent? Would it not be fair for you to count her innocent until she invites you to yield your virtue? Is it right to take advantage of one's weakness to take her possessions? The expression of a father has long been remembered. "I count the man who will make improper proposals to a girl far worse than the girl who yields her virtue. He knows only his own desires, while she must bear her own weakness with the knowledge of his wishes, making her task doubly hard. She would probably never give it a moment's thought did he not propose it, therefore the blame rests upon him."

Every man or boy who escorts a girl or woman should consider her virtue under his protection, and he blamable for any impure or unvirtuous thought or act towards her. And should she evince any impropriety, he is bound to resist it just as effectually as if he were the girl, and thus protect himself and her. There are many girls living lives of shame whose only fault was a lack of decision in standing against the evil proposal of those they respected and loved. It should be the cause of great sorrow to any young man to know a pure, virtuous, weak girl was led astray through his or some one else's wrong-doing. Every upright, honest boy and man should feel a great care for all his lady acquaintances and do all possible to preserve their virtue and purity. All men should be held to the same law of right and wrong as governs women. If you expect virtue and purity from mothers, wives, sisters, and friends, so must they expect the same from you. If you betray a girl under the promise of marriage and leave her to her shame and sorrow, you are far worse than she and should be held responsible for the same and fully as guilty as she, if not many times worse. Oftentimes for some trifling impropriety or a frankness in manifesting respect or love a girl is considered forward, and every advantage taken to betray her in order to "teach her a lesson," as the man asserts, and throw the blame upon her. Oh, how cruel! know you not that God will judge for all this?

We know that the youthful feet of our sons may be led astray by the enticements of those who live by the destruction of manhood and virtue. There should be little need to warn the youth of this degradation if they were rightfully taught from the cradle to honor and respect womanhood and virtue in their purity, and to loathe and abhor their abuse. But as there are so many who have received and entertained wrong impressions thereon, we Christian mothers would kindly and firmly insist upon every boy and young man calmly and candidly looking this most important subject of sexual temptation squarely in the face. Every unvirtuous woman or girl has been made so by the misbehavior of some man or boy. Had he retained his virtue and his regard for her virtue, there would have been no loss of virtue.

You may say, "They were equally guilty," or, "She led him on." It may be so in some cases, but facts are against the supposition that women are more ready to become unvirtuous than men. The majority of fallen women have been lured, deceived, or forced into lives of shame by the hard-heartedness of men, and are more ready to give up their sinful course, even when bound by almost impossibilities, than men are when *free* to do so. Young girls ignorant and innocent of evil have been taken to places of darkest sin, even to houses of shame, and forced by hunger and cruelty to yield their virtue to the libertine; while he is free to go and come as he pleases, she is made to believe that there is no escape for her—she is doomed to a life of shame, without home or friends, and, with no means of making a living. She abandons herself to all that is left to her, and sinks to the lowest depths of sin and shame, and after a few years passes into the dark and dreadful eternity. As woman is capable of rising to the heights of all that is good and lovely, she is capable also of falling to the lowest imagination of sin and folly and of using her powers of attraction to decoy and destroy manhood.

But, boys, stop and think! she is some mother's daughter, was once a father's pride, perhaps a loving wife or sister, and through the deceptions of base or weak men she is fallen. Perhaps she inherited the evil tendency to sexual depravity from a drunkard father (for authorities say that the majority of fallen women are daughters of drunkards) or acquired it early in the life of innocency, from evil associates or from lack of parental care. Now will any of you be blameless if you take advantage of her weakness and hasten her on in a downward course? While we hope you may all have a strong regard for virtue of womanhood, we do hope you may do your share in protecting it: and though we wish you to have a holy hatred of all sexual impurity, may you have compassion upon the weak and erring ones, shielding them from abuse and rescuing them from their evil ways.

We are heartily sorry for all who have lost their virtue through the deceitfulness of sin, and have taken to themselves the company, the degradation, the shame, and the disease of the licentious. Words fail to describe the awfulness of the consequences of such a life; one is simply lost to all that is good in this world, and heaping upon himself for all the future all that is most undesirable. Let the wisdom of God through the words of eternal truth sink into your hearts and guide you into the paths of virtue and wisdom.

"Harken unto me now therefore, O ye children, and attend to the words of my mouth. Let not thine heart decline to her ways, go not astray in her paths. For she hath cast down many wounded: yea, many strong men have been slain by her. Her house is the way to hell, going down to the chambers of death."— Prov. 7 : 24-27.

"But whoso committeth adultery with a woman lacketh understanding: he that doeth it destroyeth his own soul. A wound and dishonor shall he get; and his reproach shall not be wiped away."—Prov. 6 : 32, 33.

"Say unto wisdom, Thou art my sister; and call understanding thy kinswoman: that they may keep thee from the strange woman, from the stranger which flattereth with her words."—Prov. 7 : 4, 5.

"For the lips of a strange woman drop as an honeycomb, and her mouth is smoother than oil; but her end is bitter as wormwood, sharp as a two-edged sword. Her feet go down to death; her steps take hold on hell. Lest thou shouldst ponder the path of life, her ways are movable, that thou canst not know them. Hear me now therefore, O ye children, and depart not from the words of my mouth. Remove thy way far from her, and come not nigh the door of her house: lest thou give thine honor unto others, and thy years unto the cruel. * * * And thou mourn at the last, when thy flesh and thy body are consumed."—Prov. 5:3-11.

You see, dear boys, from these scriptures how terrible are the consequences of an unvirtuous life. It may seem attractive, as one looks upon it as the gratification of the strongest desires; but if its evil fruits are remembered, it must certainly lose much of its attractiveness. Most individuals do not go to the depths of evil all at once, but from something they consider innocent amusement to other things less innocent, until step by step they are landed at the bottom of corruption. If all who read these words of warning will abstain from impure thoughts, vulgar conversation, and evil companionship, they will have no place for sexual secret evil and will not be led to the destruction of virtue in others.

One of the saddest sights in this sinful world is a poor forsaken unmarried woman, with a little fatherless, forsaken child, trying to provide for herself and the dependent little one, while surrounded by opposition, unkindness, scorn, and ridicule, and those who would be glad to help her on a downward course of shame. Did you ever think of the awful crime of bringing poor little fatherless children into this cold, selfish world to go unprovided for? Is not the one who will do so bereft of one of the highest emotions of the natural heart—parental love? How much more worthy of love and respect is the mother who bravely stems the tide of worldly pride, and loves and cares for her offspring, filling the place of father and mother to the very best of her ability, than the one who heartlessly forsakes her, who should feel his love and protection and fill a father's place to her child! The ways of the world are so unequal that often the man may retain his social position, respect, and consideration, while the weak woman he betrayed bears shame, censure, and banishment. This comes from the wrong impression in the minds of many that we need not expect man to reach as high a standard of virtue as woman. We hope, boys, that you all may see the injustice of this worldly opinion, and keep yourselves as pure as you wish womanhood to be.

Oftentimes young men will befriend, protect, and assist women in their efforts to provide for themselves, until they have gained their respect and perhaps love, and then take advantage of their dependence to propose improper relations and transactions; and if these are met with a firm refusal, they threaten to press them by law for what they are unable to procure: and in order to avoid such trouble and misfortune, they yield to the destroyer, hoping to satisfy his demands and then claim freedom; but this step once taken, the enemy is almost sure of the victim. Though she may plead for marriage to cover her shame or to provide for her children, he keeps himself free to abandon her and his parental responsibilities whenever he may choose. Oh, the sad hearts and lives that are caused by the evil of sexual impurity! Could we Christian mothers see this going on without warning our sons of the great wrong done thereby? When men who have been guilty of these things have been "convicted of sin, of righteousness, and the judgment to come," they have found no rest, no peace, no comfort, until they renounced all their wrong-doing and made restitution as far as possible to the wronged ones, and asked their forgiveness for all that could not be righted. Sometimes they have found it necessary to provide for their scattered children, or to take to them as wives those they have so sorely abused. Oh, dear boys! take heed to your steps. You may not know where they may lead you in after years. If you ever come to God for saving grace, you will find it much harder to retrace them by righting every wrong than it would have been to walk carefully in virtue during your youthful years.

We are convinced that some who read this subject may be so hardened by sin as to laugh at the idea of appealing to boys to protect the rights of women and children: but, though you should laugh at and scorn the instruction given and the entreaty made therein, we are sure God will fasten some of its teachings upon your hearts so that in after time, if not at present, they may do you unmeasured good; for you can never escape the fervent effectual prayer of the righteous. I want to appeal to your hearts and consciences by the sad life story of a dear sister. She wants to give it to you that it may help you to see how others suffer for the wrong-doing of men, and those who should love them too well to bring them anything but joy.

Her mother sometimes left her while quite young in the care of her older brothers, who should have regarded the trust as sacred, and protected her virtue and innocency even to the risk of their lives, but instead of doing so they let their depraved hearts and sensual natures, lust after her, even to the fullest possible extent. She was prevailed upon "not to tell mamma," and thus the evil went on until she arrived at the years of accountability, when she received such a hatred to it that she never allowed it again, living a moral and virtuous life, even without Christian influence or instruction at home. She would be so glad to reach those who are guilty of this wrong-doing with an exhortation to stop and consider where such a sinful course will lead and how awful would have been the result if she had not resisted the evil. Not all would do so, and a life of deepest shame is their future portion. Sisters brought to moral wrecks, to shame and degradation, by those who in love should protect and cherish—surely the time is here when some are "without natural affection" and are "unmerciful."

Again, her virtue and strength were tried, by one who should have loved her as his own body. Shortly before her marriage when her love and respect were fully gained, the loved one instead of honoring her virtue sought to destroy it and to "humble her" before him. She being of a quiet and easy temperament and without instruction and with false ideas gathered from her associates, did not think strange of the sinful proposal but thought a refusal would end it satisfactorily. It did not, however, and after weeks of pleading upon his part, and resisting on hers, she at last yielded to him. Her remorse, shame, and dread lest some one should find it out, filled her with sorrow that cannot be expressed, or described. And, though she was so protected that no one save herself and husband ever knew it, yet there took hold of her at that time such a spirit of lust that she became a tool in his hands to do with as he pleased—yet the awful shame and fear continually filled her soul with anguish and despair. When her married life began, the sexual desire increased, until it brought much suffering, sorrow, and pain of soul, body, and mind, and ended in her husband's early death and years of sinful self-abuse. But when she came to the loving Savior, yielded her life in service to him, he took it all away and gave perfect deliverance from all sin, sensuality, and suffering. He gave a pure heart and now helps her by his grace and mighty love to live a holy and godly life in his sight.

So, boys, please take warning and do not bring the one you intend to marry into such deep sorrow or some innocent girl to a life of shame by wicked proposals and entreaties. Beware of the judgments of God, who sees all unrighteous devices and will reward each one according to his work. If you truly love some one, then prize her virtue as a precious boon instead of desiring to destroy it, and love your own manhood and virtue enough not to seek those who have already fallen and thus help to push them further into evil, instead of helping them to live lives of virtue and honor.

We may hide many of our sins and wrong-doings from the people in the world now, but in the judgment day when we shall all be judged we cannot help ourselves or hide them from any one. With what shame and remorse must we stand before all and have the secrets of our lives brought to light; and worse than all hear that awful sentence: "Depart from me, ye cursed, into everlasting punishment." Surely there will be weeping and gnashing of teeth at their awful doom.

"Prepare to meet thy God" by forsaking and repenting of sin, believing in Jesus as your Savior from sin, and obeying his instruction.

COURTSHIP AND MARRIAGE.

Most young people are interested in this subject and are forming various opinions regarding it, according to their aspirations, surroundings, and observation. We are glad marriage is looked upon with favor by the majority of people, as it was ordained of God for wise and good purposes. If rightly understood, and entered upon wisely, it cannot fail to be a blessing to all for whom it is designed by God. That there are many failures in marriage cannot be denied, when we look around us and see the mismated, the separations, divorces, and unhappy families. While some conclude from this that it is not good to marry, and that single life is preferable to married life, and so on, we want to tell you that all this comes from a failure to do all things "for the glory of God."

God has his purposes and plans for each one of us. They are for our good, in wisdom and righteousness; but if we fail to walk in wisdom and in the way of righteousness, we get ourselves into trouble. For instance, a young man may see a nice young lady whom he admires for several reasons; therefore, he concludes it will be very nice to marry her, and he begins to show her every attention possible in order to win her love and consent to marriage. She may be far different in character from what he imagined, and he may be able to see some serious faults, or may be disappointed in her way of looking at marriage; but he shuts his eyes to everything and decides to "marry her at all cost, and not expect to find an angel." In all this he has not once considered God's pleasure in the matter or whether it will lead him nearer to God and the right. In fact, he has done it all by himself. If in after years he regrets his marriage; he wonders how it came he made such a great mistake in marrying; for in other things he has done fairly well and his judgment has been quite sound.

Will you look back, dear friends, and see how much judgment you used in the consideration of the matter? Did you look at it from every standpoint? Did you think that the choice you should make would affect your whole future—for time and eternity? Did you suppose it was a step that you could ever retrace? Did you consider that the woman who is petted, admired, waited on, and deferred to will be quite different in action from the wife who must bear a heavy share of marriage duty and obligations while you are providing the necessaries of life? Did you think that the little disagreements would become less as you were constantly together? Or did you imagine as many do that if love exists it will cover up all the blemishes and remove every disagreeable feature? Love is a great power, and will do much to make life bright and happy; but there are other things to consider. Unless two characters blend together for harmony and peace, in desire, aspiration, and mutual forbearance, there is little hope of a happy life, unless salvation brings both up to a Bible standard of living; although grace from God may do much to bring order out of chaos when even one yields to its controlling power. Still our hearts long for that companionship wherein each enjoys the same things, and they appreciate and honor each other's gifts or attainments.

As life brings many changes to us all, those who marry should remember they do so with the prospect of various changes in the one loved; but the greater harmony and agreement between two when united in marriage the less probable are the changes that would annoy or destroy it.

Then when one is considering marriage he should remember to seek for wisdom from above. In order to do so he must be saved of God, to be where God will hear and answer his prayers for wisdom and the leading of his Spirit. This may seem quite strange to those who believe in the modern wordly way of courtship and marriage, but to those who read and study their Bible it will commend itself as scriptural.

Let us follow a worldly young man through this enjoyable reason. He is one who is comfortably circumstanced in life, having a good beginning in financial ways, a good education, and moral principle. To him, marriage is a very desirable state, and his imagination is busy painting in glowing colors his future in companionship with one who shall be all that is good and lovely. He looks around him upon his lady friends, but sees no one half good enough to fill the sacred place in his affections; but he thinks it will be good to associate more freely with them, in order to "have a good time" or "to learn the art of courting." His first movements are rather awkward and embarrassing to himself and friend, but he soon gets over that and has many a good time in flirting or in studying the different types of girls. He learns many things concerning the fair sex, and what he learns makes him skeptical about some of his old imaginations. His life is all gaiety and his associates of the same nature, and so he turns from one to another in the vain hope of at least finding the right one.

At last he thinks he surely is not mistaken; here is one who comes nearer his ideal than any of the others and, though she is a stranger visiting in town, he is sure he "knows by this time who is who," and so he presses forward manfully, paying her every attention and consideration, and soon finds himself happy only in her company, which he considers a sure sign of love, and so becomes very desirous of observing the same in her, which makes him more and more earnest in his wooing. At last he can bear the suspense no longer, and he with great care and in much uncertainty asks the most important question. She refuses his proposal with dignity and coldness, observing that "it is strange that a woman cannot receive the society attentions of acquaintances without them always thinking of miserable marriage." He is more disappointed and hurt than he had any thought of being, and so he mourns his fate of "unrequited love," and the casting down of his air-castles. After a time of observing her ways at a distance and with no prospect of drawing nearer to her he finds she has a number of very serious faults, that would have made their life miserable had they tried to live together.

He again takes courage and ventures to pay attention to "a modest little thing," who generally stands in the back-ground. He is surprised to find out how much she knows and how considerate and good she is in her womanly and quiet ways. He begins to think he has "found the one cut out for him," and becomes very earnest and devoted. She gives him many a quiet hint and receives some of his advances with firm resistance. But the more she does this the stronger becomes his decision "to win her or die trying." He is sure he has never seen one who came so near his ideal in every respect, and is assured a life of perfect happiness is before them. So wrapped up in his dream and desires is he, that he hardly considers the possibility of refusal, as he knows the world would say she had done well to marry one so well fixed in life. Again his aspirations are doomed to disappointment, as her friend Charley appears upon the scene and manifests his right to protect her from further unwelcome attentions. The disappointed one blames his luck, the fair ones, his own stupidity, and everything in general. Courtship becomes a serious matter, and he assumes himself: "I'll be more careful hereafter; no one shall fool me again."

It is astonishing how soon the wounded heart heals and he again takes his place in society to shine and outshine. He becomes the gayest of the gay, and decides to take things more easy. He flirts with all, making each one think for a very short time that she is the favored one; but just as this is decided in her heart and mind he is off to some other attraction. At last he meets his match in a city coquette, and is urged on and on by friends who "want to see her conquered," and so he gains the ground and the avowed affection of an unreliable woman. He thinks himself happy in his victory until preparations begin for married life, when he finds out to his consternation that she has "no love for home life," but chooses to wander from place to place in lodgings; as she "does not choose to lose her liberty of action." A stormy time ensues as he recalls her recent expressions of home appreciation, and is met with the retort that "such things were for effect, like his love for music." It ends without a wedding, and both seek other fields of conquest.

Stranger among strangers—no wonder he concludes that "marriage is a lottery," and one must take his lot; and he wonders if fate will be kind to him in placing in his way some one especially adapted to his future plans or one exactly the reverse. He sometimes thinks he could bear to make some changes to please the one who should please him, but the future looks somewhat dark. He devotes himself more earnestly to business, and waits for something to turn up to change the course of events. After a time through several changes he is thrown into the society of a talented business woman, who seems perfectly indifferent toward men, only as they can help forward her plans. He wonders if she has a heart; if she was ever courted; if she could really be approached as other women, etc., until he finds himself quite interested in her. In various ways he makes himself useful to her in business matters, and finally rejoices to see that she relies upon his judgment, and accepts his suggestions. Her reserve and devotion to business move him to fathom her character, as best he may from the business calls he makes upon her. He finds she is a woman with many womanly ways, and he resolves to woo her to marriage. It requires much effort to break through the reserve and approach her as a lover, but at length he has the pleasure of so doing. He must change many of his plans, his desires, and his imaginations, to enthrone her in his heart as queen and lady love; but he does so manfully, assuring himself that she will make up in some ways what she lacks in others. The marriage over, the adjustment of each to the usual sphere of labor begins. She finds it very tiresome to devote her time and energy to household matters, and after a time refuses to do so and wants to occupy her business station and leave home affairs to the care of others, hired for the purpose. The changes are many and very annoying, and at last he finds out that he made a mistake in taking one from her chosen sphere to serve in another. He sees when too late that it was not wisdom that caused him to seek her as a wife, but curiosity to uncover the mysterious. She has no love for wifely duties and the obligations of married life, and is only in accord with her husband in business matters. Thus the sweetness and dignity of marriage is lost in an unwise effort for worldly gain.

Thus are the majority of worldly men seeking for that which they fail to obtain. How strange it seems that such a very important subject as marriage should receive so little real wisdom of attention! While it is to many something desirable and important, it is so often considered in such an imaginative, illogical way that it fails to receive the calm consideration necessary to secure its enjoyments and blessings. As we have pictured to you the natural course of courtship among the worldly, we will try to give you the one that recommends itself to the humble followers of the Lord, who seek to do God's will in all things.

Here is a young Christian man who has given his life for the service of God in any way he shall choose to lead him by his Holy Spirit, because he realizes constantly that we are not our own, for we are bought with a price, even the precious blood of Jesus. He has committed all his interests into the hands of a faithful Friend, who cares for them in infinite wisdom, and love to him. He has learned many precious lessons of godly wisdom and has found it very profitable to cast all his care upon him who careth for us. His body is kept under by the grace of God and is brought into submission to the divine will.

As he reaches mature years and realizes that the majority of those of his age are considering getting married, his thoughts sometimes turn in that direction, and so he " takes it to the Lord in prayer " and gains the precious promise, " I will guide thee with mine eye." Knowing that God has a place for each of his children to fill in the body of Christ, the church of God, the young brother is very anxious to fill it acceptably and to do nothing to thwart God's designs. He is fully aware that God is able and willing to make known his will at the proper time; so he " waits patiently upon the Lord," and in due time finds his place in the body and is given wisdom to see that he needs a helpmeet, but still "trusts it away with Jesus," knowing he need not " seek a wife;" for " a prudent wife is from the Lord." He does not have his plans all arranged for the future and then seek to find some one willing to help him fill them to his satisfaction; but, knowing that " the Lord knoweth what is in the heart of man," he knows that God can choose, far better than he, the one suited to him and his place in life. So he walks humbly in the footsteps of Jesus day by day, in going about his "Father's business," unconcerned about the future. As he is thus occupied he makes the acquaintance of many dear, good Christian girls whom he knows would make some one happy in life, were God so to lead.

He resolutely awaits God's pleasure, and after a time is thrown by his labors into closer companionship with one whom he finds in every way congenial to himself and his field of labor. His eyes are opened to see in wisdom the hand of God, and in special prayer the answer to his inquiry is, "Fear not to take unto thee thy wife." He praises God for the good gift, and after a short period of simple Christian acquaintance he realizes a warmth of natural affection towards her and so asks her to inquire of the Lord concerning marriage, which she promises to do in the fear of God. After a time of heart-searching and deepening of consecration to the will of God she hears in sweetest whispers of love, "My child, 'behold thy husband.'" She realizes the sacredness of such a union for the glory of God, and asks him to make it doubly clear to her by giving her a true wifely affection for him. This is granted very quickly, and at their next meeting both realize the uniting of their hearts by sanctified natural affection and a high degree of companionship. Their time is not consumed in worldly ways of courtship, but each interview is seasoned with prayer and thanksgiving. A quiet wedding soon follows, and two lives are launched upon the sea of sacred marriage union, blessed and ordered by the great God of heaven. Do you look for some great failure? No; for a victory that surpasses every earthly expectation. Not that life shall be spent in mutual admiration of each other, but that it shall encourage to greater effort in the service of God, a closer walk with him, and greater strength of action for the good of perishing souls. However, there is just as much need of wisdom in all the years following, to keep in love, in sacred union of hearts and companionship as there was to first attain it. It needs its careful and prayerful consideration, its expression of love in kind and attentive demeanor one toward another, and the overflow of love in tender caresses. True love is devoid of selfishness, of the spirit of censure, of love of control, and of strife.

Is there anything more beautiful than the marriage unity when arranged and ordered by the almighty hand of God? The husband loving his wife as his own body, cares for her in tender solicitude, helping to bear her burdens and cares, and manifests his supremacy only in loving suggestions for good, as Christ does to his bride—the church. The wife reverencing her husband in tender love yields lovingly to his suggestions, emanating not from selfish purposes, but from God-love implanted within the heart.

It is true, however, that not all who claim to be Christians live happy married lives; but not all have "married in the Lord;" neither have they used wisdom and grace in their conduct toward one another. The Devil, who "goeth about as a roaring lion seeking whom he may devour," is just as ready to attack the husband or wife with his ferocious power in every way conceivable as any one else, and he knows that in so doing he destroys much good through parental influence. No one should be careless of his cunning approaches or unaware of his bold and fearless attacks. Many a home's happiness has been destroyed by a few sly insinuations that were first received with contempt, then allowed consideration, then permitted to awaken doubts, then false impressions and imaginations, until they had destroyed confidence, respect, love, and unity; and then they were allowed to wage war, anger, strife, division, and final separation and divorce.

Let each one who expects to marry or has married, remember that what is worthy of effort to obtain requires just as much effort to retain, and what is worthy of appreciation as looked forward to, is worthy of just as much approval after it is obtained. Many men who looked forward to marriage as the height of worldly happiness and whose married days have been unusually bright, often speak of it in a disappointed, dissatisfied way because it was not as ecstatic in love's impulses as in the days preceding marriage; and thus they wound the tender hearts that have done all they knew to brighten life and to keep the heart-love glowing and pure. Do they remember the hours of separation—how long and wearisome they were, and how blissful the meetings, and the almost impossible goodbys? Did you not imagine a life devoid of separation would be happier? but now that there are no separations you look back upon the joyful meetings, and wish life could be a continual bliss as pure as those precious greetings and meetings. Then try it once, dear husband, and see if it is not better to have bread and butter the year round than dry bread all the year with a few opportunities of having bread and butter as an appeasement of longing desire. Make the best of life, have a hearty appreciation for *all* that is *good*, and do not long to feast continually upon dainties, which would destroy good, wholesome appetite. By this we would not discourage the manifestation of pure affection which is natural, but we would warn each one against the unwholesome belief that an ecstacy of love or joy is essential to true happiness. True love runs deep; it seeks to shield from care, troubles, and annoyance and finds pleasure in humble service for the loved one. It appreciates each act of self-denial, exertion, and thoughtfulness as expressions of a never-diminishing affection.

How many weary wives and mothers make every day some heroic effort to please the husband as he returns weary from a day of toil. His favorite pie or cake is upon the table, although it required a great effort to still the cry of the little one and find time in the multitude of pressing cares for its manufacture. Perhaps he enters weary and pressed down with apprehension of some dire trouble that threatens the family welfare. He notices not her thoughtfulness or love, but speaks impatiently to the mischievous toddler, and eats what is before him in moody silence. She awaits his pleasure, cares for the little ones, and gets them off to bed with the promise of a nice Bible story, makes the room bright and attractive (as well as herself), and then seeks to woo him unto confidence in such a loving way that half his burden seems to have rolled into oblivion, and he really wonders where his big burden is gone as he confides it to her listening and appreciative ear, and is comforted by some strong assurance of helpfulness and trust.

Perhaps as she toils over the week's wash or is flushed and heated with her baking, the husband contrasts her appearance with what it was as he called upon her on some occasion a few years before, and a shade of disappointment rests upon his face and an accent of impatience mars his voice as he makes some slight request. But notice the happy and pleased expression that shines from her love-lit eyes as she quickly accords the favor and gives some little expression of love. The cloud vanishes from his brow and he makes an effort to banish with disdain the very thought that would lower her in his heart's appreciation. He had forgotten for a moment that no one when engaged in arduous labor is outwardly as attractive as when dressed for company. He remembers his own untidy appearance at various times and her playful nickname of "my chore boy." He is ashamed, and assures himself that "the like shall never happen again;" and so makes extra effort to atone for his disloyalty to his chosen one—yes, "the one of a thousand" for him. If dissatisfaction could always be thus "nipped in the bud," many an unhappy life would be spared its sorrow. We may also see the need of carefulness in all the affairs of life, that we may not be the innocent cause of our own troubles. Many a husband and wife forget to use the carefulness in personal appearance, in conversation, and in action necessary to retain the respect of a dear one; but injure its sensitiveness by unnecessary carelessness.

There are few who do not have some peculiarities that may be very annoying to others, and in married life these should be carefully avoided as far as known. On the other hand each one should be careful to prevent some little thing becoming a mountain, by constant dwelling upon, grieving over, and occasional mention. Where there is loving confidence and an earnest desire to please each other, there may be a proper time to speak of the little things that annoy, while often it is good to get such a victory over them in our own hearts, that they cease to appear as blemishes in the loved ones. There is, however, a right and wrong concerning everything of life, and each one should strive to attain to the right; and conscience scruples should be respected, and not dwelt upon to the harm of the possessor or to the injury of home happiness.

The endeavor of every married couple should be to elevate their married life above the sensual or sexual unto the higher plane of love, right, and spiritual union. It would be well if each one who desires married life could see the true beauty of being " married in the Lord," and would seek salvation at Jesus' feet and yield his life to the Lord's service, and thus be prepared to look unto him for direction in so important a matter. It is sad indeed to see one companion serving the Lord in faithfulness and the other in every possible way opposing every spiritual advance, or being so unconcerned about his own welfare as to grieve the other's heart and hinder the salvation work among the dear children. To avoid this it is best to serve God in the days of thy youth, and let God order the future.

There is a life of pure devotion to God where marriage seems to mar the sacredness of fellowship, the closeness of communion; and those who are thus called are happiest in their calling. A holy life of virginity for man or woman is above the reproach of the world, although it may not understand the motives or appreciate the sacrifice of the earthly for the spiritual. It does not come because they choose to shirk some of the responsibilities of life, but that they may attend unto spiritual things without distraction, and glorify God. We read of this in the Bible, and urge upon all young Christians so to walk before God that he can make clear his will to them in the matter of marriage; for *one can only serve God faithfully who is guided by him in all things.* Surely no one should take such an important step without knowing God's will concerning it.

The natural object of marriage is offspring; yet many fail to consider it while thinking of and aspiring to its high estate, while some with true love of paternity dwell in rapture upon the blissful emotions awakened in the heart by its possibilities. None should enter the marriage relation who would not take upon themselves the obligation of a parent. It may be very sentimental and attractive to look upon it as "the union of two hearts that beat as one," and "to live for each other all the days of life;" but the natural heart asserts itself within a few years, and an intense longing arises to look upon their own faces and features mirrored together into the sweetest and loveliest little one. The more natural, and highly endowed with the finest sentiments of love and the purest appreciation of sexuality two persons may be who unite in marriage, the greater will be their enjoyment in the offspring that blesses their union, and the higher will be the natural standard thereof. A child created through sentiments of love and appreciation of sexual obligations will of necessity be attuned to higher life than one born upon the low plane of lust and necessity, without parental desire and love of offspring Ah, how many are thus moored to low and degrading life from their earliest existence! The many ways invented by cunning minds to outwit nature and save unprincipled men and women from the trials and cares of parents are filling our land with very much that is an offense to the best instinct of natural man, and is meeting the severest censure and disapproval from the great Creator. The purest, highest, noblest, and most devoted parents give to the world the strongest type of manhood and womanhood in their children, but those who devote themselves to fashion, society, and pleasure never give sons of genius, or daughters of moral purity and strength of character.

Sad are many hearts, who are deprived of the pleasure of leading by the hand the little wavering ones, or of looking into intelligent faces and eyes, running over with questions, and answering them in serious earnestness, to see the glad and happy surprise mold itself into another question. All this sadness is caused many times by the evils of youthful days, or the overindulgence of marriage privileges, through ignorance or from a lack of self-control. That which is of value to us needs proper care to preserve its worth.

Now, boys, as we have given some needed instruction on this subject we hope you may receive it, and obtain a precious benefit in your lives. Pure thoughts and right living will keep you from many troubles that beset marriage. True manhood will seek for what is good and pure, and if wisdom is used in every circumstance in life, instead of desire or concern for what appears pleasurable, then the result will be much more appreciated as time passes. Sometimes individuals imagine when they marry in love and wisdom, that they should not see any faults in each other; and if they should, they begin to feel hurt and sometimes try to show it to the offender; and if it is not removed, they dwell so much upon it that it becomes a source of variance and makes them much trouble. Two persons may be lovingly united in marriage who may have some faults and differences; but these should make no change in love or harmony. Children may be very faulty, and do many things to grieve the loving hearts of parents; yet their love remains unchanged, and sometimes the most faulty one will receive apparently a greater portion that enables the parents to bear the trials more patiently. It often transpires that the abundance of affection is the power used to effect a change in the dear one. A very wicked man was converted much to the astonishment of the religious people who were used of God for his good. His testimony was that he had entirely discouraged every one, in regard to his conversion, except his dear old mother, who continued to pray for him through all discouragement and opposition, because she so truly and deeply loved him.

Now, if love can prevail over faults in other loved ones, it can for companions, who are taken for better or for worse; and it is a trick of the enemy of all good to enlarge upon the faults and try to affect that love that does exist in spite of the faults.

Once a sister said to another sister, "Have you ever thought how very sinful your husband's faults are?" The question was startling. Had she become so used to them that she had overlooked their sinfulness? It must be so, since others noticed them more than she did. Surely she must be awakened. So she dwelt upon them for several years, let the very worst aspect from them ever be present in her heart, until she began to feel herself wronged by the errors above all else. Then there was manifest in her in many ways the extreme opposite of her husband's faults, which only increased their strength and made wider the division between them. This after a time weakened their affections, and the hearts that once overflowed with tenderness and truest love were becoming so cold and indifferent that they were both grieving over the sad state of their lives. But there came an awakening for her. In a wonderful manner God permitted the enemy to allure her affection into improper channels, until with an awful horror she found herself upon the very edge of a terrible precipice of error that has engulfed multitudes—even the loathsome free love (which means love whom you will).

Nothing could have been more repulsive to her sentiments of right, and when she beheld her fallen condition her soul cried out in agony, "Oh, my God, not that, *not that!*" But it was even so. She had so dwelt upon the failings of others that she had been permitted to partake slightly of an evil that far exceeded her husband's. She was humbled into the very dust in self-abasement, and nothing but the almighty love of God drew her away from the awful horror that stood before her, and encouraged her to entreat his mercy and forgiveness to reinstate her into his favor and grace. She learned many precious lessons and applied them to her life, that brought again the natural affection to both her own and her husband's

heart and helped her to walk more humbly and in
greater wisdom than ever before. Often since the sad
experience her heart has been so weighed down by the
serious trial that it seemed there was no strength
for future progress; but the loving Lord whispered
in accents sweet, "I permitted it for the good of
souls." How can we warn others on this line but by
giving the sad experience and bringing out the lessons
that no doubt many need?

After a marriage where love and wisdom have
ruled, it is just as necessary that they continue to
govern, and allow no other power to usurp authority.
"All is well that ends well" may be wisely applied
to marriage. Often married life is begun under very
uncertain circumstances, and seemingly with all things
arrayed against it, and yet it may finally
prevail and far surpass those begun more
favorably. Then let those who are living un-
happily take courage and trust for a better time,
while every possible effort of wisdom is used to gain
the desired object. Husbands and wives are commanded by God to love one another; so if it is commanded it is possible through grace to do so, and every
unloving heart should seek that Bible standard until
it is obtained. It is a disgrace to be "without natural
affection," for it shows a hard-heartedness that needs
to be repented of before God. And I hope many will
avail themselves of the privilege and find out how
much God can do for them.

Though all may seem dark before us, the clouds

may be driven back by one move of God, and the brightness of heaven rejoice our hearts. Ye that love the Lord, remember that "all things work together for your good."

That which seems the heaviest to you now may be the means of greatest good in many ways.

>Then pray and trust, and trust and pray,
>Until they both shall win the day.

AMUSEMENTS.

It seems to be natural for individuals to seek pleasure in different kinds of amusements. Life's duties and obligations do not possess enough interest to them to afford all they desire of pleasure; therefore we see them hastening from one form of amusement to another—never satisfied with the enjoyment afforded, but anticipating it in the next.

Let me whisper a word to you boys that will make you wiser than many grown people: True pleasure is found in the path of duty. You need not seek for her, for often the more she is sought the more she eludes the grasp of the would-be possessors, or else deceives them with a mere pretense of happiness. Whatever our hands find to do we should do with our might, and find real pleasure in the doing. If one hurries through with duty in order to engage in something more pleasant, the duty fails to yield its attractions, as they are not observed. For instance, boys who are going to school may study their lessons so indifferently as to find no real pleasure therein, because they anticipate a fine time after school hours in reading some attractive story or novel with its unreal and exciting adventures.

There is real pleasure in earnest and persistent study. The mind grasps one truth after another that quickens the brain into greater activity and strength and gives desire for further instruction, which is a real enjoyment deeper than that which is found in careless amusement. The first is likened to a good meal of victuals that is quickly and easily digested, giving strength and health to the body and hope and joy to the mind and heart; while the last is like a diet of sweetmeats, nuts, and dainties that give pleasure to the taste but produce derangement of the digestive organs, and the result thereof—pain, anxiety, discouragement, and sorrow.

No one should expect to continue one occupation continuously day after day without becoming weary, for the mind and body need rest and change. These may be found in various ways without indulging in anything simply to find pleasure. There is more enjoyment in kind deeds—thoughtful and loving remembrances—than in the pursuit of happiness.

It is natural for children to enjoy play, and a certain amount is healthful and good; but let their whole time be given thereto, it loses its charm. Overindulgence in it produces a nausea similar to overeating.

As children advance in years they should have some occupation to employ the most of their time, as idleness is a source of great evil. They should be encouraged to learn to do their work in the best manner, and to find out all they can concerning it and thus become interested therein. They may be shown the worth of their labors to their parents or friends, and learn how one service deserves another. Sometimes it is well to reward faithful service in money value, thus teaching them to do business properly. Many a boy has become careless and shiftless from lack of care, and wisdom in giving proper inducements to labor. It is natural to all to desire to see some favorable results from their labors, and this is reasonable and right; for no one should wish to spend time and energy on something that amounts to nothing. Many of the duties of life, while they seem valueless in some ways, are full of comfort and happiness to others; therefore they are a necessity and some one needs to do them. Then why not you and I? And why may we not enjoy them in view of what they hold?

It seems often that boys and young men forget that they have advanced beyond their "play-days," and want to spend most of their time in gaiety. Boys "chew for pleasure," smoke "for fun," read novels "to have a good time," drink because "it makes them feel good," congregate together for mischief because "boys will be boys," keep company with the girls "to be somebody," play cards "'cause others do," and "like it," gamble a little "to be up to date," go to circus and theater for "they're all the go," "take in the races to see the stock," enter secret evils for "men are men and do as they please," go to the dance "to act the fop," etc. Now, boys, just see if you can do any of these things "to the glory of God," as the Bible tells us to do all we do. If you cannot, then rule them out of your lives.

So many things are taken up for amusement that work such great harm to the young, that we wish to speak of a few.

To many there seems no evil in a game of cards for pastime, yet those who learn to play are generally found playing instead of enjoying such diversions as improve the mind and heart. As there is great fascination and excitement about it, one is liable to neglect known duty for its enjoyment. After a time there is more interest manifest if there is a small wager at stake, such as cigars and ice-cream. It is not long until the stake is money—and the next step is frequenting gambling dens and using every strategy to win the games.

There is no evil that binds more firmly than gambling, for one who gambles will risk the last penny and beg for more from friends, in the hope that "luck will change" and he may become as rich as he desires to be, and then he will stop forever. Should he gain his desires, he immediately stakes all for greater gain, and thus is absorbed year after year by the gamling passion.

The testimony of reformed gamblers is that the evil is a severe bondage, from which few escape without the help of God through the religion of Jesus. They agree in asserting that it is a debasing, dishonorable, and wicked life; that the gambler loses the better part of his nature, his respect and love for others, which is a great factor for good in all who possess it. Gambling is one of the great evils that go hand in hand with intemperance and lust. It has been the cause of innumerable quarrels and vicious strifes that have finally resulted in the death of one and the imprisonment of the other contestant.

The one who never plays a game of cards will never be a gambler, while the one who learns to play for pastime is on the road toward one; although he may see the danger ahead and give up the pleasure before too late and save himself from such a sad fate. It is not wise to learn that which inclines to evil. Those who follow gambling to enliven their fleeting days will never accomplish much for themselves or others. Life is too short, its responsibilities too great, personal influence too extensive and certain to spend even a portion thereof in anything not strictly for the glory of God.

Another amusement indulged in by many young people is novel-reading. It is a very fascinating and injurious habit, as those who indulge in it lose interest in the common-place realities of life, and live in an imaginary world that makes them dissatisfied with the real. Often they endeavor to order their lives in such a way as they think will bring them into thrilling and romantic positions. Many boys love the tales of adventure and narrow escapes of hunters, adventurers, explorers, gold-seekers, etc., and so leave pleasant homes, good business prospects, and the advantages of civilization, and go forth to a wild, careless life that throws them among evil companions and into dangers and troubles that destroy health and future happiness. Not many can stand the wrong influence and return home bettered by their choice of life.

Another evil result of novel-reading is an almost irresistible desire to gratify the appetite for unwholesome literature at the expense of every duty and obligation of life. Days and nights are spent in following some imaginary hero or heroine through wonderful scenes and impossibilities to a bright and glowing fanciful conclusion, while all around us are the needy and suffering, the neglected and abused, who might be relieved, made comfortable and happy, by the time and energy wasted in the pursuit of happiness that lasts but for the fleeting present.

"Good deeds never die," their influence moves on through time, and only eternity can tell the grand results. Then let your pleasure be found in deeds of love and mercy, doing all as unto God.

Novel-reading is very injurious to the mind, as it produces an indifference to mental application, and the individual becomes intellectually lazy. Books of useful information lose their attractiveness, and finally are discarded for the attractive novel. The individual may attribute the disinclination for more substantial reading to weariness of mind and body from labor or from physical derangement; but the truth is the more novels are read the less are other books enjoyed, because the mind is indifferent to greater application.

Sometimes people advise the reading of light literature as a rest for the mind from the weariness of mental labor. One might just as well advise light manual labor as a rest for an overworked body. Why not take rest that is rest, instead of that which is mixed with its opposite?

Those who are good novel-readers and enter into the sentiment of what they read are wonderfully influenced thereby. The mind drifts along through the descriptive portions, becomes excited amid the dangers and fearful troubles; the heart beats quickly; the imagination is active; the sympathies are engaged, and oftentimes the whole being is convulsed with the strongest and deepest emotions, until at the close one feels as if he had been through a war, or "was more tired than if she had done a big wash." They live in the story, and when it closes, life and ambition are gone and they are ready to seek rest in sleep; but the scenes through which they have passed crowd the mind with shifting fancies, and it is long before it succumbs to sleep, "nature's sweet restorer." Even then it must wield its harmful scepter in "bad dreams" of impurity and sensuality. During wakeful hours dissatisfaction with natural events manifests itself in many ways. "Life is too commonplace; wish something would happen." "Have a notion to run away from home and try my luck in the world." "I'm tired of life, wonder how death would feel." "Wish I could die, I'm so tired of everything," "There's nothing new under the sun here; my only pleasure is in reading novels."

Do you not see, dear boys, the injurious effect of novel-reading? Suppose instead of a novel you take up a good book; for instance, one on temperance. As you read of the dreadful condition of the drunkard and his family you feel very thankful that you and your dear ones have escaped the ravages of strong drink, and your heart thrills with gratitude. Your sympathy is engaged, and you resolve to use your influence for their good. This aspiration so enthuses your being that it gives an added brightness to the commonplace duties of life. There is nothing like having some pure, unselfish motive before us to impart a love of life and duty. Each one needs "something to live for." The higher and purer the ambition the more successful will be the life. We Christian mothers see nothing so attractive, pure, and ennobling as the love of God and the desire to honor and glorify him every day in all the duties of life; "be they great or small, few or many."

You boys who have read novels until you have no ambition for living should turn to the loving Lord and let him fill you with the Holy Spirit, and there will be no lack in that direction; for there is much to do, and such precious reward for the doing that it gives a holy ambition and earnest incentive to life.

Another sad feature of novel-reading is the injury

done to the memory. This faculty of the mind occupies a very important part in each of our lives. Its power should be increased by proper cultivation, as it is very susceptible of improvement, and imparts many a favor to those who care for it in proper ways.

When anything is learned it is held by memory for future use. As reading is a means of learning important truths, the memory should grasp and retain what is read. If, however, the individual reads something that is not necessary to keep in memory, and does not attempt to retain it, then it drops from memory and is as if it had never been known. This indifference to retaining knowledge increases with very careless reading and becomes so natural that it is with great difficulty that most important items are retained for any length of time, and one "suffers from forgetfulness."

Years ago the writer was a voracious novel-reader and at times was so taken up with a novel that the facts and incidents transpiring made little impression upon the memory, and are very indistinctly remembered, if at all. The children who attended school, the places visited, the individuals met, are passed into oblivion with the novels read, while the same are well remembered when out of the novel tide of forgetfulness. When the evils of novels were seen upon mind and body and they were given up, there was an effort made to restore memory to its rightful place by strongly charging it with what was necessary to be learned and retained. This encouraged it to greater strength; but if a failure was made in not charging it strongly, the facts dropped from memory's casket, and left no trace of their existence. This became so tiresome that when it was observed to be so great a detraction from usefulness, the need was taken to God in prayer and the answer was very encouraging and helpful, and the soul is moved to thanksgiving. At times a glimpse is caught of the possibilities of a perfectly cared for mind and memory, and an earnest impulse and desire stirs the heart to sound out a faithful word of warning to the young.

Another evil aspect of novels is the undercurrent of sensuality that bestirs the sexual desires and encourages to impurity of thought and action. There are different grades of novels. Some lay claim to the highest standard of literature, and are read for their " high ideals and beautiful language." But often these same novels cover up by the beautiful language such impurity as ought to make every reader blush for shame as he catches a glimpse of it and feels its power upon the lower part of his nature. Then there are the religious novels with their false ideas and teachings, that lead souls away from the truth and blind their eyes to sin, and do them incalculable injury for time and eternity. The only safe rule for the young is to leave novels alone, and keep ears and eyes open for the good and true.

Love of amusement leads to the circus and the theater. For many people there is no greater pleasure than sight-seeing in all its forms. Their eyes are never satisfied. They are on the lookout for something new and nice.

These two amusements are very worldly and ungodly, as there is much presented that is impure and leads to the grosser evils. The stage is in direct opposition to the pulpit and the Bible. The plays performed are generally on the line of novels, with scenes that carry one into the strongest imagination and leave him unsatisfied with natural life, which is one of the greatest evils that can befall an individual. Pleasure-seekers rarely amount to much in the world; for they live for their own gratification.

Sometimes the question has been asked, "Can Christians go to the theater and the circus?" Do they want to go? For what reason does any one go? Let every one who desires to go to such places, but who thinks he is a Christian, ask himself, "Would Jesus go there?" If not, then it is no place for his followers. We know many professing Christians frequent these places and seem to enjoy themselves greatly; but they are generally the ones who do not enjoy reading the Bible, pray little, and have no burden for the salvation of souls. Their hearts are not in gospel work, and they know not what the joy of the Lord is. The professors who enjoy such amusements should examine themselves by Bible truth and see if they are Bible Christians—that is, made after the Bible pattern—for they are the only ones who have an abundant entrance into eternal glory. "Well, I wish the Bible were clearer on such things," says some one; "I never could find anything that condemned them, yet I know the most devoted Christians wonder how any one can go there who thinks he is a Christian." Listen to a word of helpfulness on that line. While there are scriptures that apply directly to these amusements to those who are truly spiritual, those who are not cannot apply them correctly. One of the works of the flesh is "revelings," another is "foolishness," and a third is "ungodliness." The world must have such things as go under these heads, and where will we find them if not in the things that do not pertain to the worship of God, or the duties of life.

In the Bible the Christian life is so clearly and beautifully portrayed that it is easily seen that worldly pleasures are left out. A man when converted is made a new creature. Behold, old things are passed away, all things have become new. That which was once loved is now hated, and that which was hated is now loved. Salvation changes the heart of man and makes it love heavenly things. The reason so many professing Christians love worldly amusements is because they are trying to serve God without a real experience in the heart. I tried this way a number of years and found it very unsatisfactory; but when I sought for a Bible experience, it so far surpassed my expectation that it perfectly satisfied every longing of my soul, and brought me joy that far exceeded the earthly; so there was found no place for worldly amusements.

Another source of pleasure is the dance. Knowing what we do about it, Christian mothers wonder how it is possible for right-minded men and women to give it sanction in their homes or public places. Can it be possible that knowing the hidden evils thereof they hold their peace for fear of the censure that falls upon those that cry out against popular evils? We hope not, but leave this with them and their God, assuring our hearts that, let others do as they may, our heavenly father requires us to sound out a note of warning to the innocent, and give an exhortation to those ensnared by its deceptions, in hope that we may persuade some to abandon forever the sensual joys of the ballroom.

At first glance the dance appears little different from many of the social entertainments of the present time; but as we look more closely we are much disturbed by some of the positions taken by both sexes, and wonder how it is allowed by those who claim right to "high-life society."

There is nothing of refinement, culture, dignity, or even common modesty in the performance of the varied figures and exciting motions. It does not require brains nor education to become a good dancer, but any one may learn in a very short time the secret of success in this "delightful recreation," as it is called.

Let us now consider some of the pleas for it, made by its devotees. "The music is attractive and inspires to motion that is most graceful and becoming." Then why not let each one move as he is inspired to by the music? But you are mistaken about the inspiration of music for motion. You learn music and motion from a dancing-master or from observing others, and then the two go together. If one learns to sing a song from playing it upon an instrument, it is natural to desire the music while singing the song. No matter how much or what kind of music I might hear, it would not inspire me to dance—for I never learned the art. When we hear fine music it wafts our thoughts above the low and coarse things of life, up to the beautiful, grand, and heavenly; and when our souls are filled to overflowing with the love of God, we " leap for joy " (not in circles and figures) to the glory of God, and give him praise. The thought of the dancer is not turned heavenward, neither do their lips speak God's praise. Their thoughts are far below his.

The next plea is: "Dancing motion is good recreation and produces gracefulness." We once had a lady boarder who besought us to permit her to bring a lady friend with her for a week "to enjoy the pure country air and rest up from the winter's dissipation." On inquiry we found she had danced most all night several times a week, and had attended parties and theaters until she was all worn out. How is that for the wholesome exercise of dancing? She was so graceful as to sleep until dinner time, and then require the daintiest food to tempt her appetite. The afternoon was "lounged away" with tales of the winter's gaieties;

not one word to show that her thoughts soared above the earthly through her great endeavors to shine. Mothers send their children to dancing-school to make them graceful, but the result is they marry below themselves in social life and manifest a boldness that is far from graceful.

Another plea is: "Dancing is far better than many other amusements, as all its doings are before the eyes of many, and nothing imprudent can occur." There is just where the great mistake is made; for those who engage in the dance must first lose that fine sense of propriety and the essence of modesty that protects them from improper conduct. Those who have entered dancing-schools have been shocked by the positions taken by the dancing-master, but have assured themselves that "there is no harm intended, for so many good people countenance it, or they would not dance." If a woman would permit her gentlemen acquaintances to take the same liberties with her when alone in the parlor, they would have reason to believe she would welcome further approaches toward impurity.

Men know and admit that the tendency of the dance is to sexuality, and in it they find much that gratifies their lower nature; but let one center his affection upon a lady, and he becomes very loath to see her in the embrace of some other man; so he tries to obtain a promise from her to dance with none but himself. This shows clearly that they know there are feelings and emotions aroused that should be confined to those most closely united. It is sometimes termed jealousy, but that covers the ground for effect. Men also know and admit that the best partners are those who yield themselves up to their own movements and feelings and partake of " all that lust could desire except the overt act of crime." "The whole dancing system is contrived for the purpose of sexual enjoyment outside of marriage," and is " a school of vice and an allurement to the house of prostitution." "In order to overcome intemperance the saloons must be closed by the prohibition of the manufacture and sale of strong drink, and to overthrow sexual corruption through the houses of prostitution there needs to be a strong strike made against its source—the dancing-school."

Now, boys, you know you have a great warfare with your fleshly desires, without stimulating them by such amusements as lead you into deeper and stronger evils. Those who dance know they have greater respect for women who do not dance than they have for those whom they see in the lustful embrace of the libertine, and are free to talk about in the most vulgar manner when by themselves, after the ball is over. Those who have respect for womanhood should strive to shield women from the disgrace of the dance and its sad results. Men stirred to the depths by lust are not slow to take advantage of opportunities for its gratification with the innocent, and plan their destruction in many sly and subtle ways. Dancing-masters acknowledge the downfall of their pupils caused by the seductive power of libertines, who infest dancing society as fine society gentlemen, as a means of reaching the innocent to satisfy their own desires and entice them to the brothel for money reward from its keeper.

It is stated by good authority that "two-thirds of the girls who are ruined fall through the influence of dancing." Who of you wants to lend his influence to this kind of business? Who wants to be so inflamed with sexuality as to enter this field as a destroyer of woman's virtue, or follow her to the lowest depths of shame in houses of prostitution that curse our fair land?

Oh, can it be possible that any of our boys, *our dearly beloved sons,* would ever aid in any way the downfall of *our daughters or sisters?* O boys, awaken to your manhood, gain control of yourselves, and never be found in any place where you would not want to take your mother or sister. Are you not glad there are many women and girls who do not yield to impurity? Then be worthy of their regard and affection.

The impurity of dancing makes it a most harmful pastime; not alone for the moral, but for the physical man. One may labor every day of the week and be so refreshed by the night's rest that he feels no evil effects. But should he dance a few hours each evening, "for exercise," he will quickly see the difference. The close contact with the opposite sex in arousing and continuing strong excitement of the passions makes it, according to the claim of physicians, "the most harmful exercise for both sexes." The dance would lose its popularity if it were confined to one sex, or to married people. Life is cut short by the dance; many physical evils arising therefrom, especially with women. The average "length of days" for the excessive male dancer is thirty-one years. If dancing does not always lead men to the loss of virtue through adultery, it increases the development of sexuality that finds present relief and future destruction in secret vice (or self-pollution) that causes most of the sexual ailments of men, and brings them to utter wretchedness.

The only way of escape is to be not enticed into the meshes of this net of lust and destruction, because it outwardly appears fair and is endorsed by fashionable high-life society, but weigh it well in view of eternal judgment.

Dancers often admit that their pleasure in dancing is overbalanced by the remorse of conscience, and the displeasure of God resting upon them in their quiet hours or during the silent watches of the night or when death stares them in the face. It is a very enticing pleasure, and all need the help of God to understand its allurements or to enable them to give it up. The very strongest desire for it may be taken away by the salvation of Jesus, and other joys found that far surpass the earthly.

There are other sources of worldly pleasure we might mention; such as play parties, socials, festivals, picnics, etc., that are endorsed by many who disapprove of the foregoing; but there is great need of carefulness in drawing the lines between sin and righteousness. Some who have gone into the grosser evils have been led there by the lesser ones, which have as " little foxes destroyed the vines."

Everything that makes people gay, frivolous, and foolish, makes them careless about spiritual things and drives away the Spirit of God, who is seeking to draw men's hearts unto himself, that they may find in him more than the world can give—even joys eternal. How many times we hear the testimony of men and women who have tried to drown the voice of conscience and grieve the convicting Spirit of God by going deeper into sin. Some have done so to their future destruction, while some have only partially succeeded, and were at last drawn unto God. It is not safe to choose our own way or to seek for our own amusement and joy.

Let us look at it fairly!

The drunkard finds his pleasure in drink.

The lustful finds his enjoyment in the gratification of lust in secret vice or adultery.

The card-player finds his pleasure in gambling.

The chewer and smoker, in tobacco.

The society devotee, in the dance, modern courtship, the theater.

The formal professor, in parties, socials, festivals, and picnics.

The Christian finds his pleasure in God, and Christian good works.

No one can intermix worldly pleasures with Christian duty without a reproof from God in some way; for he shall hear a voice saying, "This is the way, walk ye in it," and if he is seeking to do God's will, he will make inquiry of God before he enters into anything of which he is the least uncertain. "Whatsoever ye do, do all to the glory of God." How can any one glorify God in seeking for pleasure in worldly ways? We wish to show the boys that there is no need of these things; for the joy of God—the peace and love that passes understanding—is far superior to what you can find in worldly things.

May God bless you all with such a longing for the good things of God that you may seek him earnestly with all your heart.

AMUSEMENT'S JOY.

O joy of earth, how fleeting thou !
  With all thy boast, how very small
Are all thy gifts? not one we tried
  Could ease a pain, or e'er let fall
On any one, a blessing sweet;
  But ever keep the richest joys,
The purest peace, and gracious meat
  From hungry hearts that take thy toys.

O fickle one, how very false
  Are all thy charms, thy promise too!
Though thou art sought in dance and waltz,
  In cards of chance and pot of stew,
In races great, and circus fair,
  In halls of feast, or lodges grand,
Thy promise strong is never there;
  For all is treach'rous, shifting sand,

You seem so good—so very glad
　To lure the mind and earnest soul
To brighter things, and give the sad
　A taste of good in frolic's goal—
But ah! beneath this *seeming* good
　There lies a poison, strong and vile,
That robs their life of holy food,
　And gives them taste for worldly guile.

Your parties gay but lead to balls,
　And they through dance to secret vice,
To social evils, shameful falls,
　That prove to us they're never nice.
Your games of chance to gambling lead,
　To strife and fight, and then to shame
Behind the bars, to prison's feed,
　To loss of all, yes, even name.

Your gayest times o'er stage and song
　But lure the mind to baser things.
Through acts and parts and comic wrong
　There flows a power that ever brings
The heart to hardness more and more;
　And conscience, voice is hushed in shame,
Until the soul the wrongs adore
　And yields in gladness to the same

Again, you say in accents sweet,
　"Oh, rest your mind in novels rare,
And find in love and honors mete,
　A balm for woe or loveless care!"
In this you know must ever lie
　The power for harm to soul and mind,
By giving thought and wish to die,
　Or causing them the false to find.

AMUSEMENTS.

Oh ! would they all could clearly see
   You are a fraud and never do
Delight yourself in what shall be
   Of good to soul, and ever woo
To nobler life and love of God,
   To peace and grace and heavenly goal,
To righteous paths the Savior trod,
   To good to body, mind, and soul.

Your path is far below the true;
   It clings to earthly selfish life,
And vainly tries to have us sue
   For what is given in worldly strife:
But Christian love and heav'nly grace
   So far exceed your ev'ry gift,
That they have won a precious place
   Within the heart—a holy rift.

This keeps us from the joys of earth,
   And lures us further day by day
Within the realms of gracious worth:
   Oh ! keep us thine, dear Lord, we pray,
And feed our souls on heav'nly joys,
   That we may serve in pure delight,
And give no place for earth's alloys,
   But walk in love and holy light.

BUSINESS.

We turn from amusements to business, and hope many of our sons will follow us with pleasure and profit, not only in the reading, but in actual living, that they may find how much better it is to find the joy of duty than the pleasure of amusements.

Upon men falls the responsibility of providing a living for helpless women and children, as well as for themselves. This is no little matter, as the welfare and happiness of the dear ones is dependent upon it. Whatever is worth doing is worth doing well. He should try to succeed in order to "provide for his own," because it is a God-given obligation.

While we are not to be troubled or bear burdens about temporal things, yet a certain amount of thoughtfulness and care are necessary for any undertaking if one would be successful in life.

As this duty stands before boys and young men, it is right to prepare themselves therefor by cultivating business principles and right rules of action. One who labors indifferently and unwisely may never rise to the proper standard of business capability. Life is a sphere of action, and we should all remember that we come not here to pass through this world "on flowery beds of ease, but to fight to win the crown," and labor for our own and others' welfare. Good honest work is good for all, developing the physical system, thereby strengthening the mind, and aiding or preserving the morals; for "Satan finds some mischief still for idle hands to do."

Then, boys, let us look the future bravely in the face and prepare for action. Let us make up our minds there is work before us—perhaps for many years, maybe for only a few; and whichever it should be, our portion of work ought to be well done. It is a hard thing sometimes for the young to think they must work the majority of their days of life; for they love play and amusement so well that to have no work would seem a great favor. Often when left to themselves this idea prevails so largely that they form habits of idleness that are hard to overcome.

There is just so much to be done in this world to properly provide for all mankind; therefore there must be a proper portion for each individual. If one shirks his duty in labor, some one or more fails to be properly cared for, or else his portion of labor falls upon some one else perhaps less able to do it. Take a family for example. If the father is careless, and indifferent to labor, the mother and children are lacking the comforts of life or must put forth greater effort by taking a portion of the father's work. Many a mother washes for a living, while the husband "knocks about" attending to trifles; although he is far more able to labor hard than the wife with her family cares, and his lack of ability to provide comes from indifference to duty, and a dislike for manual labor. Of course this is unjust and must be put away when one serves the Lord.

Again, the father may do his part as provider fairly well, but if the mother and children are indifferent to their responsibilities, many things are left undone that would assist him in his efforts and accomplish much for their own welfare and the good of others.

Oftentimes we see a father and mother equally diligent in business in their different spheres, but the children are "born shirks." The parents take pleasure in their labors, and when the children manifest such a strong dislike for work, they do not feel like compelling them to labor, and hope it will not be so when the children are older. Sometimes their hopes are realized and sometimes they are not, and when too late the parents see the folly in bringing them up in idleness.

Not long ago I read the advice of a noted woman to parents. It contains several good things that may help our sons. She said: " Parents should give each child a portion of home care, then notice the kind of work he prefers, and give him an opportunity to do all he can of that kind of work if possible, while encouraging him to learn to do all kinds well. "

Children need to have some one to use decision for them in accomplishing some things that to them are difficult. Oftentimes they become discouraged, give up, and despise that work ever after; because they were unsuccessful in accomplishing it; but let them be encouraged and perhaps assisted, or some attraction pointed out to them; and when it is finished there is perfect satisfaction, and they say, " Well, I believe I'll like to do that when I learn just how." Their labor should be changed, as one kind becomes tiresome from monotony, and because it tires one set of muscles. Fortitude and perseverance are often quite deficient, and parents should supply the lack by firm decision to accomplish what they undertake. It is good also to have them labor with parents who will give them something to think of while they work, and thus the time passes pleasantly.

Little ambitions and inducements are great incentives to labor. If calculations are made and a small percentage of profit is given for faithful service, it encourages an interest in the business engaged in and helps to acquire ability therein. Sometimes we see young men leave home who have never had the handling of money or been taught anything regarding its worth or expenditure. There is just as much to be gained by carefulness in the outlay of means as there is in obtaining it. Therefore young people should be allowed to earn money for clothing, and then be instructed in a wise purchase, that "they may have lack of nothing." If they are taught to keep accounts and live within their income, and not let every attraction lure them into debt or to an unwise outlay, it will be of great advantage to them in after years. If they see they cannot have everything they desire, then they will do some thinking before they make a purchase.

Some people think it savors of stinginess to be careful in the use of money; so when they have any they are flush and use it indiscriminately, just as their impulses run.

How would you boys like to have the following? Mother goes to town, and because it is your birthday and she loves you fondly, she brings you several very nice presents, beside candy and nuts, and you have a good time for a day and look at your presents joyfully; but in a week you are in sore need of shoes to protect your feet from the cold and ice, and a pair of mittens to work in frosty mornings, and some books for school, and perhaps other things. Mother says, " How I wish I could get them for you, but I have no money now; so we must wait till we can sell something or you can get some work to do." Do you not think she would have expressed her love and care for you better if she had remembered your future needs and brought you home something useful? And then, if your needs were supplied, she might have brought you some little thing you had expressed a desire for or something that would help you in some way? Oh, yes! we all should look away from thoughtless impulse and desire and use wisdom in all the affairs of life. That is one way to express our love—by thoughtful consideration.

Let us look at it in another way. Suppose children are needy? The father can make a dollar a day every day he will work, but he stops every few days and "lays off, to have a good time." Thus, perhaps he fails to procure about a fourth of the necessaries of life. You would all say he was selfish and unkind, in his carelessness. Suppose he does work every day and gives the money to the mother to purchase what the family needs. She buys a part—say three dollars' worth—then she makes a treat of something unnecessary to some one, that costs a dollar. Thus she continues spending one dollar needlessly for every three that she uses wisely. Is this not the same as the father working only three-fourths of the time? And is it not just as unkind? This principle is at work everywhere. There is greater lack of care in spending than in making money, by both sexes. There is just as much need of self-control on this line as on any other; for the desires of the flesh will lead astray whenever possible.

It is very nice sometimes to make some self-denial in order to give to others, and the Lord would have us use wisdom in so doing. A mother may deprive herself of some nice warm garment in order to give her boys some skates for their pleasure. It may not be wise; the mother may take cold, be sick, require help, and make quite an extra expense for the husband to bear; or the boys may so delight in their skating as to neglect work or study, and thus form bad habits. If the mother should deprive herself of something that will not expose her to sickness, and procure something for her boy's spiritual and intellectual good, the blessing of God would rest upon it and prove a blessing to all.

We may deny ourselves even necessaries in order to help those more needy, and not experience any serious inconvenience in so doing, when it is done in wisdom and not as a mere impulse without forethought. Again, one is always safe in doing what the loving Lord may lead to do, knowing he never makes a mistake.

There was a missionary who went to visit a needy family. To encourage them to trust in the Lord in their need, he repeated several scriptures, and told them a number of instances of wonderful answers to prayer. He was about to leave the house, excusing himself from giving them temporal aid on the ground that what he had in his pocket was in wisdom laid aside for clothing, which he intended buying immediately because much needed, when he was arrested by a voice saying, "Why don't you practice what you preach? Why not you do the trusting, and let them have the money? He hesitated a moment and thought it over. If some one should do the trusting, why not he as an example of faith to them? He drew out the money and handed it to them, saying, "I was to use this for my winter's clothing, but you may have it; I will trust the Lord for more." They were astonished, but recovering from it, said, earnestly, "If you can trust for your clothes, we will endeavor to trust for the supply of our needs.

When he returned home, joyful in his strength of

faith, and willing to wait God's own time to supply his need, he found a small parcel awaiting him, which proved to be a much-needed pair of gloves. When he attempted to put them on, something prevented, and on examination proved to be a roll of money—double the amount given away. He used his portion for clothes, and with a heart of thanksgiving carried the rest to the needy family, who were so affected by the loving-kindness of God that they yielded fully to his service, were strengthened in courage and faith, and were soon supplied with work to support themselves, and means to assist the mission work they loved so well.

The instruction of the Bible is to "labor, working with his hands the thing which is good, that he may have to give to him that needeth." To some this is hard work, as they want to lay up their treasures here. If we remember that giving to the poor is lending to the Lord and laying up treasure above, and is a real fruit of holy love, then that will help us to do all things for God's glory and not to please ourselves.

Now, boys, we do not doubt that you would all like to be "good business men in order to have what you want;" but are you just willing to be good business men and have what you need? Are you willing to labor hard for even your needs? We fear some of you are not; for there is a great desire at the present time "to take life easy," "make money without work," and "make a living by my wits." Now let us think a moment. Can any one "take life easy," and make a success of it in every way? You answer, "No." Those who try to do so shirk some responsibility, and prove unfaithful to their obligations. Can any one make money honestly without some kind of labor? You answer again, "No;" and this too is a fact. Those who think they make money without work are simply taking other people's money by some fraud; but still that often requires an effort that is greater than common labor, and proves a greater strain upon the one doing it. Besides, no one who does this is acting wisely or honorably, or can do so long without serious results to him here or in eternity.

Is it possible to make a living by one's wits in an honorable and just way? Yes, you say; for you are thinking of intellectual labor, which has a good compensation in many forms of business. But that is not what is meant. One who makes his living by his wits is using them in some swindling, cheating, sharp doings, etc., as this comes on the line of making money without work, and is dishonesty in the worst form. So now we bring it to this point: Each one must labor in some way in order to fill his place in life in justice.

Some work with their hands, and use very little mental ability with it, and so form the lowest class of workers. Others work less hard with their hands, but use their reasoning powers and judgment so well that they accomplish more in many ways. There are some whose mental work is more severe and overtaxing than any manual labor could be, and receives a proper reward.

Perhaps you are thinking of some people you know who do not work for their living, and you wonder where they belong. We will class them as butterflies—they sip the nectar from every bud and flower, and give nothing in return. Their money makes their living, and withholds from many the opportunity of being well provided with homes and suitable employment. The Bible says, " Woe unto you that are rich; for ye have received your consolation."— Luke 6 : 24 "How hardly shall they that have riches enter into the kingdom of God!" * * * "Children, how hard is it for them that trust in riches to enter into the kingdom of God! It is easier for a camel to go through the eye of a needle, than for a rich man to enter into the kingdom of God."—Mark 10:23-26. Those who are rich are to be willing to distribute, ready for every good work; so their riches would not long remain to them.

" Well," you may say, " if we cannot be rich, there is no need of working—there is no incentive to be good business men." Oh, yes, there is, dear boys! There are many paths of duty that are fairer than the path to riches, or to self-gratification.

Love is a wonderful power; let it induce you to be as diligent in business as you can, then properly care for your dear ones. Right is far above wrong; be earnest workers because it is right. Honor is worthy of esteem and attainment; and labor assists toward honor; for faithful labor is honorable, while idleness is dishonorable in this sinful and needy world of woe. Be laborers together with God, and let your toil assist precious souls to eternal glory. What can be more grand, more worthy of approval, or can do you so much good now and hereafter?

"Well, what can boys do toward helping themselves to become good business men?" They must be *good* boys, and aspire to a good honest business; learn to love labor, to be diligent, punctual, persevering, thoughtful, and accurate. Now let us see what that means. To love labor is to take pleasure in exertion, both physical and intellectual. It takes away the shirking from what would be unpleasant effort, and makes it agreeable. To be diligent means to waste no unnecessary time, but apply one's self to business earnestly. To be punctual means to be prompt in meeting your engagements; and especially, to be at your post a little ahead of time rather than a minute behind, if you are working where there is a stated time to begin. To be persevering means very much, as it is to be not discouraged by the many things that seem to oppose progress in our labors, but to toil on patiently, knowing success must follow wise labor. Thoughtfulness will see many improvements, ways of economy of time and labor, and make variations in what would be dull routine. Accuracy will make careful calculations in business ventures, in outlays and incomes, and keep accounts straight. If you begin on this line while young, you will soon see a real beauty in faithfulness to business.

Some of you, as you look around, and see so many out of work yet good, willing workers, may think there is no chance for you; for there are too many working boys already, and you will aspire to something higher, although you are very uncertain as to what that will be. " There is always room at the top " means there is in every business occupation room for those who are most efficient laborers. Thus it means, " What is worth doing is worth doing well." May this be your motto, and bring you success.

This reminds me of an experience told many times by a dear one. A man with a family of children and wife entered into a western city during the drouth of 1860, with only a few cents change in his pocket. He was a good mechanic and had no doubt of finding work to support his family. He immediately began to seek for it earnestly, but found none, as there was little being done, because of the very dry summer. One large, fine house was being built, but all the workmen were engaged. No one had taken the contract for making the window sash, and it was still open for bids. Our mechanic was not slow in casting in his bid, at the lowest possible figure, and was given the work. He did it faithfully, wisely, and well, thus showing the building contractor his ability as a workman, and when the grand staircase was to be built, he was given the work, because of the fineness of his workmanship, and thereafter had no lack of employment.

Another point is willingness to do the best one can under adverse circumstances. Many good workers will never lower their wages, no matter how necessary it is to have work, and so fail to believe that "half a loaf is better than none." There are always opportunities of aiding others by giving service at reduced prices, and steady employment at lower wages is worth more than an occasional job at high wages. Another thought is this. Many only "labor for what *they* get out of it," and if they are doing work for some one they take no interest in it only so far as they are concerned, and their disinterestedness cuts short their engagement. Natural hearts are very much alike, and are moved by the same impulses. Let a bright, cheerful, willing boy or man take hold of a piece of work, take an interest in it, make suggestions, do it faithfully and well, and be not afraid to do a little more than his share of labor; and the heart of his employer if it be not adamant, will be touched with the same feelings, and he will cheerfully grant the little favors that help along in all our lives; for no one lives to himself, but we are all more or less dependent upon one another. If one may choose his helpers, the choice falls upon those who make themselves necessary and modestly pleasant.

There is remembrance of a boy who entered a store as an errand boy. His work was to make fires, open boxes, sweep, and dust, which he did faithfully, placing goods in neat and effective shapes, arranging windows in attractive style; and then opened and shut doors, carried out goods, held horses, etc., making himself generally useful. The merchant's trade revived, and the boy became a necessity to him, to supply what he lacked to be successful, and for which he could afford to pay well. Many boys had stepped over this opportunity, because they did not see it or failed to do more than necessary, or took little interest in their employer's business. Wherever you are, boys, make yourselves useful in doing well what is to be done. Have a real strong spirit of helpfulness, so no one will fear to ask favors of you.

Visiting the home of an acquaintance, the lady was strong in praise of a young preacher who had lately made his home with them for a short time. She said laughingly, "Why, he just anticipated my every wish—was there need of water, it came so quietly and easily that no one dreamed he was acting chore boy;" or if the fire needed replenishing, he saw it first, and did it just right. His room was kept in perfect order, and nothing of his was left in the way of others. He was certainly his mother's helper, and a grand, good one." Often boys and young men would like to help around the house, but seem to know so little about it that they fear to make an attempt. If they will just whisper the wish to the one who cares for them, she may be able to show them how to be helpful to her, and thus form good ways that will assist others wherever they go, and make life's pathway more pleasant. Notice how others do the things you would like to do, and then do them in the same way or in a manner that will recommend itself to them as more appropriate.

It is a fine addition to any one's education to be able to do easily the home duties that often are left undone when sickness attacks the housekeepers. How many times a weary mother, barely able to move around, must perform the necessary work for strong husbands and sons, because they do not know how to get a meal, wash dishes, or sweep! How nice it is when a bad headache lays mother or wife aside, to know that the work will move forward much the same as usual, and is not piling up for extra effort when the illness is past. Now, boys, when your mothers desire your help, give it to them freely, for you do not know how much it assists them, or how useful the training may be to you in later years.

One mother, who was spending a portion of her time in assisting her husband to provide for the family, and who had several sons but no daughters, was teaching them to perform housework as perfectly and as easily as if they were girls, and remarked that she was trying to make good husbands for some mother's girls, and hoped they were making good wives for her sons. This is the thought. How nice it is to be able to more than fill our own little sphere, and be ready to extend it to others in general helpfulness! We hope the brothers and sisters who read this will learn to exchange work; that will aid them in the future. Not long ago a sister said to her brother, "If you will wash the dishes, I'll pile up wood for you." The exchange was made, and pleased both as a relief from routine work.

Now, boys, we would not conclude this subject without urging upon you the necessity of being extremely honest in all your business transactions, and applying the golden rule in all your dealings with others. "Honesty is the best policy," even in dollars and cents; and when it is counted in morality, there is little to exceed it in value. An honest man is one who can be trusted. He is just, honorable in all his dealings, and above deceit and unfairness. He may not appear to be as prosperous as those who are not careful to be honest in business matters, but he is solid and worthy to be relied upon at all times; and if capable, will succeed in his undertakings; for men in general appreciate honesty when in their favor.

A choice of occupation should be carefully considered, and wisdom used to decide; for the one for which each one is best fitted, and that seems most congenial to taste and circumstances of life, will assist him in spiritual things and be a means of aiding others. In fact, one should be perfectly satisfied that he is in the place God designed he should occupy for his glory. One can be just as fully consecrated to do God's will and just as earnest and faithful a steward while on the farm, or in a shop, store, mill, or office, as if he were in gospel work, as long as he abides faithful in the calling to which he is called. There are many ways by which we may assist in salvation work. Those who are blessed with business ability and readily make money should remember not to hide their talent, but improve it to God's glory. As long as we obey the gospel precept " Diligent in business, fervent in spirit, serving the Lord," the business part will not outrun the spiritual and make one worldly or covetous, but tend to advance the soul in the grace of God. It is necessary, however, to be ready to change positions, to lay down arms, and to move forward at the command of the Captain of our salvation. Sometimes he takes his reinforcements from the different stations of life and places them in the forefront of the battle to urge forward the force to victory. Keep your heart and ears ready for the call while you are doing with your might what your hands find to do, as unto God and not unto men.

Business need not hinder the soul in communion with God or prevent wonderful victories of faith from attending your personal efforts for the good of souls. Oftentimes God's children are pressed down with the fear that honest and earnest effort in business will detract from their spirituality; so it is left in careless indifference that prevents diligence, and so little is accomplished.

Awake, dear ones, to earnestness! If you are not called to " stand upon the walls of Zion," then stand in your place, fill it well as a living sermon to those around you, and send forth the ammunition of war against sin, in the shape of holy literature and free

Bibles for the poor, and speed on his way the gospel messenger, that he may reach the unknown thousands that have never heard the precious gospel of salvation from sin, and backed up by earnest prayer and devotion it may accomplish more than those who go half-heartedly and with little faith into the wide gospel field.

Now, dear boys, we have considered many of the subjects of life, and looked at them from reason's point of view and in remembrance of the judgment day. Now we come to the subjects that more closely pertain to eternal life, and as you have no doubt been interested in the previous lessons, we know you will be in what is to follow, as it leads us to higher and holier themes. May God bless you and make them a power for your eternal good, is the prayer of Christian mothers.

THE MOTHERS' HOPE.

Our mothers' hearts so loving, true,
Are praying much, our sons, for you,
That you may guide your feet aright,
And shun that dark and awful night
Of sin and woe that tries so well
To wreck your souls in endless hell.

If you will heed in youthful days
The voice that ever for you prays,
Then you are wise, and shall not come
To terrors great, that's promised some,
Who turn from right and choose the wrong,
To walk in joy amid the throng.

Then take your place beside the right,
And enter boldly in the fight
For God and truth and heav'nly land,
That stands before the praying band,
Who strive to win to truth and grace
Our sons, that they may win the race.

RELIGION—TRUE AND FALSE.

We come to the most important subject that can engage our attention. That man is a religious being inclined to worship and serve something he considers a god, cannot be denied, as we look about and see various nationalities of people performing religious services pertaining to the different beliefs that exist in the world. This shows that the Great Creator endowed man with a religious principle that should, if properly used, lead unto the true and living God, that made heaven and earth and all that in them is. In doing so, the loving Father has done all that could be done for man, and leave him a free moral agent responsible for his decisions and actions. It is a great thing to be given the privilege of choosing our future destiny—to be able to make choice of good or evil. Upon no other basis could God in justice and mercy set before us life and death, reward and punishment. Only upon this plane of moral freedom could man be reached with a plan of salvation that would prepare for a glorious world of purity.

As we look out upon this wide world with its laws and harmony, and see how all are to work for good to man, we know positively that a great mind planned all for a wise purpose; for all his works are in wisdom. This makes us desire to know more of him who hath spoken to our souls so plainly in the wonderful works of creation.

Another thought that is of great benefit to us, if we will receive it, is this: The mind and power that created the universe and arranged so well for the good of man would know that we as thinking beings would wonder, and desire to know about the Creator, and so he would meet that need in some way for man's benefit. He has done so in love by giving us the Bible, and its record is this: " In the beginning God created the heaven and the earth." It is so emphatic, so concise and to the point, that we have no need to doubt; but as we read the Bible further, we find that after man was created God walked and talked with him in the Garden of Eden. As men lived to great age the generations that followed must have conversed freely over the wonders of God's creation, and his dealings with man. However, as we read we see that for many years God continued to talk to those who trusted in him, and gave them needed instruction that they obeyed.

This record inspired by the Spirit of God was given by Moses who lived 1,460 years B. C., or over 2,500 years after the creation. A part of this record covers a period of time for which there was no other account kept—no profane history—but we see from other portions of the Bible, including Christ's and the apostles' teachings, that the record given by Moses is correct, as it was accepted by them, and many portions repeated in their teachings of truth. Another proof we have of the divinity of the Bible is that its promises are verified to those who meet the conditions of reception. For instance, it says, "Come unto me, all ye that labor and are heavy laden, and I will give you rest." Let an individual, pressed down by sin and sorrow, decide to love and serve God, and accept this promise as his, it is very soon fulfilled to him, and his burden of sin and care is removed and he is made happy in the love of God. In old times God spoke through the prophets, and their prophecies were fulfilled at the proper times. Many are the prophecies of the Old Testament concerning the coming of a Savior, the circumstances of his life, and death upon the cross; and they were all fulfilled to the very letter. Thus we know the teachings of the word of God are strong and true, and must be fulfilled.

Now, let us go back in thought to the record God has given of himself. Speaking through a prophet, he says: "Look unto me, and be ye saved, all the ends of the earth; for I am God, and there is none else."—Isa. 45:22. Speaking to Moses in the burning bush, he said, "I am the God of thy father, the God of Abraham, the God of Isaac, and the God of Jacob."—Mark 12:26; Ex. 3:6. "And Jesus answered him, The first of all the commandments is, Hear, O Israel: The Lord our God is one Lord: and thou shalt love the Lord thy God with all thy heart, and with all thy soul, and with all thy mind, and with all thy strength."—Mark 12:29, 30. From these scriptures we see plainly that God wants us to recognize him as God, and to love and serve him. Now comes the question in many hearts: "Why should we love and serve him?" Because it is right; he is our Creator, a great and good being from whom we receive all our blessings. We love, honor, and serve our earthly parents—how much more ought we to do the same to our heavenly Father! Let us see what more we can find in the Bible concerning him. "God is love." "God is light, and in him is no darkness." "There is none good but one: that is God," "the only true God." "God is a Spirit."

Now, dear boys, from these few short scriptures we may learn much about our God, and why we should love him. Let us examine them carefully. "God is love." Love is good, pure, and worthy of honor; so if God is love and we honor love, we will in reality honor God. Again, "God is light." Do we esteem light more than darkness? If God is light, we must honor him because he is so much better than darkness. Again, "There is none good but God." So we find he is good. Do we love goodness? If so, we should honor God, as he is all that is good and pure, and not one of us can be good without his help. He is "the only true God." As he is the *only* God, and is a true God, he is a peculiar being—there is none like him—and as he is true, we need not fear to believe and trust him. Again, we find "God is a Spirit." "Oh," says one, "that is so mysterious that

I cannot comprehend it." Well, let us see. Here are two boys going home from school. One of them carries the books for a little schoolmate, helps several others over the bad places, does all he can to make them happy. The other boy knocks off the little ones' caps, runs off with their dinner pails, and finally pushes one upon a wire fence, hurting him cruelly. He teases and torments all who will heed him, thus bringing them sorrow. What would you call those boys to distinguish them by their actions? "Oh," you say, "the first one was *good* and the other was *bad*." That is right; for "even a child is known by his doings, whether they are good or bad." Now a bad boy is letting a bad spirit move him to badness, and has a bad spirit; and a good boy is letting a good spirit move him, and therefore has a good spirit. God is a spirit of love, light, goodness, and truth. He is all love, all light, all goodness, and all truth; therefore worthy of our highest regard and love. Added to this he is "all-wise," "gracious," "merciful," "just," "faithful," "almighty," "eternal." Combine all these qualities, and we see by faith the most wonderful being that our minds could conceive of. Indeed, we cannot to any degree comprehend him in all the attributes of his character.

Now, boys, did you ever think lightly of God? Will you try to understand him better? Look here! You play with your schoolmates in perfect freedom, act as you please, speak as you please, and look as you please. You realize you are on the same level, all children together. Now, let a teacher, preacher, or stranger be with you, and you feel a constraint. You know they are above you and know more; therefore your respect for them is greater, and makes you feel your littleness, and you keep quite still and do not draw their attention to yourself. Now, if you should come into the presence of a governor, a president, or a king or queen, you would feel more backward, would recognize their greatness, and have very great respect for them. This is natural. Now, as we have contemplated the character of God, we ought to have great respect for him; that is, give him honor and esteem. We can do that naturally—realizing our dependence upon him, and being grateful for mercies and blessings—without really obeying the first commandment, to love him with all the powers of our being; but we cannot truly love him as we ought, without first comprehending his greatness, and love toward us. "We love him because he first loved us."

Now let us look again to his word, the Bible, and see if he wants man to recognize him through his works. In the nineteenth Psalm we find this most beautiful language: "The heavens declare the glory of God; and the firmament showeth his handiwork. Day unto day uttereth speech, and night unto night showeth knowledge. There is no speech nor language where their voice is not heard. Their line is gone out through all the earth, and their words to the end of the world." From this language we may know that through the greatness and wonders of the universe he speaks wisdom to every human being, and would have him stop and consider the great reality of life. As we behold the works of God, the thoughts come: "Oh, how grand! how wonderful! Surely a mighty hand has formed all this. What for? Why am I here? Is this all? How may I know more? Surely not only a wise but a loving hand formed all things—yes, even myself. What does he want of me? I would love to know more of him—the great Creator." We dwell upon it. God is near and knows the desire of the soul; he gives precious thoughts and the desire is strengthened until it overreaches all other wishes, and the soul is seeking after God. "Because that which may be known of God is manifest in them; for God hath showed it unto them. For the invisible things of him from the creation of the world are clearly seen, being understood by the things that are made, even his eternal power and Godhead; so that they are without excuse."—Rom. 1 : 19, 20.

The soul recognizes the eternal power and Godhead of the Creator through his works, and the soul is brought to humbly seek to know more of him, and the promise is: "And ye shall seek me, and find me, when ye shall search for me with all your heart." Yes, "God will move mountains" and "work wonders" to bring souls to the knowledge of his will, when they desire to know it.

Oh, dear boys! how many of you are seeking to know God? If you had the opportunity of making the acquaintance of a renowned person who could grant you many favors, you would not be slow in doing so. You may know God. You may so love him that he will be unto you more than treasures of gold and silver—yea, more than life and all else. When God is so willing to reveal himself to mankind, is it not sad that all do not seek to know him?

Let us look further and see what God's purposes are concerning us. In Rev. 4:11 we are told that God is worthy to receive glory, honor, and power; for he has created all things, and for his pleasure they were created. As we are the workmanship of his hands, we are included in what should give him pleasure. So now as he is an almighty, an all-wise, and an all-good God we can see how great is our mission. As one who is good must delight in the good, it is necessary that man should be good, to please God.

If we read the account of the creation, we see that man was placed above the earthly creation. The ground was his to till, the herbs were his for food, the animals were given him to name and to use for different purposes. The sun and moon were to give light, heat, and fruitful seasons; and to speak, in unison with the rest of creation, of the great and loving Creator.

Again, remembering the creation, we find man was made in the image of God, who "breathed into his nostrils the breath of life, and man became a living soul." As God is a Spirit, and "a Spirit hath not flesh and bones," it could not be that man was made in outward appearance like God; so the image must be in something else. Man could be made in the image of God in *purity*, and we find this is what was meant; for the plan of redemption brings him back to purity and to God. As he is in the image of God and a living soul, man is a much higher being than any of the others created; even if they had equal intelligence, which they have not.

God placed man in a beautiful garden, and gave him instruction regarding the fruit therein. There was one tree of which he was not to eat, but all the rest were for his use. There are two great powers in this world—one is good, the other is evil. God stands for the good, and the Devil for the evil. When God gave instruction to man not to eat of that fruit, it was good that he should not. He was a living soul in purity, and if he would eat of that tree (the knowledge of good and evil), he would become responsible for the evil. In partaking of the forbidden fruit he disobeyed a righteous God, partook of evil, and became impure and a transgressor of right. A punishment followed; for the decree of righteousness was, "In the day thou eatest thereof thou shalt surely die." As it was not an instant, literal death, it must have been a spiritual one, according to the scripture "The soul that sinneth, it shall die." What an awful fall! from purity to sinfulness, from a perfect man to an unholy one, from one who had never partaken of evil to one who now knew its exceeding sinfulness in the eyes of an all-wise, almighty God.

We see also that the Devil in the form of a serpent deceived Eve, until she believed him rather than God; but she found out when too late what a sad mistake she had made in so doing. Many are to-day doing the same thing—heeding the sly, subtle words of evil rather than the precious words of truth. May the Lord help you to see how very necessary it is that each of you love the right and hate the wrong.

Because of this great fall of our first parents all their descendants have been born impure in heart. They have inherited the fallen nature, or inclination to evil. This was a great misfortune, starting the whole human race on the way to eternal death. But God, in love and mercy, provided a plan to save humanity from such a sad state.

As the result of doing evil is death of the soul, God's plan was to provide a Savior who should suffer death for every man and make him free from the result of his wrong-doing; that is, make the soul that was dead in sin again alive in righteousness. Let us illustrate this point so you will all remember it for your good. You have no doubt seen a dead person, and know what a great difference there is between the dead and the living. The dead are helpless; they cannot move, speak, or use any of the powers of a living person. Should some one try to make a dead man stand upon his feet, he would have to be propped up from every side. And should one try to make him move, he would only do so as far as he was made to. This was very clearly demonstrated to us a few years ago by a little home incident. The children had a pet cat. She had never had a family of her own; so she one day innocently stole another cat's kittens, which she tended with the utmost care; but not being able to supply them with their natural food, they soon died. Her grief was pitiful to witness; she would rub them, turn them over, lick them long and tenderly, move them about with her feet, try to give them food, and whine and cry so piteously that we all felt very sorry for her. When the last one died, she carried it to us and laid it at our feet, and went through all her endeavors to make it alive; every few seconds looking at us so pleadingly, as though she thought we might help her in her loving efforts. We expressed our sympathy to her as best we could, and tried to show her that we could not help her bring it to life; and then we gave it decent burial before her eyes, to try to help her to understand that the principle of life was gone and could not return, no matter how much we wished for it.

How often has the human heart been wounded almost to death by the loss of loved ones, and a most passionate longing has arisen therein to woo the dear ones back to life; and if intensest longing, ceaseless caresses, and sweetest of names could have done so, not many would be lying in the cold and silent grave. If the death of the body is so great an event when the length of days is numbered at threescore years and ten, what must be the great reality when a precious immortal soul dies to purity and loses its spiritual life? Men may weep over the death of the body, but the great God weeps over the death of the soul; the hearts of loved ones are wrung with anguish over the loss of natural life, but the gracious Savior, the angels of heaven, and the Holy Spirit grieve in divine sorrow over the soul's eternal death.

Dear boys, can you now see that when a man sins, chooses evil instead of good, and the life of the soul departs, nothing he can do of himself can bring it back? He is in a hopeless condition, unless some greater power can again restore the life back to the dead soul. This is what God intended to do when he promised that the seed of the woman (Christ Jesus) should bruise Satan's head. This also was what was meant when God said to Abraham, "In thy seed [Christ] shall all the nations of the earth be blessed." —Gen. 22:18. And this was God's purpose. "When the fullness of the time was come God sent forth his Son, made of a woman, made under the law to redeem them that were under the law, that we might receive the adoption of sons." God wanted to redeem (or buy back) fallen man to his lost purity, and restore life to dead souls. Only in permitting the penalty for sin to fall upon some one else, could justice be sustained in mercy. Let us illustrate this.

Here is a person who has disobeyed the laws of the land and has killed a fellow man. The penalty therefor is death upon the scaffold, and the justice of the law can only be sustained by its enforcement. The man has a sick wife and helpless children, and his brother's heart is moved in compassion; and as he sees the criminal is truly repentant and would not do the like again and he knows more of the extenuating circumstances of the case, and remembers his brother's extreme kindness to himself when in trouble, he proposes to take his place and suffer in his stead. This is permitted, and the innocent suffers death for the guilty. The price has been paid, the offender is free —the sacrifice has been made, the man is redeemed unto life.

Nothing could restore to life dead souls but for some one to take their penalty, and suffer death for their redemption. This God did when he sent his only begotten Son into this world to take upon him the form of a man, and suffer the ignominious death upon the cross. "He tasted death for every man." Thus full redemption was bought for every man; and God designs that every one should enjoy his presence in glory eternally. The plan is perfect, the whole world of mankind is free as far as the plan of redemption is concerned.

Let us remember again our illustration concerning the condemned man and his brother. Suppose when the brother proposed to suffer in his stead, that the convict did not believe him, and "did not think it was true," or was "too simple" or "something or other." When he sees his brother bound, led forth to death, and then the jailer leads him to the prison door and tells him he is free, if he still is doubtful and does not take his freedom, you would consider him unworthy of the sacrifice that had been made, and that he held his liberty at little value, and you would think him "a very foolish fellow." And so he would be—his liberty was bought at a great price, and is worthy to be accepted gladly.

So it is, dear boys, in regard to spiritual life. The price was paid that makes all souls alive in Christ Jesus, but they can only have it as they receive it by faith. They are told they are free; they are urged to take their freedom; but they hesitate to take it. Do they value it aright? Ah, no! they are not worthy of it; but mercy pleads, the love of God draws them, and some yield and prove the truth that the precious blood of Jesus cleanses from all sin, and redeems the soul back to God in purity.

Wonderful! *wonderful!* surely thou art a God of love, mercy, and justice. Man might be deficient and overlook one of these and conceive of different plans, but the true, all-wise, almighty God must combine the three, for which our hearts should give him praise. We are sure if your hearts and minds have followed us through this subject, you must be convinced of the reality of the religion of Jesus Christ.

There are some, however, that are skeptical regarding what they cannot investigate with their natural senses; therefore they sometimes consider this religion "too superstitious." They do not discern the difference between faith and imagination. Faith is simple trust; if our judgment is convinced of truth, it is easy to believe it. Whereas, imagination is something unreal that one may conjure up without any effort of the reasoning powers, and which the mind retains regardless of judgment. Faith has something to rest upon, while imagination has not. Some people are more imaginative than others, and let their mind drift into any channel it wills, without restraint of reason or justice, and then accept as true their various thoughts and suggestions. This gives room for many false ideas to arise, which are often attached to religion and make its presentation very unreal and unreasonable to those who weigh everything carefully.

So we see the need of carefulness in receiving or not receiving different teachings. It is very strange how wise, thinking beings will allow false and very harmful teachings to be received as religion. This brings to mind an expression heard somewhere, "People love to be humbugged," and it seems as though it is true at first thought regarding spiritual things; but when we consider it more carefully, we see it is because they do not properly consider those things pertaining to eternal life and happiness, but think because " there is the mysterious in religion it is unnecessary to try to understand it," and " one might as well believe one thing as another." This is unwise. There are mysteries in nature—some things that are very strange, and which we cannot "reason out" but must admit their existence and reason around the facts. For instance, we cannot comprehend the power of the earth to afford different substances for the growth of different kinds of vegetation. Nor can we know why it is necessary to have heat, moisture, and sunshine to make plants grow, yet we know it is true, and when we plant them we plan that they shall have what they need as far as we are able to provide it.

We may not understand all the "whys and wherefores" in the religion of Jesus, but we can plainly see the facts and comprehend their importance, and leave the rest unto God to make clear to us in his own good time. Another thought is necessary also. The natural man cannot understand spiritual things as fully as those who have become spiritual through the reception of life to the soul.

You know there are often those among you who make sport of religion, and deride certain teachings because they seem foolish to them. But just remember for your own good that when they are so doing they are simply fulfilling the scripture: "The preaching of the gospel is to them that perish foolishness, but to those who are saved it is the power of God." It shows a great weakness in people to deride what they do not comprehend.

It is only natural after the lapse of 1900 years that the religion of Jesus should have attached to it in various ways in the minds of many, such things as do not recommend it to their confidence; but let each one throw down all past teachings and come to the Bible for instruction, and receive the precious truths in an actual experience of life in the soul, and these false ideas and notions will flee away and the true will stand out in bold relief as the most beautiful and perfect religion that could be conceived; because God's thoughts are far above man's thoughts.

The false religions because they are the thoughts of man are found to be far below the true. They are the conceptions of hearts filled with sin, and their sensual joys, and their promises of future happiness must partake of that fallen nature. One of them permits its believers to live in sin, do very many wicked things, live most ungodly lives; and then occasionally confess these sins to a man, who gives them some penance to perform to make their forgiveness sure with God. Also, the regulations of this religion permit such arrangements as lead to the most depraved and licentious transactions.

Other religions promise a future of sensuality to the faithful adherents, because their conception of enjoyment rises no higher than their depraved hearts. Idolatrous superstitions and worships attract many people by their fanciful and earthly devotions. Some of the worshipers are very devoted and zealous and undergo great hardships and privations to gain the favor of their gods, as they imagine, when we know that "an idol is nothing" but the work of man's hands. There is also the worship of natural objects, as the sun, moon, stars, and animals. It is a great pity that man does not more perfectly "seek after God." These false religions cannot satisfy the soul, and many of their teachings are repulsive to the better part of our human nature. Let us remember again that God speaks to every individual through the wonders of creation and the longings of the soul; so every one is without excuse. The heathen are a law unto themselves, their conscience accusing or excusing them. It is the precious privilege of man to carry the good news of salvation in Jesus to all these idolatrous nations, for their present and eternal good. What must be the sad state of those who turn from the true unto the false because of self-will or desire! All around us, even in what are called Christian lands, are forms of worship that partake of heathen idolatry.

We realize that God wants us to warn the boys from entering the doors of deception and evil through what seems to many very attractive, because of its innocent appearance and the promise of good. Every city, town, and village has as many different lodges as it can support. These claim to give special benefits to their members. These benefits with few exceptions are very small compared to the money and time invested therein, and are such as but few have need of—especially if Christians. We refer to the promises of assistance in times of sickness; for Christians will care for the sick according to the scriptures without any reward. The time, money, and effort used to sustain the lodges is very great, and the good done among the sick and needy is almost imperceptible. The lodge spirit of charity is very far from the Bible standard, which is to do good unto all men as we have opportunity. If the money, time and effort employed in lodge work were applied directly to the relief of the sick and needy, there would certainly be much more good accomplished. If a young man will apply himself to labors of love and kindness without desire for reward, he makes provision for himself in the hearts of others and in the mercy of God. Oftentimes sickness is permitted to come upon us to make us more sympathetic toward others, and we should do good, hoping for nothing again. Lodge *charity* is no charity; for in most cases it is more than paid for in lodge dues and service, and it is so considered by the members. Often have we heard the remark made by the sick, " The lodge ought to help me; for I have done more for it than it has for me." Often our hearts have been saddened to think how much more good would be accomplished if what societies require for their existence were used for the spread of the gospel of salvation.

There is another sad feature of society and lodge work. Many professing Christians will be more zealous for lodge obligations than for religious service, while others claim that " the lodge is good enough religion for them;" and thus precious souls are being destroyed through this lodge influence.

Again, some of the lodges have forms of worship; and while they lay claim to the knowledge and worship of God, their service is so mixed with idolatrous performances and beliefs that it is more heathenish than Christian, and meets the censure of God in dishonoring his holy name and gospel truth They leave out the name of Jesus our Redeemer, and yet profess to prepare men for the "Grand Lodge above," which is, to say the least, one of the worst forms of sacrilege; for "there is no other name given under heaven or among men whereby we must be saved."

Lodges are directly disobedient to the teachings of the gospel. We are told to "swear not at at all; neither by heaven; for it is God's throne; nor by the earth, for it is his footstool; neither by Jerusalem, for it is the city of the great King. Neither shalt thou swear by thy head, because thou canst not make one hair white or black. But let your communication be, Yea, yea; Nay, nay; for whatsoever is more than these cometh of evil."

All the lodges we have heard of have some form of oath to administer to the candidates, and the higher the lodge the greater and more terrible are the oaths, and penalties for the revelation of their secrets (which are no secrets, since they have been revealed). This alone should deter any one from entering their portals; but this is not all; the lot falls upon some of the members to fulfill these terrible penalties upon those who break their oaths, to reveal, for others' good, the workings of lodgism, which is the most brutal murder minds can conceive. The death of men who have made revelations, and the sworn statement of those who have done the terrible deed, and the sly and cunning threatenings of others have established the fact beyond doubt. In coming to Jesus for salvation these awful things have had to be acknowledged and forsaken in order to obtain forgiveness from God. The administration of these awful oaths, the contemplation of their fulfillment, and the secret admission that it is necessary, to enforce the lodge regulations, have a very strong tendency to produce hard-heartedness and to cause men to look upon such things with complacency instead of with horror. So we are not surprised that lodge members count the opposers of lodgism as "fanatical." You cannot touch a lodge man in a more tender spot than to speak against his lodge—it becomes his idol.

The principle of lodgism is directly antagonistic to a republican form of government; for they run politics for their own advantage, whenever possible. Many of the wisest and strongest statesmen have raised their voices in opposition thereto, because of the tendency to weaken the nation by the defeat of justice and mercy.

There is no greater hindrance to the administration of personal justice than the power wielded in the lodge by members defending one another "in all cases, not excepting treason and murder." Often has the verdict of the jury been changed by the endeavors of a brother lodge man, and the innocent have suffered in the defeat of justice. This power extends to religious organizations as well as to commercial circles—favoritism and promotion depend upon being a member of some lodge, and those who oppose it are persecuted and belittled as far as possible. While speaking to a minister who claimed to preach the gospel, he said a preacher who was not a lodge man stood no chance of obtaining good positions, but was sent to the inferior or backwoods stations. A politician admitted that much of the political wire-pulling was done in the secret lodge room. Many of the fair, strong, young men who have gone down under the curse of intemperance took their first glasses of strong drink at the lodge meeting or supper or banquet. Many a mother, wife, sister, or daughter has arisen after the midnight hour to receive from the lodge an inebriate loved one, and many a home has sorrowed because "lodge meeting" came nearly every night in the week, and gave the home circle little opportunity to enjoy the society of fathers, husbands, brothers, and sons.

Surely then, we mothers have a right to cry out against the lodge that would usurp our place in the hearts who have promised to "love and cherish." Sometimes the excuse is made that they entered the lodge for the protection of and provision for loved ones, "in case of death removing the support and stay of future years." Those who trust in God need no such provision; for he careth for the fatherless and the widow. Should any one "do evil that good may come"? The idea of a man being under obligation to provide for the future of his family, after his death, is absurd, and savors of the strongest unbelief. The desire to do so has placed "burdens grievous to be borne" upon many frail shoulders, and has hastened them to the tomb, or has induced them to enter secret lodges for future benefits, or to insure their lives for the same purpose. If a man uses the ability and wisdom he has, in business effort, and then cares for his body properly and trusts God for health and prolonged life for his family's good, he has done all that is necessary, and escapes many hurtful lusts and trying circumstances.

Many of the young enter these institutions without examination and with the desire to use them innocently for their advancement in business matters. Others think they will get much for little by paying small dues, and then receive a large amount to settle upon some one or more. This often fails to work as planned, and sometimes is the cause of death and destruction through evil desire when death brings more than life. It is not right to place this temptation before any one, no matter how pure and strong.

O dear boys, will you not more carefully consider these things and avoid all that would have a tendency toward evil in any direction? The word of God speaks plainly to those who would be Christians: "Be ye not unequally yoked together with unbelievers; for what fellowship hath righteousness with unrighteousness? and what communion hath light with darkness? and what concord hath Christ with Belial? or what part hath he that believeth with an infidel? and what agreement hath the temple of God with idols? * * * Wherefore come out from among them, and be ye separate, saith the Lord, and touch not the unclean thing; and I will receive you."

Here we see that those who serve God are forbidden to be unequally yoked together with the wicked. Now, it is clear that in every lodge there are unbelievers, unsaved, wicked men, who know not God and who *will not* serve him. Then how would it be possible to be in a lodge without disobeying this scripture?

The church of God must fearlessly proclaim the whole truth of the gospel against everything sinful. As it does so, and does not yield to the seducing and overpowering influence of wicked men and evil works, he who would serve God faithfully and gain the benefits of his salvation must square his life by the gospel and forsake every man-made institution of sin. It is natural for men to want to receive the benefits of the religion of Jesus, while clinging close to the things that delight the natural heart. This is why there are so many close counterfeits of the true religion. Often only those who live the closest to God and trust him for wisdom can discern between the true and the false. We cannot mingle the two together—it is take the true and discard the false or take the false and discard the true. Which shall it be for you? We cannot serve God and be partakers of the Lord's table and the table of devils, but must choose this day whom we will serve. "If God is God, serve him; if Baal, serve him."

Now, dear boys, as we know you are concerned about these things, we have desired to present the truth so as to win you to the service of God, remembering this scripture: " What shall it profit a man, if he shall gain the whole world, and lose his own soul." May each dear son be awakened to examine well the path of his feet and incline them unto wisdom's ways and to the living God.

SALVATION IN JESUS.

In connection with "religion true" we must dwell upon this salvation that is found in Jesus our Savior. You remember man's hopeless condition after his fall into sin, and how God moved with compassion promised to provide a Savior to redeem from that sorrowful state of soul-death, and as many of you have heard of the birth of Jesus, we will only state it briefly, and you may all read the exact account in the Bible in the Gospels.

After God had made the promise of a Redeemer for fallen man, all who knew God and trusted in him looked forward to Christ's coming as the great event in the history of man; and those who trusted and obeyed God's direct commands were counted righteous; for their " faith was counted unto them for righteousness." Their souls were alive through the atonement that should be made. They walked and talked with God, and received his instruction and blessing. Many prophecies concerning Christ were given to them, which were all fulfilled at the proper time. Our Savior came from the courts of heaven and took upon him the form of a man, that he might suffer man's trials, endure his temptations, and conquer his foe, the Devil, who had so deceived and injured him through his fall into sin. Nothing more beautiful can be imagined than his humble birth and lowly life which he lived in this world, and through his death and suffering brought again spiritual life to the souls of men.

The immortal part of man, the soul, must have an existence somewhere throughout all eternity. In the pure state in which he was created that existence would have been with God in eternal glory in heaven; but when his purity was lost in partaking of evil, then that existence must be in the opposite—even with the Devil in eternal death in his abode, which is hell, which was prepared for the Devil and his angels (those who serve him). When the redemption was made that bought man back to purity of soul, it also restored him to *all* that was lost—eternal life in heaven with God. And while we should desire purity more than all else, we may look forward to eternity in glory as a very precious privilege. Some seem more anxious to get to heaven than to be pure in this life and honor God by a holy walk and conversation. This ought not to be; for we should love God more than to seek only for our own good. Many souls went down to eternal death because they would not heed the voice of God and look forward to the atonement of Christ for the sin of the world; and some are doing the same thing now; because they will not heed the instruction, and believe that all may have life through Jesus the Savior.

For three years before his death Jesus preached the gospel of the kingdom, and offered salvation from sin to every one who would receive the atonement for sin through faith in him as the Savior. Many believed on him as the Redeemer, and obeyed his teaching by repenting of and forsaking their sins, and trusting him for spiritual life. He sent out preachers who went into every city preaching the good news of salvation in Jesus, and all who believed it received its fulfillment in life to the soul and health to the body; for " he healed all manner of sickness and disease among the people; for God was with him in power, working wonders in the sight of men." Notwithstanding all this, men hated, rejected, and persecuted him, and were ready to destroy him, because the truth upset their false religions and reproved them for sin and iniquity; because their deeds were evil, and his good and pure. The wicked cruelty of men was unable to do its pleasure until Jesus said, " The hour is come when the Son of man must be betrayed into the hands of men." " Then laid they their hands upon him," and hasted him away to mock trial and to cruel crucifixion—the most solemn and sublime hour in the history of the world. The " King of kings " and the " Lord of lords " hanging between earth and heaven to make a way into its celestial portals for poor fallen man! And while they reviled and derided the Son of God, the earth was darkened—the sun hid his face in shame—the rocks rent, the earth quaked, the graves were opened, and the veil of the temple was rent in twain from top to bottom, revealing to the world that a mighty work had been wrought for man.

O ye faithless ones! what more could the God of heaven have done to prove his love and faithfulness to you, in that wonderful hour of Christ's humiliation and death? Stand still, dear ones! look upon the scene, let your hearts and minds take it all in and retain it there, until it shall melt you into tears, into submission and humbleness, and into strongest belief of the truth, and then into salvation in Jesus. Then will you *know* that "*his name is Jesus because he saves his people from their sins.*"

After his sufferings and death upon the cross he was taken and laid in a new tomb hewed in a rock, and a great stone was placed at the door and sealed with the king's seal, and guarded by the soldiers. On the third day he triumphed over death and the grave, and "rose from the dead," according to the prophecies. The rocks could not hold him; the king's seal could not prevent him; and the soldiers could not restrain him! "Praise his name, all ye people!" "Rejoice with the voice of triumph." Our God reigneth! Though it seemed to the scorners that they had demolished every claim to the divinity of Christ by placing him upon the cross, yet they were only fulfilling the scriptures and giving him the opportunity to bring to naught the reasonings of men, and prove himself the very Christ. So now the scoffers may reject his atonement and scorn his salvation from sin, but the time will come at no very distant day when he will come in all his glory, with the holy angels with him, and "then shall every knee bow unto the Lord and every tongue confess unto God." After his resurrection he appeared to his disciples and they were convinced of his resurrection and testified to it even unto their enemies. Forty days he tarried with them, and as they were together without the city he was parted from them and went unto his Father—even unto God. The clouds received him out of their sight, and they returned unto Jerusalem and were continually in the temple praising and blessing God.

As we contemplate the atonement of Christ that brings man back to the state of purity from which he fell, through the subtlety of Satan, our hearts should be moved with love and gratitude, and we should desire him as a friend and companion all through our earthly pilgrimage. When we were talking to you upon companionship we advised you to choose for friends those who could help you upward and forward to true manhood. If it is necessary to have friends while in this world, no one can help us so much and be so true and steadfast as our Savior. And this is what he desires to be unto us: one who loves, saves from sin, gives life, comfort, strengthens, bears burdens, sustains, and takes home to glory. Thus would he be more than all unto us. "Companionship with Jesus here, makes life with bliss replete." There is nothing can help our sons to true manhood faster and more perfectly than acquaintance with the Lord our Redeemer; because his salvation begins at the root of the trouble and makes the heart pure, and thus the life becomes pure and Christlike. The individual is raised up from the earthly to the heavenly. His heart being pure and having heavenly aspirations, his desires are higher; his mind becomes more active and dwells upon godly wisdom, applying it to his life until he is able to walk in the footsteps of Jesus, who did no sin neither was guile found in his mouth.

Now we hope you all will inquire as others have done, "What must I do to be saved?" Yes, we hope and pray that you may realize your need of a Savior, and come to him that your souls may be made alive. It is very sad to think that any of you are going about with souls that are abiding in spiritual death, when a loving friend is near to give you life. Let us think of it real soberly and use an illustration to make it forcible to our souls. Here is one of you who has lost the use of a right arm. Another has no use of one of his feet, and still another has been made blind, while a fourth has become deaf and dumb. How sad to see you thus disabled! Do you think your parents would spare any expense to give you the right use of your members that are dead to you? Ah, no! How many parents have labored, hoped, saved, and prayed, that they might afford the best medical skill in the hope of restoring to their children the use of their different members that have been diseased and helpless! Sometimes they have succeeded and sometimes they have failed. And whichever way it turned, their hearts were moved with the strongest emotions toward their dear children, in joy or sorrow. Here are several boys who through accident or sinful practice have lost the right use of their minds. What grief rests upon the parents! Dearly as they love their children, they would sooner have seen them laid in the silent tomb, or would willingly have borne any amount of suffering or privation; but here is their trouble and little can be done. Day after day and year after year they must bear their sorrow and see their children helpless as babes. Oh, yes! it is a dreadful thing to have dead members as portions of a living body, and more dreadful to have dead minds incapable of comprehending life; but more awful than all this, is it to have souls dead in sin—away from God—and not realize the sad state they are in, and so make no effort for their good.

Awaken, boys, and see your need; because others are careless about their souls is no reason you should be. You ought not to drift along just because others do. In fact that is one of the Devil's ways to destroy precious souls. Because others are indifferent to their eternal good the enemy suggests, "Religion cannot be true, because many do not heed it." You know, boys, there are plenty of things *you know are true* that many people do not heed. You know it is true that an education is good; but some refuse it, and "have no use for it," saying, "It is foolishness," and "waste of time," and so on. You know it is true that intemperance unfits man for the best of life, and yet many do not believe it, and fill drunkards' graves. Their doing so does not prove the facts untrue, but their lack of wisdom. You see we must not follow others to do evil. It is right to consider the welfare of the soul, and we should do it regardless of what others do. If we wait to decide what is right, true, or wise, until others agree upon it, then we will wait forever. We ought to make a wise decision on every vital question, in order to help others. The more we try to shirk the responsibility of making a decision the more responsible we become. In the salvation of the soul we may know the truth; for it makes us free from sin. It simply *proves true*, the same as two and two are four.

"Well," some of you say, "If I knew it was true, I would seek for it, but it seems so unreal and so far away that it seems I cannot be earnest enough about it." Yes, that is often the reason precious souls go on year after year indifferently; they are waiting for something wonderful to happen to make them put forth an effort to obtain eternal life. Oh, how strangely we do act sometimes! Did you ever get what you most needed or desired without putting forth an effort to obtain it? Anything that is worth having is worth striving after. The more we desire something the more apt we are to strive for it earnestly. Some one says, "I thought it was a gift from God."

It is, dear boy; but we must be in condition to receive it—not that we can make ourselves worthy of it, or in any way make our hearts better; but we must come in God's way so we can trust for it.

Now, we believe some are really interested in knowing how to obtain the salvation of their souls; so we are going to give a few lessons, taking this theme step by step. Our next subject will be Conviction; as it is the first step. Let every one who knows he ought to be a Christian begin to study his Bible. Please read all the scriptures you can find on sin, and the story of Jesus' life and death.

Salvation in *Jesus!*
  Then how can you doubt it?
Oh, honor his name!
  And think much about it.

Salvation in *Jesus!*
  It sounds sweet and holy;
So humble yourself,
  And come meek and lowly.

Salvation in *Jesus!*
  We know you believe it;
Then open your heart,
  And gladly receive it.

Salvation in *Jesus!*
  You say you "can't doubt it;"
Then praise his dear name!
  We'll sing it and shout it.

Salvation in *Jesus!*
　You now "*do believe it;*"
You *yield* and you *trust*,
　And *fully receive it.*

Salvation in *Jesus!*
　So now you ' have found it;"
Just *praise* the dear Lord,
　And *gladly resound* it.

Salvation in *Jesus!*
　How perfect its fitness;
In love, and in truth,
　May each be a witness.

CONVICTION.

Every individual has a standard of right by which he judges the actions of men, and is quick to approve or disapprove—often without due consideration. This standard of right is modified generally by circumstances and influences of life, although it is often much higher than individual surroundings.

This voice from within is known as conscience, and is by many considered the rule of action in all life's transactions. While the world would be much better if every one did as well as his conscience dictates, yet as conscience is subject to influence and education, it is not to be depended upon as a guide in all circumstances.

Generally the conscience of those who have had little or no moral teaching is much below that of others who have been well instructed in moral principles. Here also the influence of parentage is very great. Parents who do not heed their conscience to do right as far as they know, but who "follow their inclinations," or "let their natural disposition run away with their judgment," generally have children who are low in conscience, and follow in the way of all evil. For the sake of our loved ones, if for nothing else, each individual should live upright and after the dictates of his conscience, if not after the teachings of Christ.

Let us illustrate this. Here are two boys in a large family of children, who were born under apparently the same circumstances. The parents are morally good people, who give clear moral teaching to their children. These two boys, being the oldest in the family, are most of the time under their father's care, and he instructs William, the older, to " give up to brother, as he is younger;" and as William begins early to find pleasure in yielding his wishes to others, he readily complies, and the younger child, George, soon looks upon it as his right to have his own way. This encourages selfishness, and soon what he *feels like doing* is what he does, regardless of others' desires and rights, and thus his evil nature is encouraged and the voice of conscience is not heeded.

William listens to instruction, forms decisions for right principles, and has a hatred of everything false and impure, and every necessity for decision in right and wrong appeals directly to his conscience, and he says, " I believe this is right, so I'll stand for it."

While George continues to walk after his own desires, his brother's better life compels him to see that he "ought to live better;" and while he does not yield to its dictates, his conscience reproves him for his low life. Though he may reason himself into the belief that his ways are worldly-wise, yet the voice of conscience rebels against it; so really he is not satisfied with himself, and cannot help being somewhat unhappy. If he fights against his conscience and forcibly resists it, there may settle upon him an indifference and hardness that is called ease of conscience; which seldom "asserts its right to be heard" or to his consideration. This is very dangerous ground.

No one is wise in living below his conscience, or in considering it a safe guide of action in all circumstances. If we are uncertain as to our course of duty, the only safe and sure guide is the Bible. For instance, it has become popular teaching, among moral and religious people, that when a married couple cannot live pleasantly and peacefully together they may separate, procure a divorce, and marry again. The Bible says that Moses suffered people because of the hardness of their hearts, to write a bill of divorcement and to put away their wives but that from the beginning it was not so." Further teaching is stronger even than this; for if divorcement is obtained, it causes one or more to live in adultery by recognizing the marriage of those divorced, as the Bible does not. Many have lived moral and religious lives, but being ignorant of this higher standard of right, they were not condemned in conscience until the standard of truth was raised. So you see our only safe guide is the Bible, and in order to understand it we need to be spiritual by having the salvation of Jesus.

Besides our conscience strivings we have the Spirit of God troubling us on account of our sins. If it is best and necessary to heed the voice of conscience, it is better and far more necessary to listen to the Spirit of God, who comes to us in our better moments with wooing tenderness trying to draw us unto God in love and mercy. Also, God speaks to us through his word, to show us how sinful we are. If we cannot realize the need of salvation, we should study the Bible and let God tell us: " All ye, like sheep, have gone astray." " The heart is deceitful above all things, and desperately wicked; who can know it?" " If our hearts condemn us, God is greater than our heart," and condemns us also.

You know, dear boys, that you do many things which you know are wrong—your conscience tells you so. The word of God tells you the same, and the Spirit of God pleads with you, saying, " Come unto me, all ye that are heavy laden;" and as you think of these things you know you do " feel real mean." Every time you have done wrong since you " knew right from wrong," you have stained your soul with sin and made yourself a transgressor against God. You were just as blamable as Adam and Eve when they disobeyed God by eating of the forbidden fruit; for you have disobeyed his holy commandments. Every time you gave way to such feelings as anger, hatred, selfishness, covetousness, pride, and selfwill, you were living after your evil nature and committed sin, and are accountable to God for each one. Oh, how many times each one of us has sinned, and how the sins pile up, and stand as mountains between us and God! When we see this as we ought to see it, there is a heavy burden upon us. We are convicted of sin. We realize God is displeased with us; and while he loves us, he cannot make our souls alive in righteousness until we give up all our sins. So the great responsibility lies with us. God is waiting—Jesus is ready—only we hesitate to give up sin. If we yield, we shall obtain salvation. If we do not, our hearts become harder and evil more pleasant, and God could in justice leave us to ourselves—lost.

Boys, let us think more earnestly, and use our every-day wisdom. Here is our nation; it makes laws by which each individual that lives therein must abide or be punished. This is right, you admit, and say quickly, " If any one does not like our laws, let him go somewhere else where he is better pleased." Suppose some people do not like our laws, but like our people, climate, and other things about our country, and are determined to live here, what must they do? You say, "If they want to live here, let them be subject to our laws, whether they like them or not." That is right, but suppose they come to stay, yet will not obey the laws? You say, " Then let them be punished; for our laws are good." That answer is right also.

Now, let us apply our lesson. There are two great spiritual kingdoms in the world—the kingdom of righteousness, with God as king; and the kingdom of evil, with the Devil as king.

Each of these kingdoms has its laws, and each king would like to have all the inhabitants of the world dwell in his kingdom: " but people have their likes and dislikes," so some abide in one and some in the other.

The kingdom of righteousness has a beautiful country, lovely future prospects, a pure people, and a holy King. In order to preserve this nation and sustain its standard of excellence it has some very strong and pure laws, that are unchangeable. The inhabitants of the other nation look upon our happiness and future prospects with longing desire, and they would like to enjoy them with us; but they do not like our laws—they look unwise and not right, etc. In their nation each one thinks he does as he pleases and is enjoying himself greatly, but every little while his pleasures are turned to sorrow; for the king's imps fall upon him, cruelly afflicting him—sometimes even unto death.

The people are so blinded by their personal-liberty ideas that they think their ways will turn out all right after awhile, and they console themselves with the thought that they "have no such strict laws as that other nation." If we look carefully, we may see what they do not see. Their king says to them, "You may have your own way, do as you please;" but to himself he says, "I will have my way whenever I WANT *it* and in the end"—and the *end shall be destruction*. Whenever he thinks they are having too good a time he sends out his imps to draw his reins with the utmost cruelty. Whenever his subjects begin to long for the other country he spreads before them new attractions, which please for a time—but

end in sorrow. Some of these people get tired of
this kind of freedom, and finally see how their king
is deceiving them, and through much effort cast off
his yoke and flee to the other kingdom; and then they
say, "Why, all the laws are just right—everything
is agreeable." So they are well pleased to abide, and
wonder how they could have been so deceived into the
belief that there were no laws, and each was having
his own way, when now they see so clearly that the
laws of that land were Satan's own plans and desires
for each one of them, which he fulfilled to his own
satisfaction without their consent.

Some of the loyal subjects in the kingdom of evil
decide they will improve things, they will take some
of the most agreeable laws from the kingdom of
righteousness and unite them with their own desires to
receive the future benefits of righteousness, and thus
harmonize the two kingdoms to suit themselves.
They draw off to one side of Satan's kingdom—so
close to the other that they seem to enjoy some of its
prospects, and flatter themselves that they have
"found an easy way to heaven." They are not in
the kingdom of God, for they do not obey its laws;
so they are still in the kingdom of Satan and will receive his future prospects—eternal death. This little
province is *false Christianity*."

Now, remember your former answers and see where
it will bring us. If the people of this little province
do "not like our laws, let them go somewhere else."
If individuals want the privileges of our nation, "let

them obey the laws whether they like them or not."
"And if they will not keep them, let them be punished."

Boys, this decision means everything to you. You must make decision in favor of one of these nations. Most of you are abiding in the kingdom of unrighteousness, and your king is the Devil, and he is deceiving you with the idea that you are having a good time, when you are often most miserable. Your conscience, the Word of God, and the Holy Spirit are telling you that you are not acting wisely, and you look over into the kingdom of righteousness and desire its favors and future prospects of heaven; but when you look to its laws and think you must give up sin and the pleasures of the world, you draw back, and say, "Oh, I believe it will all work out right some way;" and so you stay in Satan's kingdom, and let him deceive and allure your precious souls to eternal destruction, and all because you do not like the laws of righteousness. Now let your own answers condemn you. "If they do not like our laws, let them go somewhere else," and give up all the bright prospects of eternal joys. But if you want the blessings of righteousness, then "obey the laws whether you like them or not." "And if you will not obey them, then let you be punished."

"Why must one give up sin to be a Christian?" Because sin is the transgression of the law of righteousness. And you remember the first transgression was simply partaking of evil. If you could be saved without giving up sin, you would enter right into it again and be as bad as ever. But if you decide against evil and give it up entirely, then you will not expect to do evil, and salvation will keep you from it.

Sin is not nice, sweet, pretty, or good; what do you want of it? Salvation is nice, it makes men and women nice in their behavior in every way; it is also pretty; nothing more lovely than salvation; and it "beautifies the meek:" it is good; for it makes all who receive it good. Then give up sin and take salvation full and free.

Conviction is not a very agreeable feeling to anybody; for by nature we all like to think we are pretty good, and to have others believe the same; but there is nothing more necessary for our spiritual good than a real deep and thorough conviction of our sinfulness. Sometimes when God begins to reveal our hearts in their awful sinfulness we begin to shrink from it and compare ourselves with others who, we think, are "so much worse" that by the side of them "we are pretty good." It is not wise to do so; for we may grieve away the Holy Spirit and be left to our own goodness, which in the sight of God is "filthy rags."

Every unsaved soul should encourage conviction by carefully considering all his sins and trying to see them as God does. Did you ever think as you "do some little meanness" how a Holy God looks upon it? You know it is mean, little, low, and indecent, even in the sight of moral men; and you know you do not measure to your standard of a man; but oh, how impure, unholy, degrading, contemptible, and defiling it appears in the sight of a holy and wise God no tongue can tell! but we may *feel* it, if we allow conviction to run deep and plow up all the hardness within our stony hearts.

I remember once "allowing my thoughts to run wild," and then awakening in horror to behold the awful sin that lay upon my soul. The sight of it caused the most intense agony, and when I thought how God looked upon it there seemed to be no life in me. My heart almost stopped its beating, and my soul could only moan, "O Lord, forgive! O Lord, have mercy, and blot out my sins and remember them no more forever!" At first it seemed but one sin, but as I looked upon it I could see one great sin with a score clustered around it; and I did not wonder that one transgression was enough to sink the soul to eternal destruction. This caused such intense suffering to my soul and body that my eyes became a fountain of tears and my voice one long, low moan of despair. The Lord of heaven and earth spoke in tenderest accents of love and mercy to my soul, assuring me of his willingness to forgive and save. And as I received pardon by faith the sorrow and sighing fled away, and I was drawn nearer to God in true humility and self-abandonment than ever before, and then God flooded my soul with love, and gave me the joy of salvation. Oh, that every one of our sons might realize the exceeding sinfulness of sin, and the joys of sins forgiven!

We will give you several letters from those who

have forsaken sin to follow in the footsteps of Jesus. May you read them carefully and learn some precious lessons that may help you to serve Satan no longer, but turn to the living and true God.

DEAR BOYS:

I believe God wants me to write my testimony and tell what he has done for me, to encourage others to seek him.

When quite young, the power of evil fastened upon me in bad habits. Being ignorant of the result thereof, I continued therein a long time, until life became miserable indeed. It is true where the word of God says, "The way of the transgressor is hard." Oh, what a burden sin is! At times I would resolve to do better and quit my evil ways in my own strength, but it was only for a little season; all was in vain in that way, and the longer the habits continued the worse they became, until my whole body was wrecked, and my soul was in a lost condition. I would look back over my life and exclaim, "Oh, how worthless!" and then look into the future and see nothing but pain and death. I came to the point that I could see myself as I really was—full of sin and wickedness. Something must be done. What could I do? Oh, how wretched I was! Jesus said when here on earth, " Come unto me, all ye that labor and are heavy laden, and I will give you rest. Take my yoke upon you, and learn of me, and ye shall find rest unto your souls. For my yoke is easy, and my burden is light."—Matt. 11:28.

Truly, I was heavy laden, and needed rest, and here was a promise of help. Was I too bad? In Luke 19:10 Jesus said, "The Son of man is come to seek and to save that which was lost." And Isaiah said, "Come now, and let us reason together, saith the Lord; though your sins be as scarlet, they shall be as white as snow; though they be red like crimson, they shall be as wool."—Isa. 1:18.

Again, in Rev. 22:17, it says: "Whosoever will, let him take the water of life freely." So I could but come to Jesus and give myself as a servant of righteousness, and as I did so, God for Christ's sake forgave me my sins, and I found rest to my burdened and sin-bound soul. Life had now strong future hope. Praise God for deliverance from my evil ways! for he changed my nature to serve him and walk in the paths of the righteous, which I found were "peace;" and I could live a pure, sinless life in this world, and have a bright hope of the future. I cast all on Jesus, obey the word of God, and he does the keeping. He not only saves my soul, but heals my body, and I enjoy very good health, for which I praise him, as all glory belongs to him.

I write these few lines with a deep sympathy for those in sin, especially those in bondage to evil habits as I was, and pray God to bless them to the good of many; for deliverance is free to all, for "whosoever will, may come."

Jesus came to save the lost and set the captive free. Will you let him set you free?

Your loving brother,
C. D. Orr.

DEAR BOYS:

It is with a heart filled with love and gratitude to the dear Lord that I write my testimony for his glory and your spiritual welfare.

God for Christ's sake forgave my sins at the age of nineteen, and I was regenerated and received the witness of the Spirit and could look up in confidence, crying, "Abba, Father." He saved me from gambling, card-playing, theater-going, tobacco-using, and a multitude of other sins. The desire for them is all gone, and God has kept me four years, and gives me abundance of grace to live pure and holy in this present evil world. I have had precious victory, but must confess that it has taken much secret prayer, self-denial, and strict obedience to the word of God; for this is the only ground upon which he has promised to keep us.

It is with joy I am drawing water out of the wells of salvation, and if you will repent and turn from your evil way, you can have this same joy, and spend eternity with God if you are faithful.

My prayer is that God will bless the unsaved readers of this book with deep conviction of sin, that they may turn unto God for forgiveness of sin, and receive the riches of his grace in the salvation of their souls.

Yours in Jesus' love,

Alexander Carswell.

If your conviction is not as deep as it should be, you may ask God to convict you more deeply. You should all seek God because it is right. Some have taken conviction for conversion, and without having a real change wrought in the soul by the spirit of life, have gone on day after day and year after year "trying to serve God," while they were under the power of sin in their hearts, and could not be as good as they wished to be, and so were often found sinning against God. It is sad to make a mistake any time, but how much worse when it is in regard to the salvation of the soul!

Now, boys, walk very carefully when you come to this point. Do much praying and study the word of God, earnestly desiring to know the way of life, and God will help you to come to him aright.

The next step in salvation is repentance, and we will have it for our next lesson.

CONVICT OUR SONS.

Convict their hearts, dear Lord, of sin,
And let them feel its weight;
Oh, show them, Lord, how bad they've been,
And help them "see things straight."

Convict them of their sinful ways.
  And show them how sin's pow'r
Has ruled their lives and spent their days,
  And tries to gain this hour.

Convict them, Lord, of sins so great,
  That stand upon *thy book;*
And help them all their ways to hate,
  And to their future look.

Convict them, Lord, of righteousness,
  Oh, make them see its need;
Then show thy love and graciousness,
  And help them strive indeed.

Convict them, Lord; oh, let them not
  Go down to endless woe,
But point them out their awful lot,
  If on in sin they go.

Convict them, Lord; you've *promised* to,
  We know you can and will.
By faith we know you surely do,
  And promises fulfill.

REPENTANCE AND CONVERSION.

When John came preaching the gospel, to prepare the way before Jesus, he taught the people to repent and "bring forth therefore fruits meet for repentance," which meant that they were to be truly sorry for their sins, give them up, make confession and restitution to all they had wronged, and confess their sins unto God.

It means more to repent than many people believe, as it includes the making right of all wrongs that lie between individuals, and such a godly sorrow for all evil-doing as will make one hate the very thought of again partaking of it.

If conviction of sin is retained and allowed to do its work in the heart, it will lead the soul to repentance. There will be a decision to give up every sin, so far as one is able of himself, and a willingness to nevermore walk in disobedience to God.

In coming to Jesus for the salvation of my soul the Devil brought to remembrance everything that could possibly come against me in the Lord's service, and made it appear so great that it seemed it would be almost impossible to serve him. But in carefully considering it I was made to see that this was the only chance of gaining heaven or of pleasing God; so the decision was made to serve God if I had to be almost continually on my knees in prayer because of my great trials. Firm in this decision, I retired to rest at night and on waking in the morning my soul was made so happy in the love of God that I could truly feel that all my trials would be as nothing compared to what I should receive, even while here in this world of sin. In the years that have passed since that time it has proved true.

Some dear souls will give up all their sins but one or two, and try to get saved while clinging close to these. For instance, a boy would like to be a Christian if he could be one and continue his using tobacco and reading novels. He is willing to give up card-playing, drinking, and bad company, but does not see how he could give up the two darling pleasures. Either one of these would make one disobedient to God; for the Word says, "Whatsoever ye do, do all to the glory of God," and no one can do these things and expect God to be honored thereby. Instead of that his cause is disgraced by those who do them and profess to be God's children. Others can give up such things, but do not like to be numbered with such a plain, peculiar people; for they cannot give up their worldly reputation. These things hold people to the service of Satan; for they cannot see why they cannot be Christians and hold to those evils.

You see, boys, they are not willing to bear reproach or to deny themselves for the good of their souls. Each one of us must be willing to "count all things but loss for the excellency of the knowledge of Christ Jesus my Lord."

Looking the matter over carefully and prayerfully and reading the Bible with earnest desire to know the way of life, the soul becomes heartily tired of his sinful life and decides to give it up. Then he sees he has some wrongs to make right—has been unkind to father and mother, and must ask their pardon for it, and then be reconciled to those from whom he has been alienated by his own proud ambitions. Then he remembers a sly and ugly transaction that requires great effort to make right. At last it is all done, and he feels much better; and the promise rises up to God, "Whatever more you show me from the past I will gladly make right." The past being made right as far as he is able to do it, he comes to God heartily sorry he has spent so many years in sin and folly and that he has so displeased a wise and good God.

He abhors his past life. Its doings seem darker and darker, until he realizes he is "chief of sinners," and is not worthy of God's love and mercy; and yet he wants it more than tongue can tell, and he feels he must seek for it as the pearl of great price. He knows nothing more to do, and cries out in anguish, "O my Lord, I give up the world. I have done all I know to do, and if you do not save me, I am lost." In this earnest heart-cry he recognizes the Lord as the only means of salvation, and rests upon him. So he is really believing on him as the Savior of the world. The loving Lord whispers, "Ye believe in God, believe also in me." "He that cometh unto me I will in no wise cast away." Why! that means him. Now he can believe that Jesus is his Savior, and as he thus believes, joy and peace come flooding his soul with the glory of the Lord, and his lips speak the holy praises that stir his soul. The dark night of sin is past, the light of salvation shines into his soul, and he is confident that his sins are forgiven and his name is written in the Lamb's book of life. His soul is full of sweet peace and joy, and he wonders why the whole world does not come to Jesus. He will try to tell it to everybody; for he is sure if they knew how blessed it is to be forgiven, they would surely want it. He finds some who want to talk about it, but have no earnestness to receive it, while others are perfectly indifferent. He has surely found something of great value—nothing he ever had suits him so well, and he could sing forever: "Oh, happy day, when Jesus washed my sins away," or, "Take my life and let it be consecrated, Lord, to thee;" "Take my heart, it is thine own, it shall be thy royal throne."

Some are so troubled about faith, and wonder how it is and why it is, that one must be saved by faith. They can understand repentance and restitution, as well as yielding to God, but hesitate to "take it by faith" as they are instructed. Well, let us see if we can explain it. Salvation is something we cannot see with our natural eyes nor handle with our natural hands; so when God offers it to us there must be some way to take it.

We believe there is such a thing as salvation, for we read of it in the Bible, hear of it from Christians, and see the effects of it in their lives; and so we know it is a reality, though not observed by natural sense. As it is a spiritual substance it must be received not by the hand of the body but by the hand of the soul—*faith*. It is not seen by the eye of the body, but by the eye of the soul—*faith*. It is not felt by sense of touch, but by the touch of *faith;* and these are as *real* as the natural senses.

The eye of faith sees the precious gift, the hand of faith takes it home to the soul, and the touch of faith realizes its presence there as a saving power.

Thus the soul dead in trespasses and sins is made alive in Christ Jesus. The divine life comes into the soul, and we are " born again," " born of the Spirit," " born of God," redeemed from the power of sin and made righteous.

Now what kind of life will this man lead? Will he " sin every day in thought, word, and deed "? or will he obey the Savior and " go, and sin no more?" It must surely be the latter; for the word of God says, " If any man be in Christ, he is a new creature; old things are passed away; behold, all things are become new." There is, therefore, now no condemnation to them which are in Christ Jesus, who walk not after the flesh, but after the Spirit. For the law of the Spirit of life in Christ Jesus hath made me free from the law of sin and death."

In our sinful life we were many times, if not all the

time, condemned by our hearts for wrong-doing; but now since we are in Christ, that condemnation is gone, because we do not walk as we did before salvation came to our souls; but being made alive by receiving his Spirit of life, we walk after that Spirit which has made us free from the law of sin. The sin that is in the heart would naturally bring forth evil fruit, but the Spirit of life gives victory over sin, and it must not bring forth its evil fruit—sins of omission or commission.

Then let us see how it works. The drunkard is saved from drunkenness and as he is a new creature he does not drink liquor, but uses his money for good purposes, and loves and protects his family instead of being a disgrace and burden to it.

The lustful man is saved from his passions and low desires, and finds enjoyment in the service of God and acts of kindness to others. The covetous man is saved from his covetousness, and gives to the poor and needy, while his time is given to good works. The angry man rules his temper by the grace of God, and becomes patient and loving.

Though they all may feel weak, unworthy, and impure in heart, they realize no condemnation, but desire to live closer to God and to become holy in heart. While they know all their sins are forgiven and they are born of God, they may feel the need of being "filled with the Spirit."

This first work of God's grace—conversion—removes our transgressions as far from us as the east is from the west, and brings us back to the state of innocency from which we fell when we committed our first sin. As we look upon a little baby we think it very sweet and innocent, and sometimes individuals think it is *pure;* but when we observe it closely, we see it is not pure; for in its innocency it manifests impure feelings, and it is not long until it gets angry, and uses its feet and hands to fight, as well as it can. Thus it manifests the carnal nature inherited from the fall of Adam, and which naturally brings forth evil fruit and makes its life impure and unrighteous. The little babe does not know right from wrong, and so is innocent before God of transgression. When it gets old enough to comprehend good and evil, it will not long remain innocent, for it will follow its inclination to do evil.

Forgiveness brings an individual back to the state of innocency. All his past sins are forgiven, and he stands as though he had never done wrong. There is not a single sin held against him to come up in judgment—all is forgiven and forgotten, according to God's word, which is truth.

The converted man, woman, or child must keep so humble, prayerful, and obedient that he does not commit sin. The Bible says, "He that committeth sin is of the Devil;" that is, every one who knowingly transgresses God's law of righteousness sins against God, partakes of evil, and loses spiritual life out of the soul, and so belongs to the Devil's kingdom.

No matter how good a Christian one may be, if he

yields to temptation and commits sin, he loses salvation and becomes a sinner, and must come back to God through repentance or be lost. One sin separates the soul from God just as fully as a dozen. One cannot be a Christian and a sinner at the same time, but is either "saint" or "sinner," according to God's word. There are a great many who claim to be good Christians, loving God with all their hearts, and yet say they "sin every day in thought, word, and deed," and we have no doubt they do; for we see them doing many things which God's word forbids, and which are sin for any one of good understanding. The mistake they make is in counting themselves Christians while under the power of sin. They have some desire to do right, and try to do it, but fail because they are not born of God. I have been in this place myself, and tried to serve God nine years in this way, and ought to know what a miserable, hard life it is. It looks very attractive to a great many who want to get to heaven without making any self-denial or being very much different from the worldly people. They are willing to give up some things that they consider real wicked, but their "little besetting sins" such as untruthfulness, deceit, lustful thoughts and desires, covetousness, worldliness, pride, fashion, sectism, foolishness, and jesting, they cling to as things they must do all their lives, because they "are so weak."

Dear souls, it is not because you are so weak, but because the heart has not been changed by divine grace. "Ye are still in your sins." I was wonderfully surprised and pleased when after that long nine years of formal religion I found Jesus in salvation and was given victory over my evil nature and my controlling (or " besetting sins," as they are called) were vanquished foes. No more could they bring me under condemnation and make me feel that I was the " meanest, most sinful Christian living;" but I knew as long as I obeyed, was watchful and prayerful, God's grace would keep me from sin.

Now, boys, the Christian mothers hope you may get the right kind of religion—you will if you come to God aright—so you may be made free from the bondage of sin and all evil habits, and " have a good time " serving God in the victory of faith and grace. To be converted means to be turned around; and one who has been doing evil is turned about to do good instead of evil. If salvation could do no more than many religious people claim, it would not be worthy of honor or of the blessed Savior who gives it to us. In order to honor God we must lift the standard of his salvation.

Now, we have here several letters from those who have been saved, and they will tell you some very important things, which we hope may accomplish much for your good.

DEAR BOYS:

Knowing that Jesus loves you all and is not pleased in any of you going down to everlasting death, I want to tell you of some of his dealings with me, and something about how I have treated him. I trust it will help some of you to give your hearts to God soon; for while you are young is the best time to be saved.

"When I was about ten years old the Lord convicted me of my sins. I knew I ought to yield to God then. I was attending a meeting, and felt I ought to go forward and give my heart to the Lord. Then I thought of how the people would look and laugh at me, and then I would not yield to God. I grieved the Holy Spirit, and he ceased to strive with me as he did. Then I went on for years, getting harder and harder in sin. I came near death several times while unsaved. Once I had the diphtheria, became very low, and did not know but I would soon be in eternity—and unprepared. I became very much concerned about it and had my mother pray for me, but oh! it is so very dangerous to put off our return to God until we get down to death's door.

I became worse and worse, was unconscious. If I had died, my dear mother would have conforted herself, thinking her son was saved and with Christ. Instead of that, boys, I would have gone down to hell a lost soul. You may wonder how that could be after being so much concerned about myself, and asking others for prayer in my behalf. It was this way: In order to be saved, a sinner must "repent and believe" the gospel. I did not repent then, but was only afraid to die. I knew in my condition that I was unfit for heaven and would be cast into hell.

Repentance means much more than merely having a fear of going to hell. I was not sorry for my sins; I was only afraid of the punishment for them. Oh! I am so thankful God had mercy on me and spared my life at that time. Afterward he helped me to a real Bible repentance, and I believed on the Lord Jesus with my heart, and "his peace came flooding my soul," and I knew " the past was under the blood," and my name was written in heaven.

" Now is the accepted time, now is the day of salvation," while you are young is the time to begin to obey God.

Your friend in Christ,
C. H. Tubbs.

Dear Boys:

I believe the Lord would have me send you my testimony, as it may be a benefit to some of you, and thus please and honor him.

I am praising God for his faithfulness to me. Truly the Lord has been long-suffering. He has not dealt with me after my sins; nor rewarded me according to my iniquity. For as the heaven is high above the earth, so great has his mercy been toward me. (See Ps. 103:10, 11.) Praise his dear name!

Five years ago this fall the Lord first spoke peace to my soul, and forgave my sins, which were many. It was on this wise: While hearing the precious gospel preached, God's love to fallen man, the Holy Spirit convicted me of sin, made hell and everlasting torment appear so real, that I trembled under the thought of being banished in outer darkness from the presence of God through all eternity. Oh, how glad I am that God made a way of escape from eternal destruction, and that he so loved us that he sent his Son into the world not to condemn it, but that through him the world might be saved; that "whosoever believeth on him should not perish, but have everlasting life." Hallelujah; I am so glad I yielded to the Spirit's call. Vile as I was, enslaved to lusts and passions, bound by the fetters of sin, the Spirit and power of God have set me free. That was Jesus' mission in the world. God anointed him to preach good tidings unto the meek, sent him "to bind up the broken-hearted, to proclaim liberty to the captives, and the opening of the prison to them that are bound." "To appoint unto them that mourn in Zion, to give unto them beauty for ashes, the oil of joy for mourning, the garment of praise for the Spirit of heaviness; that they might be called trees of righteousness, the planting of the Lord, that he might be glorified." This he did while here on earth, and he is the same Jesus now. He is just as willing to help you, save you, and keep you as he was those who came to him and obeyed him while he was here in the flesh, and is just as able.

I was born in Sweden, and my parents being Lutherans, I was brought up in the Lutheran faith and doctrine, being sprinkled when a child (for baptism), confirmed at the age of sixteen, and taken in as a member of that denomination. All this did not bring salvation to my soul; for Jesus says, "Ye must be born again," and, "Except ye repent, ye shall all likewise perish." Repentance includes sorrow for sin, forsaking *our* ways, making wrongs right to all our ability, forgiving those who have wronged us, and confessing our sins to God—like the prodigal in Luke 15:18-21 —and then we can believe with our hearts unto righteousness, and look upon Jesus as our Savior, that he paid the penalty of our sins.

Though I was a "member of the Lutheran sect in good standing," I had fallen into the grossest sins in the sight of God, and although I was looked upon as "a model young man" by many (so I was told), I was vile and wretched in the sight of God; for he knew all my secret sins and thoughts—while man only looked on the outward appearance, he looked on the heart. He showed me my past life and my heart, and truly I had a bad record. The grace of God was able to make a new creature out of me, "for where sin abounded, grace did much more abound." Hallelujah! God will do the same for you, if you will let him, by meeting the same conditions, for he is "no respecter of persons."

If you have been brought up under certain religious training and customs that do not meet the requirements of Almighty God, and that by still practicing do not give you the satisfaction of knowing you are a child of God and having his constant approval, by his Holy Spirit in your heart, I would ask you kindly for your good, to forsake the traditions of your former teaching, and the doctrines and opinions of men, and search the word of God for yourself. Seek God with all your heart and obey his precepts, and you will find to your own satisfaction that God will do just what he promised, by sending his Spirit into your heart, crying, "Abba, Father," giving you the sweet assurance that you are his child.

After my conviction I began to desire and seek for a pure heart. I consecrated my life fully to God's service, and I believe with all my heart that as I walk in the light of truth, obey the leadings of the Holy Spirit, he applies the blood of Jesus to my heart, cleansing me from all sin. Praise, honor, dominion, and might be to God and the Lamb forever and ever!

I had formed many bad habits in my sinful life, which had to be broken. I began using tobacco when nine years old, and was a slave to it. Many times I would try to quit (what I called " swear off "), but it was only a resolve to be broken, until God saved me.

The night I first made a start to seek God in earnest I threw my tobacco away, but in my own strength. The next day I went about fifteen miles from home after a load of potatoes, and as it took longer than I expected I had to go without my dinner, and I did not have tobacco; so you may imagine how I felt. I had no experience of salvation, as I had not known how to meet the conditions, but had made the decision that I was going to be a true Christian. About one o'clock I could endure my tobacco-craving no longer, and so begged some of a man who was with me. You know tobacco-users are great beggars, and if they are ashamed to beg, they will steal it if they can. This had been my lot. Oh, the deceitfulness of sin! Commit one sin, and then another to cover it up. I had to make these wrongs right in order to meet the conditions of salvation. I made a decision I would quit tobacco by the help of the Lord; and so thought I would get some gum to use as a substitute for awhile, but the longer I chewed the gum the more I wanted tobacco. So I made up my mind 'I would trust the grace of God as a permanent cure, and the appetite left me. It was cheaper than the "Keeley Cure," and ever so much better. Bless the Lord!

Joking, jesting, and using idle words was another bad habit I had formed, and though I had quit many long before I was saved, such as swearing, there was one expression commonly used that I will tell you about; that was "You bet." I do not remember using it more than once since my conversion. I was walking in company with another boy when I used it. As soon as I realized what I had said, I confessed my fault to the boy I was with and told him I thought it was wrong to use it. Read Matt. 12:36, 37. And so I found with all my bad habits, that if I was overcome in temptation or through weakness, if I confessed right then and made the wrong right, it helped me to overcome. And so it may be with you.

May God bless every boy and young man that reads these few lines, and help you to shun the path of sin and vice and live a holy, chaste, and upright life before God and man, is my prayer.

Your brother in Christ,
Emil Kreutz.

Dear Boys:

A good man said:

> " God bless the boys,
> Who make the men."

I join in a hearty " Amen " to that poet, and while I purpose, God helping me, to write so I may edify the boys, I wish also to interest them.

I presume you will all be pleased to go and see a boat launched, although some of you have already the start of me, and know all about it. However, there is something so grand about it that all will enjoy the scene. While we have been coming, many things have met our view which speak loudly and lovingly about God who made all things and has bestowed them upon us to enjoy. Everything speaks to us of his great love for us, and I trust our hearts are now turning toward him in praise for these many mercies and blessings given us.

See! Here we are. Already a large crowd has gathered, and " big and little " people seem to enjoy the sight. The vessel is all ready. See the long timbers under her, and the strong men around her ready at a moment's notice to push her off, with the help of those large pullies attached to her. Now the word rings out—" Ready "—and every man moves his pike-pole at the same time, and splash, goes the vessel. Our hearts seem to stand still while we wait to see if she goes up or down. Then she comes right side up. Is she not a beauty? See the clean, white decks, and everything about her bespeaks taste and strength; but I have heard people say that they test these boats, and if there is one knot-hole, or bad place in the lumber, or flaw in building anywhere, no matter how strong otherwise she is, they call the boat only as strong as her weakest place; because that place may be sufficient to sink the whole thing. Evidently they have found a weak place in this one; for the men are measuring the water in the boat, and there is more than her allowance, and the men are at the pumps while she is being towed away to the "dry dock," where she will be tested and repaired, then rigged out for the sea. Soon the clean, white sails, lifeboats, life-preservers, and many needed things will be added, and then we could safely take a trip on her.

Now, I think you will see the application I wish to make. Every one of our lives is as a boat launched upon the great, wide ocean of life, and many of them are fair and beautiful to look upon, but God who knows all things sees not as man sees. The Psalmist felt the weakness of his bark when he cried out to

God and said, "Behold [or look], I was shapen in iniquity; and in sin did my mother conceive me."—Ps. 51:5.

If you turn to Rom. 7:15, you read what Paul thought of the strength of his vessel. Not one of those who shall land his bark upon the beautiful shores of the heavenly land but what has had to run into God's great " dry dock " for repairs—yes, even to be fitted up with the Spirit of life—for " all we like sheep have gone astray." But " God has laid upon him [Christ Jesus] the iniquity of us all." He says in John 1:9: " If we confess our sins, he is faithful and just to forgive us our sins, and to cleanse us from all unrighteousness." Praise God for such deliverance. It is through repenting of our sins and faith in Jesus Christ that we get over this ocean of life without sinking to the bottom.

We can have the white sails spoken of in Rev. 19:8. Our lifeboat is Jesus Christ. He is our all in all, blessed forevermore.

You, dear boys, have begun your voyage, and do not think that you can attend to your souls' needs later on; no, *now* is the promise to you, to-morrow will never come. To-day if ye will hear his voice, harden not your heart.

Be sure to pay attention to your soul early in life, and make mother your confidante; for none can understand and appreciate so fully " the boy " as his mother. None watch with so much interest and hopefulness each change in his life as he unfolds into manhood.

How many times we hear a mother say with joy beaming in her face, "This is my boy." Happy that boy if he rightly esteems and sweetly acquiesces to the will and wishes of his mother.

A dear crippled boy, who had never known what it was to be strong like other boys, and of whom the best physicians had said, "He cannot live longer than eight years," but who was now nearing his sixteenth birthday, while conversing on the word of God, which he daily read, and had been reminded by the Spirit of the command and promise in Ex. 20:12 and Eph. 6:1-3, said earnestly, "Mamma, I just believe that is why I have lived so long—because I have always obeyed my parents." He was assured by his loving mother that doubtless it was so. He has often expressed the hope of living until Jesus comes to be glorified in his saints. Acts 1:11. I am reminded of a small child, of whom I read, who had early learned the lesson of obedience to parents. Seeing a very aged man, white-headed with years, feebly passing her on the street, she said, "Mamma, I think that man must always have done what his papa and mamma told him." Being asked "Why?" she said, "Because he has lived so long." These are sterling truths. May you all take them home to your hearts. They will have a blessed influence upon your lives.

Let me exhort you, dear boys, to seek the Lord early. "They that seek me early shall find me." In this God implies that he is more easily found by the young, and when we remember how life's cares, evil ways, and selfish desires fill the lives of older people, we know it is true. Therefore wisdom says, "Seek him early." I have seen some remarkable conversions among children in early youth, and nothing can be more beautiful than the faith of these young desciples. One dear child who had a change of heart at four and a half years, awoke crying, and said, "Mamma, I'm so wicked." She had been taught from her first little talk about Jesus that "all we like sheep, have gone astray," and she realized her sinfulness. Her mother at once lifted her to the floor and knelt in prayer, telling her that by faith we are now the sons of God; and by a simple act of child-faith she believed, and received the witness of the Spirit that she was the Lord's, and her after-life bore testimony of this fact. At an early period of her life I saw her with her arms around the neck of an unsaved aunt, of mature years, pleading for her to come to this same Jesus who had saved her. When she neared her fifteenth birthday I stood by her death-bed, and said, "You are suffering, my darling?" She faintly whispered, "Yes—but—it—is—all—right." Praise God for such a dear Redeemer, who, while he is high and lifted up, condescends to the weakest of his creation who will come to him.

A wonderful faith in a sweet child of five I once witnessed. He was converted and healed. His conviction was great. He was truly contrite in spirit, and not until the witness shone in his heart, shining all the darkness away, did he cease to weep. Finally he broke forth in singing loud and strong, with joy in his face:.

> "Hallelujah! I have found it,
> What my heart so long has craved;
> Jesus satisfies my longing,
> By his blood I now am saved."

And for a long time he sang a chorus or verse of different hymns as the Spirit brought them to his remembrance. He became remarkable in his life of faith. God seemed to take this babe and show to many that "it is not by might or power, but by my Spirit, saith the Lord." At one time he was left a week with a friend while his mother was attending a meeting. On her return home as he sat on her knee with her arms about him, the friend said playfully, "Come now, you have been with me a whole week and had whatever you asked for and have not said a word about pay. What are you going to do about it?" With a look of surprise and deep thought he looked at one, then the other, and exclaimed: "Oh, I know! Give us this day our daily bread." To this answer the friend assured him, "I have been well repaid." His faith was that God would pay his debt to her, as he had promised him daily bread.

I could cite many instances of the wondrous love of God in illuminating the mind and proving good the word, "A little child shall lead them;" but unless you come to Christ, seek him with all your heart, all will be useless, and our entreaties vain. But I believe some who read will seek and find mercy before it is "too late," and come in their youth. Begin now to call upon God for salvation, and may God help you all, is my prayer.

Yours in love,
Aunt Ella.

PURITY.

We are wondering how many of our sons appreciate the lovely, beautiful, and pure that surround life's pathway. Probably more of you do so than we might think; for hid away in the recesses of most natures is a "better self" that gives honor to that which deserves it.

If we let this "better self" lie dormant and do not encourage it by improvement, we need not expect its development or that it will to any great degree manifest itself in our lives. The farmer boy knows that if a field of corn is not properly tended—the weeds removed, and the soil made mellow by cultivation—the corn will be puny and small, and yield but little.

Supposing each one of us had access to a very large flower garden, filled with every variety of flower, and we were given the privilege of choosing one hundred different kinds for our own pleasure and profit in our small flower garden, and some of us would quickly make selection of the most bright and showy flowers, without considering their different characters and qualities; while others would deliberately choose such as would give a succession of blossoms, would endure severe winters, would be nice for bouquets, for the

sick-room, and would gladden the eyes and diffuse
their sweetness through all the months of the year,
which would you think made the wisest choice?
Every one of us is doing this every day of our lives;
for life is a flower garden that has every kind of flower
growing within its borders, and some are choosing to
admire, select, and cultivate the coarsest, most showy,
and indifferent ones rather than to consider more carefully and make a wiser choice.

If an individual should prefer the bright, gaudy,
coarse sunflower rather than the pure, white, delicate,
and fragrant water lily, we would consider him very
deficient in taste. Now, if any one makes choice of
something impure, coarse, deficient of almost every
quality of beauty except its bright appearance, and
cultivates it in his life, he is doing the same thing. For
instance, in life's flower garden is the coarse flower
of selfishness, which has a bright, gay appearance and
promises much enjoyment; for to have one's own way
and every wish gratified looks as if it would be the
best choice in life; but in choosing this flower we refuse unselfishness, one of the purest, most delicate,
and richly perfumed flowers of character and life. Its
delicate beauty and purity make it most lovely in all
the circumstances of life.

Again, the highly colored flower of fame attracts
the eye of many and seems to be a very desirable acquisition for even the smallest garden of life; for men,
women, and children in every sphere are living for
and in the good opinion and "speech of people,"

while their lives are barren of the choicest and purest flower of humility.

Some of these flowers leave a very poisonous effect upon other plants growing near, so that their lives are short or they bear imperfect flower or bud; for we have seen good, wholesome characters that bid fair to become most lovely, entirely spoiled by an ill-savored plant that was carelessly allowed to grow, or was held in high regard by the possessors.

So, dear boys, make a wise choice of your flowers of character. Take time for consideration. As we look upon you we may know something of what you are choosing, and if we should tell some of you, perhaps you would be much surprised and somewhat ashamed. Will you watch your actions and see what kind of flowers you are cultivating?

There are natural flowers that are quite pretty which grow upon the most obnoxious weeds. When the writer was a little girl, several of us children had the pleasant (?) task of cutting pinpsum weeds that grew in an unused cattle-yard. The flowers were white and delicate-looking, but exhaled a most nauseating and disagreeable odor. The seed-pods were pretty to look upon, but " pricky " to touch, and when they burst the multitude of small seeds flew in every direction, thus sowing for the future. It was thus very necessary that they be destroyed before maturity, or they would soon fill the farm, and the evil spread to friends and neighbors.

Sometimes we see such fair flowers of character in

others that we are apt to think they are using carefulness in making selection of their flowers, but upon closer observation we see the blossoms are only weed flowers; for the root is a weed root and the plant's appearance is coarse and impure, and its seed scattered everywhere to the detriment of friends and neighbors. Did you ever see a boy who made friends wherever he went by being kind and attentive to all he met; but who used the friendship thus gained for base and selfish purposes, and for the injury of friends? This is surely bearing weed flowers, which may for a time deceive but are sure to reveal their true character in the end. Surely we should not want our life gardens to bear aught but purest and best flowers, such as will prove a blessing to others. How sad to see time and space yielding briars and thistles instead of lilies and roses! And how much sadder to think of hearts and lives bearing obnoxious and poisonous weeds that run to waste their own flower gardens and pollute those of others!

Look to your hearts and lives, boys, and begin at once to grow flowers of grace, beauty, and purity. You may enter the garden of the Lord and procure seeds, slips, and roots of the most precious varieties, and have your hearts well stocked with virtues rare and lovely. The only way to effect this is to receive the grace of God into the heart to its fullest extent. We might place a few very choice plants in a garden; but if there were any weeds or any ugly or imperfect plants therein, we could not consider it a perfect or lovely garden. So, though you may have religion enough to show forth some precious flowers, you need to have all the evil seed destroyed, all the evil plants rooted up, and the very root of evil removed by the perfect salvation of Jesus. When this is done the heart is made pure, and the life actions become pure; for if the fountain is pure, the water that flows therefrom will be pure also.

We said we believed many of our sons appreciated the pure and lovely. Sometimes we have seen rough and coarse looking men admire and love the beautiful flowers that grew in their dooryards or be tender and loving as any gentlewoman to the tiny babe that claimed a portion of their hearts. But oh, how precious would it be if that finer life could pervade the individual and remove all the coarseness!

We are glad that the religion of Jesus meets every need of the soul and life, so that its work is perfect; for it purifies the heart, strengthens mind and body, elevates, ennobles, and purifies every thought and action.

We have tried to draw your minds to what is good, pure, and lovely—to bring out your better selves—and help you think for what will be of value to you; for you know we are apt to drift along with the tide of life, below the standard of excellence. The coarse part of our being is apt to have the ascendency over the finer, more beautiful, and pure.

Probably many of you have wished you could bring your lives up to the standard of right, but have not known how. Sin is what is defiling to the natural man. If he could have it removed from the heart so it would not spring up in ungodliness, then he would keep victory over evil.

Let us look deeper into this subject of salvation, and see how much God has promised us. We have seen how Adam was created in the image of God in purity, and how he fell from that grand estate unto sin—impurity—how we, being born in that impure state have an inclination to walk in evil ways, although our conscience and better self know it is better to seek for higher and nobler things. You have seen how conversion brings us back to God in innocency and his grace gives victory over sin, so that we love righteousness and desire to be perfectly pure in heart, for man's soul is never satisfied until it reaches the standard of creation—*purity*. The Bible says, " Blessed are the pure in heart, for they shall see God." " Unto the pure all things are pure: but unto them that are defiled and unbelieving is nothing pure; but even their mind and conscience is defiled." From these and other scriptures we learn that the heart is made pure. Man in his natural state is sinful or impure, but in his saved state he is pure in heart; so it must be that salvation gives him purity.

Now, dear boys, how many of you so dearly love and admire what is good, pure, and lovely that you will desire this most precious gift from God—purity of heart ? Is it not very good to think that he will do so much for man after all his evil doings? Oh, yes! we ought to love him dearly for his mercy and love toward us.

Our last lesson brought us into the life of innocency. Sin had been forgiven, and the soul was rejoicing in the love of God, but was often catching a glimpse of a higher and purer life. While the soul had victory over sin, there was a longing to be pure in heart. Sometimes during a strong temptation the heart was made conscious of the impurity within it. There was an inclination toward worldliness, pride, ambition, or strife that made it hard to keep a perfect victory over sin. There was a foe on the inside of the city as well as on the outside, and you know in such a case there is greater danger of defeat. The foe of impurity would seek to betray the soul into the temptations of the king of evil—the Devil.

After an individual is converted he begins to bear fruit for God. He has quite a degree of love to God, for the Holy Bible, and for his neighbors. He also has peace with God; for his sins are all forgiven and he has given up rebellion and opposition to God's will. His joy is great; for he is much pleased in his Lord's service. He has quite a degree of long-suffering and can bear quite patiently the faults of others. His gentleness is noted by all his friends, who once bore much from his harshness and cruelty. His goodness is developing day by day in walking in the light of truth. His faith increases as he uses it in offering up his petitions to God for present needs. His meekness causes him to bear with patience the scoffs and ill-will of all opposers. His temperance makes him peculiar in this world of overindulgence. And thus he brings forth his fruit of the Spirit of life, which is acceptable to God.

This life of grace is far above his old life of sin, and he praises God with joyful lips for his loving-kindness and mercy that have brought him unto this blessed state of justification. As he sometimes realizes the impurity within his heart, he seeks communion with God, and by more earnest devotion strives to have such victory of grace as not to allow it to manifest itself. As time passes he comprehends that he cannot procure freedom from it in this way; for growth in grace cannot grow out the evil stump.

Just here he needs faithful gospel teachers to show the Bible way; for this is a part of their mission according to the scriptures. "And he gave some, apostles; and some, prophets; and some, evangelists; and some, pastors and teachers; for the edifying of the body of Christ; till we all come in the unity of the faith, and of the knowledge of the Son of God, unto a perfect man, unto the measure of the stature of the fullness of Christ." From this we see positively that Christians are to be so edified by the teaching of the word that they come through the knowledge of Jesus unto a "perfect man"—unto a full-sized Christian through the fullness of grace that is in Christ—for this is God's provision to bring man back to his pure state through the favor of Christ's salvation. When we see that conversion does not do that, then we know there is more to follow; and when the converted man hungers and thirsts for something more than he has received in conversion, it is evidence that there is more to attain; and when he realizes that his heart is not pure, and there is an intense longing to be in perfect harmony and accord with God, that too is an assurance of something more that is necessary for the Christian's good and it also designates the need, which is purity.

From the converted soul a prayer ascends to heaven, " O Lord, help me to love thee with all my heart, soul, mind, and strength, and my neighbor as myself." The soul is conscious of its need; and if it is allowed to assert its desires and seek God for their fulfillment, it will reach the coveted treasure—purity. Many dear souls have thus fought their way through ignorance, opposition, and worldly wisdom to the precious gift of cleansing in the blood of Christ; and those who do not are apt to live very unsatisfactory lives, battling with impurity and temptation, or eventually go back to sin. God made provision that the converted should move right through the wilderness up to the precious land of Canaan—heart-purity—and those who do not, spend many years in a wilderness of doubts, fears, and backslidings. By this we would not lower the standard of conversion, which is a glorious work of God in making the soul that is dead in sin, alive unto God in righteousness; but God's purpose was to have the gospel teachers so instruct the converted as to urge them forward to the *fullness* of salvation—*purity.* When this is done the converted state is a high state of grace, and the soul realizes the approval of God in each step forward, and rejoices in the prospect of higher attainments.

This purity of heart is known by different names, such as Christian perfection, second work of grace, the cleansing, perfect love, the indwelling Christ, and the Bible names sanctification, or baptism of the Holy Ghost. These all indicate different phases of the salvation work; so we will see what we can understand from them.

The first title is "heart-purity." The heart is the seat of evil. "The heart is deceitful above all things, and desperately wicked; who can know it?" Out of the heart proceed evil thoughts, murders, adulteries, fornication, thefts, false witness, blasphemies; these are the things which defile a man. The evil nature in the heart bears all manner of sinful action, and when it is regenerated, or "born again," by divine grace, it receives power from God to have victory over its sinful nature. In other words, the unrighteous tree is cut down and must not spring up into evil action; but the root of evil is still there, and, if not kept down by grace through watching and prayer, would bring forth its evil fruit—sins.

When the soul seeks and obtains purity of heart the impure element is cleansed away by the blood of Jesus; that is, the atonement removes it from the heart, and it is made perfectly pure and holy, so there are no evil-tree roots to spring up into evil doings.

Christian perfection means that grace of God that makes perfect Christians. When one is converted he is a Christian, but is not a perfect one until the soul has received the *full* salvation in the cleansing of the heart from sin, or until he is brought back to the state of heart from which Adam by transgression fell —even to the image of God.

Sometimes people think this is too high a state to be attainable here in this world, but expect it for the next. Do you not know that this world is the state of probation, and here is where we must prepare for heaven; for heaven is holy, and nothing unclean can enter its sacred portals? If man contemplated making himself perfect, it would be right to consider its accomplishment presumptuous; but when Christian perfection is acknowledged as a gift from God, and received by faith, it removes every cause for complaint against its attainment as the "height of presumption," and makes the experience one to be sought and received by every Christian.

As we look upon the works of God we see many things that proclaim him a "Master Workman," capable of achieving anything that will honor him by its perfection; and we cannot see how an imperfect or impure Christian can honor him so well as a perfect and pure one.

Again, men make many things that are termed perfect, such as machinery, houses, and homes; and nature produces fine specimens of animals, suited for all purposes. Then why should not the mighty God make such Christians as shall honor him by the purity of their hearts and lives?

Surely, dear boys, when you think of it in this way you must admit that it is quite necessary that God magnify himself by a salvation that perfectly saves every one of those who desire it.

This experience is termed second work of *grace*, because it is through God's favor, or grace, that we may enjoy its blessings. No one properly converted thinks of giving himself any credit for the possession of that experience, as it is simply God's gift received by faith. So, also, in this term "second work of grace," all the honor is given to him who performs both first and second works.

The cleansing also designates the work as one that gives all the honor to God. That man's heart needs a cleansing you have already seen from its sinful condition, and that he is unable to perform that work has also been established by those who have tried to do so; and the more they strove the more they became conscious of their need of help from a higher source. The Bible asks and answers one of the most important questions, in the Psalms, which is as follows: "Wherewithal shall a young man cleanse his way? By taking heed thereto according to thy word." If we listen to the teachings of the gospel, it will lead us to the way of cleansing both heart and life.

We were telling you a short time ago what kind of fruit a converted man bore, and now we want to show you something more about fruit-bearing. In the fifteenth chapter of John, we read: "I am the true vine, and my Father is the husbandman. Every branch in me that beareth not fruit he taketh away; and every branch that beareth fruit, he purgeth it, that it may bring forth more fruit." In another verse Christ says: "I am the vine, ye are the branches. This purging of the branches by the second work of grace, or the cleansing, brings them into condition to bring forth more of the same kind of good fruit that is manifest in the converted. They have more love—realize they love God with their entire being and their neighbors as themselves. The peace and joy are multiplied, and long-suffering is increased even unto joyfulness; for what was once patiently endured, as a necessity, he now rejoices in as a privilege. Gentleness, goodness, faith, meekness, and temperance are so increased and increasing that it astonishes even the possessors, and the praise of God is welling up from full hearts to consecrate utterance. Thus is borne the fruit of the Spirit in "rejoicing evermore, and praying without ceasing."

Because of the abundance of love and fruit the experience is called "perfect love;" for the entire being is filled with love divine that makes all else sink into utter nothingness, and Jesus is enthroned in the heart to wield his scepter of love over all that is good and pure. Therefore it is often called the experience of "the indwelling Christ." Jesus said to his disciples, "If a man love me, he will keep my words: and my Father will love him and we will come unto him and make our abode with him." This he does in the person of the Holy Spirit, the Comforter who comes to abide forever in the hearts that are fully cleansed.

The Bible terms "sanctification" and "baptism of the Holy Ghost" mean so much that we will more perfectly consider them in the next lesson. In dwelling so lengthily and earnestly upon this subject of purity we have desired that you might behold its value and loveliness, and be encouraged to press into its experience. It should attract every careful observer, and be a strong inducement to every religious person. What could be more admirable than a pure heart and life with all its attending graces?

You will not, dear boys, toss this beautiful, most precious and delicate flower of God's garden aside and choose the sunflower of worldliness, will you? and thus rob your hearts and lives of their exquisite influence and power. God grant you may not, but esteem God's gift as the very highest good for all men.

> Purity is a precious blossom,
> Heavenly gift and gracious power;
> Lovingly its tendrils bind you,
> Longingly it woos each day and hour.

> Purity—oh, the precious treasure!
> Holiness, love, and counsel sweet,
> Entreat thee and invite thee,
> Coming now thy heart to meet.

PURITY.

Purity—oh, thy holy greatness,
Heavenly love, and wisdom too !
Comforting Spirit, the anointing,
Lowliness and meekness woo.

Purity—can you slight it ever ?
Purity—your longing heart's desire.
Purity—choose it " now or never."
Purity—the Holy Spirit's fire.

BAPTISM OF THE HOLY GHOST.

You may all take your Bibles and read all you can find upon this subject; for we are decided to teach nothing but gospel truth, by the help of God.

Many times in the teachings of Jesus we may read the promises he made in regard to sending the Holy Spirit upon those who loved him and obeyed his word. We will only quote two, and you may search for the rest. "If ye love me, keep my commandments. And I will pray the Father, and he shall give you another Comforter, that he may abide with you forever; even the Spirit of truth, whom the world cannot receive, because it seeth him not, neither knoweth him; but ye know him; for he dwelleth with you, and shall be in you."—John 14:15-17. "But the Comforter, which is the Holy Ghost, whom the Father will send in my name, he shall teach you all things, and bring all things to your remembrance, whatever I have said unto you."—Verse 26. From these scriptures we see the Holy Spirit was promised to man after his conversion, and while living in obedience to his teachings. The Spirit was *with* the converted, but should be *in* them as an abiding presence directing their footsteps into the way of truth.

We find this promise fulfilled to the disciples who

met in the upper room after Christ's ascension, as recorded in the second chapter of Acts. Each one of the 120 present was filled with the Holy Ghost, according to the promise given many years before by the prophet Joel: "And it shall come to pass in the last days, saith God, I will pour out of my Spirit upon all flesh; and your sons and your daughters shall prophesy, and your young men shall see visions, and your old men shall dream dreams; and on my servants and on my handmaidens I will pour out of my Spirit; and they shall prophesy." When this was fulfilled to those gathered together at that time, the wonderful event was noised abroad and many came together to see if these things were so, and when Peter preached to them, they were convicted of their sins and asked what they should do to be saved, and the answer was: "Repent and be baptized every one of you in the name of Jesus Christ for the remission of sins, and ye shall receive the gift of the Holy Ghost. For the promise is unto you, and to your children, and to all that are afar off, even as many as the Lord our God shall call." From this we learn that the promise of the gift of the Holy Ghost is to all who repent and obey God. If it were not for such forcible teaching, we might think that only a few could receive this great blessing; but when it says " as many as the Lord our God shall call," then we know it is for every one of God's children. If we search further, we find many instances where others received this Holy Spirit baptism.

Now, boys, let us think. The Word speaks of the Father, Son, and Spirit as the Godhead—one divine person with different spheres of work. God is our Creator; Jesus, the Redeemer from sin; and the Holy Spirit, the Comforter and Teacher. When God promised that the Holy Spirit should come into the hearts of men, he made the greatest promise that could be given unto men.

Just think! The divine being, the great God, promises to dwell in us by the Holy Spirit, and "guide us into all truth;" to be a witness unto us that the heart is made pure and free from sin according to the scriptures. "For by one offering he hath perfected forever them that are sanctified. Whereof the Holy Ghost also is a witness to us." "That I should be the minister of Jesus Christ to the Gentiles, ministering the gospel of God, that the offering up of the Gentiles might be acceptable, being sanctified by the Holy Ghost." "And God, which knoweth the hearts, bare them witness, giving them the Holy Ghost, even as he did unto us; and put no difference between us and them, purifying their hearts by faith." These three texts teach clearly that when the Holy Spirit comes to the soul it is a witness that it is perfect, sanctified, and purified, and that it is done through faith. These three terms signify the same thing—purity—for the perfect man is one who has a perfect heart, made so by a cleansing from all imperfection—sin—and "sanctified" means "to be made holy, or free from sin; to be cleansed from moral corruption and pollution; to be made fit for the service of God, and the society and employments of heaven;" and "purified" means to have been purged from moral defilement; therefore "a vessel unto honor, sanctified and mete for the Master's use, prepared unto every good work." Sin being removed from the heart, the Holy Spirit comes in to be the controlling power in the heart and life.

Let us see if we can make it clearer by illustration. If you wish to accomplish anything, your mind or will gives direction to the different members of your body and they obey orders and fulfill your desires. Suppose you want to write a letter. You decide to do so, and your hand obeys the will and reaches out for the material; and as you dictate, the hand forms the words and sentences. Just so the heart is brought under the control of the Holy Spirit, and desires and acts in harmony with its wishes; and as we know the Spirit of God would only dictate holy thoughts and actions, therefore the life is pure. For instance, if one receive some injury from another, the natural impulse of a sinful heart is to "pay back in the same coin," but when the Holy Spirit controls the heart, the impulse is to "return good for evil." How many times we have heard the expression, "I just hate that man, because he played me a mean, ugly trick." He that hateth his brother is a murderer." Therefore the Spirit of God prompts the feeling and expression, "O God, have mercy upon that poor soul; for he knoweth not what he is doing."

The natural man says, when he comes in contact with the poor and needy, "Each one must fight for himself, let him rustle for a living;" while the saved man filled with the Holy Spirit heeds the voice, " Inasmuch as ye did it to one of these ye did it unto me," and bears his brother's burden by supplying his need. Oh, boys! it is so precious to have the very last particle of hatefulness, ugliness, and sinfulness taken out of the heart, and it filled with the Holy Spirit of God.

When the experience was shown to me in the preaching of the word of God, it seemed almost too good to be true; but when its truth was assured to my understanding and heart, a wonderful longing possessed my soul to obtain the gracious benefit, and I began to inquire the way to gain it. It was the pearl of great price to me, for which I was willing to give all I had, and while it was necessary to do that very thing, it was far above anything that could be given by mortal man. Its worth could not be estimated in natural things; it is far above the conception of the natural heart as well as above the price of earthly things. It is a blood-bought gift, the most precious that God could give to his saved children. Oh, how we Christian mothers do hope some of you may seek to find it for your present and future goods; so we are going to try to tell you how you may obtain it.

The first necessity is to be clearly converted and walking each day in the narrow way of truth and righteousness, keeping the commandments of God as far as they are known, and seeking earnestly to know them by a diligent study of the Word. The next great need is to know the Bible teaches heart-purity and the baptism of the Holy Ghost; and the next is to realize the heart's need of it; and the next, a firm decision to obtain it; let the result be what it may.

We have given a number of scriptures that should convince any unprejudiced mind and soul that there are two works of grace wrought in the heart by the Spirit of God. The first is the forgiveness of all actual transgressions; and the next, the cleansing of the heart from all impurity.

You are invited to search the word of truth a little further with us. In the seventeenth chapter of John in Christ's last prayer for his disciples he asks God to "sanctify them through thy truth," and again, "sanctify them that they all may be one as we are one." Here we are taught that, although the disciples were "not of this world, even as I am not of the world," he wanted God to sanctify them, that they should have the unity of the Spirit of God.

We see very often that the natural, or carnal, nature is prone to make division. In 1 Cor. 3:3, Paul tells the Corinthian brethren, "Ye are yet carnal; for whereas there is among you envying, and strife, and divisions, are ye not carnal, and walk as men?" He could not count them spiritual, but carnal, even babes in Christ. This explains it clearly: if the disciples should be sanctified, it would remove the carnal nature, and they would be filled with the Spirit of God and thus be one as God, Jesus, and the Holy Spirit are one. That is just what a perfect salvation does for Christian people—the very last remains of division are removed, and the blessed unity of God pervades the soul.

Another scripture showing the need of the Christian to be cleansed from impurity is 2 Cor. 7:1:— "Having therefore these promises, dearly beloved, let us cleanse ourselves from all filthiness of the flesh and spirit, perfecting holiness in the fear of God." Here the brethren " dearly beloved " are exhorted to perfect holiness by a cleansing. Holiness is begun in conversion and perfected in the purifying of the heart, and reception of the Holy Spirit.

When one sees how clearly the Bible teaches the need of a purging from sin, he begins to look to his heart to see the need, and beholds in different ways his lack of purity. In my case I could clearly see that I did not love God with all my heart, soul, mind, and strength, and my neighbor as myself; therefore I was deficient. Again, I saw when God wanted me to be reconciled to my neighbor, that while I knew it was right to be in love and harmony with all, I was not humble enough to be glad to do his will in seeking to woo them unto love and good-will; and there was an inclination to variance, and a withdrawing of myself from hearty friendship.

My heart was melted into tears of sorrow, and an intense longing to be Godlike in every way possessed my soul. I knew that whatever good there was about me was from God, and whatever was contrary to godliness was of myself; so the cry arose to my lips from the depths of my soul, " O God, kill me all out. Cleanse me and make me clean."

In Rom. 12:1 I read: " I beseech you therefore, brethren, by the mercies of God, that ye present your bodies a living sacrifice, holy, acceptable unto God, which is your reasonable service. And be not conformed to this world; but be ye transformed by the renewing of your mind, that ye may prove what is that good, and acceptable, and perfect will of God." " This is the will of God, even your sanctification." I presented myself entirely to God, was willing my soul and body should be brought into perfect accord with the will of God in every particular. In order to do this I must lay down my will, and take the holy will of God. Oh, how unholy my own nature seemed, and how anxious I was to get rid of the root of sin, that my heart be made pure!

I was very sure that God would do his part when I had done mine. It was made very plain to me that a Christian could make a deeper consecration of himself to God than a sinner could, who was seeking forgiveness of sin, and that was the need of being a " living sacrifice " presented upon the altar Christ Jesus; and when the offering was fully made, the promise should be fulfilled: " The altar sanctifies the gift."

It is natural for us to have some desires, aspirations, and ambitions for ourselves and friends that may not be in harmony with the will of God concerning us. For instance, a man with a family may be striving to procure a comfortable and pleasant home and give his sons and daughters a good education. This may be all right in many cases, but for some who have such desires God may have a special gospel work that would interfere somewhat with these plans. He may call him as a preacher, evangelist, or teacher; and if his heart is too much set upon his own comfort and pleasure, he may call loudly for a portion of his means to carry the gospel to heathen lands. Therefore to yield all our desires and ambitions to the will of God means very much to all of us. We must stand ready at any time for God to change all our ways and wishes to suit himself.

You know, boys, when a man enters the army he gives up his previous avocations and stands ready to obey the officers' orders in every particular, whether it is to hardship and death or to pleasure and profit. Just so must every soldier of the cross of Christ be ready to fall in line of duty at any moment; he is to have no will of his own, but yield to the will of the Captain of his salvation. As long as the heart is not entirely pure there will be an inclination to choose our own pleasure and profit instead of seeking to know and do God's will perfectly. Therefore, to very many, if not all, it means very much to "die out," that is, to yield up all interests to the will of God. The child often has a great struggle to yield to the wishes of his parents, and the stronger his will the harder it is to yield; and sometimes it is done outwardly, while the heart chafes at the restriction. The converted man will often yield to obedience, while his heart is not in perfect harmony with God in his requirements; but when an entire consecration is made he realizes God will require nothing of him but what shall be for his good, although he may not see how it is to work out to that end.

It meant very much to me to present myself a living sacrifice; for I wanted to live in ease and comfort, to walk in pleasant paths while in this world; to have many friends, and to " have the world's good will " to quite a degree. While I had something of victory along this line, yet " to be willing to be anything or nothing " required a wonderful yielding up to God.

The first trial that came to show me my great need on this line was in this way: I went to the altar to seek for purity of heart and the baptism of the Holy Ghost, and while kneeling there it came to me that I could more perfectly give myself to God by holding up my hands. I wanted to do so, and yet the thought of doing anything peculiar before a large congregation held me bound for some time. I prayed earnestly and asked God to help me and make the way plain before me, but could get no help until with my heart crushed and bleeding my hands went up slowly to "please God," and as they reached their utmost height, the Lord blessed my soul with victory, and I cared naught for " what the people say." My reputation was given to God, and I could rejoice freely in the victory, even should the world call me foolish. As different things were brought to my remembrance by the Spirit, I yielded my will to God. It seemed I was going down, *down*, DOWN—losing sight of everything but God and his will. At last I came to the place where I could say, "O Lord, I have done all I can; take me and sanctify me in thine own way. Then the Spirit deepened my consecration by showing me the real sufferings of lost souls, while he took me through the vale of humiliation; and "I with Christ am crucified" was pressed upon heart and mind. God had done what I asked him to do—"kill me out"—for the old nature was crucified, put to death, and could trouble me no more as long as I remained consecrated to God's service.

I was conscious my heart was pure, and looked up to God in confidence to finish the work. Then the words, "If ye then, being evil, know how to give good gifts unto your children, how much more shall your heavenly Father give the Holy Spirit to them that ask him?" came to me with the assurance that if my child asked me for aught I could give, it should have it immediately, and as I, one of God's saved children, was calling upon him for the Holy Ghost, he must be even more willing to give him unto me; and so I could look up in faith that God did then and there give me the Holy Spirit and seal me all his own. As I believed this, my soul was flooded with the glory of God and realized the Spirit's blessed presence. Oh, how precious was that hour! All the Lord's! A perfect consecration had brought a perfect salvation. I was now where I could truly love God with all my heart, and bring forth much fruit to his glory and praise. I could realize that my strongest desire was:

> "Oh, to be nothing, nothing, only to lie at his feet,
> A broken and emptied vessel, for the Master's use made meet."

My heart was in perfect harmony with God. If he said, "Go ye," my heart said, "Yea, Lord;" and if he said, "Suffer ye," the same glad response filled my soul. My time was the Lord's to do his will and seek to save souls. My ability was his, to use in any way he desired. And my loved ones were his, to do with as seemed to him best! "Not a sparrow falls to the ground without his notice, and ye are of more value than many sparrows" was realized in his love, and the strong confidence that my desires taken to him in prayer should receive his care and he would do better for me than I could ask or think.

How we should praise God for the blessed privilege of being "all the Lord's," thus pure in heart, sanctified, meet for the Master's use, prepared unto good works, sealed by the Holy Spirit—in short—*kept by the power of God*. Oh, dear boys! may God help you to see its beauty and seek for the baptism of the Holy Spirit. And though the world may deride and scorn, let your bravery be manifest by "counting not your life dear unto yourselves," but live for God.

It takes more true courage to be a faithful Christian than it does to face the enemy in battle. And though you may never hear the applause of the world for your deeds of valor, you may hear what is far better—the voice of God in welcome: "Well done, good and faithful servant; enter thou into the joys of thy Lord."

THE LIFE OF FAITH.

HAVING entered into the holiest by a new and living way, we are to live by faith in the Son of God. Often individuals think if they only become Christians all will be well for time and eternity, and seem to think they can drift along the rest of their lives, enjoying what they obtained by earnest effort. This is a great mistake; for the Christian life is one of activity, of earnest effort, and of wonderful battles and victories.

If an army were to march on day after day in ease and plenty, it would never develop its powers of endurance nor achieve anything for its country's good or for its own promotion or honor. But let it meet the enemy in battle and by its bravery, endurance, and wisdom defeat the foe—it wins the applause and honor of the world, and perhaps accomplishes something that is considered of value to its country.

Just so the Christian must meet the foe in battle to prove himself worthy of his Commander or to become a strong and valiant soldier. His enemy is on the alert to attack him in his weakest place and try to capture him for his own pleasure and advantage. If the Christian knows his weakness and fortifies himself by receiving grace and strength from on high in every time of need, he may escape the snares and powers that come from the enemy; and as he claims by faith and obtains victory, he is better fitted for the next encounter. The implements of his warfare are not carnal, but mighty through God to the pulling down of strongholds.

The Christian is not always on the line of defense to preserve himself from the enemy, but he boldly, in the name of the King, takes possession of the foe's strongholds. Sometimes the battle wages hot and heavy and fierce and long, but if he by faith presses the battle to the gates he is sure to win a victory; for the almighty God is on the side of right. If you will read the eleventh chapter of Hebrews, you may see some of the victories of faith, which should stir your soul to a real activity for God through faith. Let us look along the line of Christian living, and see what use there is for faith, remembering that it is simply a childlike trust in the promises of God.

A firm belief of the scriptures brings a hearty conviction of sin, which brings repentance that leads the soul to conversion through the act of faith in receiving the salvation promised by Jesus, in which the soul rejoices exceedingly. By faith he sees the Lamb of God bear all his sins away and give him a heart to serve God. After conversion he wants to walk in obedience, and from the teachings of God's word he sees the need of being baptized to fulfill all righteousness, and, accepting the duty by faith, he obeys the word and is "buried with Christ in baptism." Here he may meet the foe in battle array, insinuating and contending that " sprinkling or pouring will do just as well;" but he meets the enemy with the sword of the Spirit and forces him back of his entrenchment of unbelief with the word of God: " And they went down both into the water, both Philip and the eunuch; and he baptized him." This makes the foe shift position with: " The ordinances were all nailed to the cross.' But, Mr. Foe, twenty-five years after the crucifixion Paul taught the Corinthian brethren, saying, " Keep the ordinances as I delivered them unto you;" and he then more perfectly instructed them concerning the Lord's supper, which was delivered to the disciples on the eve of Christ's betrayal, with the injunction: " Do this in remembrance of me, until I come again." And again, Mr. Foe, *after* Christ's crucifixion and just before his ascension his commission to the disciples was: " Go ye, therefore, and teach all nations, baptizing them in the name of the Father, and of the Son, and of the Holy Ghost." This victory of truth through faith strengthens the believer, and he more fully sees how the enemy is trying to deceive the people, and he becomes more watchful and prayerful. Being baptized, he realizes the answer of a good conscience and rejoices in the truth that has been made so clear and plain.

He begins to realize that his heart is not pure, and seeks to draw nearer to God and to understand his need more perfectly. He reads, " Blessed are the pure in heart," and while he is enjoying the possibility of a clean and pure heart, the enemy appears in the form of a religious friend, with the assurance: "There is none good. We all sin more or less every day." Certainly, Mr. Devil, we admit the fact that none of us are good of ourselves, but God's salvation makes men "just," "righteous," "good," "holy," and fills them with the Spirit, which would surely make them good and pure in heart. The Word says, "He that sinneth is of the Devil," and you will find that the ones spoken of as not being good are those who have said in their hearts, "There is no God." "Yes, Mr. Devil, I read of holy people in the Bible, and that is what I want to be; and if one can be holy, every one can, who will." You say, "That is making ourselves equal with God and is mockery; and tho one who does is not humble"? That is just as you try to see it, Mr. Foe; for you are trying to persuade people every day (and succeeding pretty well) that they are plenty good enough for heaven without getting converted or without obeying the commandments of God; and now you want to crush those who are looking to God to prepare them by a perfect salvation for that pure, holy, and heavenly place, God's eternal abode, by taunting them with "lack of humility," and "bigotry." We want to cut off your head forever with the sword of the Spirit. "Follow peace with all men, and holiness, without which no man shall see the Lord."—Heb. 12:14. "The oath which he sware to our Father Abraham, that he would grant unto us, that we being delivered out of the hand of our enemies might serve him without fear, in holiness and righteousness before him, all the days of our life."—Luke 1:73-75. Surely one must press his way through the unbelief, rebellion, and darkness of the Devil and the world and " walk in truth," if he would be cleansed from all sin. The Devil fights the experience of sanctification or purity because he knows those who gain it are being made " strong in God," and will be hard to reach by his snares and deceptions. We ought to praise God that he has made the way so plain that we may behold the seductions of the enemy and beware.

The Christian after gaining this victory of faith and becoming " the temple of the Holy Ghost " is better fitted to " fight the good fight of faith and lay hold on eternal life " through the promises of God. As the " anointing which he receiveth teacheth all things," the Word of God is illuminated and its meaning made clear and plain, to those who seek to " know the truth." Therefore, it is not long before he reads the thirteenth chapter of John and begins to inquire concerning the expression "If I then, your Lord and Master, have washed your feet, ye also ought to wash one another's feet." After prayer and meditation it seems so clear and plain that he says to himself, " That surely looks as if it means for Christians to do what the Lord did. But here comes the foe saying in accents soft and low, "O dear soul, that means you are to be humble enough to do so in sickness or death; it is a lesson in humility." But the true Christian thinks, "Why, my heart was always humble enough to do anything for the suffering. Surely it means more than that; and then the language clearly asserts that it is something to be done, and as humility is a grace of the heart, it cannot be done, but must bear its fruit in action. It surely means just what it says—"wash one another's feet." And though the opposition comes strong from every quarter, the more I pray over it and read it on my knees before God, the more I am convinced it is an ordinance of God's house, the church. This verse—" If ye know these things, happy are ye if ye do them "—assures my heart that washing the saints' feet is included with the Lord's supper. Oh, how precious this victory of faith against the doctrines and teachings of men! Yes, I realize the humility of Christ in my heart that makes me willing to do just what Jesus did—" wash the diciples' feet." Now I know if I believe and practice this, it will be a line of division between myself and those who oppose it; but I hear the voice of Jesus saying, "What is that to thee? follow thou me," and the response of my heart is, yea, Lord, "I will follow thee even unto death."

Here comes another twist from the enemy: "Oh, that was 1800 years ago, and people were not as refined then as now, and it seems to me it is too shocking to modesty; yes, even vulgar and indecent to take it up as an ordinance in the congregation of God. Besides, they wore sandals those days, and needed to wash oftener." Oh, Mr. Deceiver, I have caught you! "Man shall not live by bread alone, but by every word that proceedeth out of the mouth of God," and Jesus said in his last commission when sending forth preachers to all nations, "Teaching them to observe all things whatsoever I have commanded you; and lo, I am with you alway, *even* unto the end of the world." That thrust of the sword of the Spirit has cut you through and never more can you fight this battle with my soul. Jesus Christ is the same yesterday, to-day, and forever. He does not change his way to please even extremely refined people. "Whosoever therefore shall be ashamed of me and of my words in this adulterous and sinful generation, of him also shall the Son of man be ashamed, when he cometh in the glory of his Father with the holy angels."—Mark 8:38. Oh, how strong I feel in God; my shield of faith is lifted up and the enemies' darts shall not penetrate it for my soul's destruction. Fare ye well, dear friends and foes, God doth hide me in his pavilion from the strife of tongues, and I am seeking not mine own glory but the glory of the Father in exalting his word by keeping its instruction.

The Christian presses forward joyfully trusting in the God who never lost a battle. Soon he comes to a stronghold—" many doctrines." "There are a multitude of good people who believe many different doctrines, and each party or division claim to be right and walking in the truth of God; and can you reject any of them because they differ from you?" Oh, Mr.

Devil, how cute you are! No, we will not reject them because they differ from us, but because they differ from God's truth, and come under the condemnation of teaching for doctrine the commandments and traditions of men. Let us see what God says about it. Please turn and read Matt. 15:1-9, and you will see that because a religious people who claimed to know God departed from his instruction and taught the opposite of truth they were told they had made the commands of God of none effect by their traditions; therefore his censure was given in these words: "Ye hypocrites, well did Esaias prophesy of you, saying: This people draweth nigh unto me with their mouth, and honoreth me with their lips; but their heart is far from me. But in vain they do worship me, teaching for doctrines the commandments of men." How firmly this teaches against wrong doctrine and impresses the obligation of knowing the truth. Here are several more scriptures that are equally forcible: "For there are many unruly and vain talkers and deceivers, specially they of the circumcision; whose mouths must be stopped, who subvert whole houses, teaching things they ought not for filthy lucer's sake. * * * Wherefore, rebuke them sharply, that they may be sound in the faith; not giving heed to Jewish fables and commandments of men, that turn from the truth."—Tit. 1:10-14. " Now I beseech you, brethren, mark them which cause divisions and offenses contrary to the doctrine which ye have learned; and avoid them. For they that are such serve not our

Lord Jesus Christ, but their own belly; and by good words and fair speeches deceive the hearts of the simple."—Rom. 16:17, 18.

Now let us see how many things we may learn from these verses. In the first place, men may worship God with their lips, and their hearts be unsaved or far away from his true service, and though this may seem good and honorable, Jesus said their worship was vain, or of no value to them, because they taught the commands and teachings of men instead of God's teachings. Now let us illustrate this point, to make it more forcible. Suppose when a mother leaves home for a month's absence, she lays out several books and says to her daughters, "While mamma is gone you may be lonesome, and it will be very nice for you to read an hour a day in these books. You will see I have marked portions that are very necessary for you to learn soon for your good. Be nice girls, and do as mamma wishes."

On her return home she says, "Well, daughters, how did you enjoy your reading?" "Oh, mamma, dear, we were so busy playing, for a few days, that we forgot our lessons; and then brother got his new book, and said it would do just as well to read in it; and then John said we ought to hear the war news, and so he read awhile every day to us; and so we have not looked at those books you told us to read to keep us from being lonesome—you don't care, do you, so we got along all right?" "Well, children, let us look at those books and see what *you* think about that.

Here is the first lesson, a very nice piece telling how a family of girls learned to keep house, and at the close is a note from your mamma giving you her love and telling you to 'look in the pin-box and see what you can find for each of you.'" Little hands soon find the box and bright eyes quickly spy "a dime apiece for something nice." "Oh, *oh*, how we wish we had had those dimes the next day after you left, for we went to town and could have had a nice time shopping!" "Here is the second lesson, telling you how to be happy, and a note saying, 'If you have been good girls, you may visit Edith for a couple of hours.'" "Oh, my! oh, dear! we wanted to go, oh, so much but thought we better not unless you said so." "Well, girls, take the books and see how much you have missed by disobedience." They do so and find a nice pleasure awaiting them after each lesson, and at the close these words: "If you have been faithful in your lessons, I will, if possible take you with me next visit I make." See the children's faces covered with tears, and hear their lamentations. Then see the regret and sorrow on the mother's face as she says in loving tones, "So much you have missed by taking your own and other's ways, instead of doing as your own dear mother wished you to do." Now, boys, for the lesson to you. There is a precious reward in the learning and practice of every scripture, and if any one leaves it out or puts something different in its place, he loses the reward; and at the end of life fails to receive the approval of God, or his welcome into heaven. Oh, how bitter will be the regrets of those who have received the teaching of men instead of the instruction of God!

Now look back to the scriptures quoted and see what more we can learn. Paul was instructing a young preacher when he said, "There are many unruly and vain talkers and deceivers whose mouths must be stopped," because " the teachings of men turn from the truth." If there were false teachers at that time, so soon after the pure gospel was delivered to the church, then there is more likely to be more at the present time, when, according to the scriptures, "because iniquity doth abound the love of many shall wax cold;" and it is especially foretold that " in the last days perilous times shall come," and besides many ungodly things they shall do, men shall " have a form of godliness but deny the power thereof;" and we are told, " From such turn away "—clearly showing that God's children are expected to know the truth, and distinguish false teachers, and even " instruct " and " rebuke " the " opposers," " if God peradventure will give them repentance to the acknowledgment of the truth."

Looking back to our scriptures again, we notice the entreaty of Paul's language to the Romans when he said, "Now I *beseech* you, *brethren, mark* them which cause divisions and offenses contrary to the dictrine which ye have learned, and avoid them." From the strength of the language used we see the necessity for doing so. Only in a real strong opposition to everything contrary to the pure gospel doctrine could it be preserved pure. You know if one associates with those who do evil in any way, he is apt to become affected thereby and lose his strength of resistance against the evil, and may in time be encouraged into it, the same as his associates. If one worships with those who teach false doctrines, he is apt to lose his strength against them, and finally the spirit of truth, until he is blinded to the truth and receives the error. Certainly our text must be obeyed in order to please God, and the verse following makes the necessity very clear: "For they that are such serve not our Lord Jesus Christ, but their own belly; and by good words and fair speeches deceive the hearts of the simple." This is so strong that it seems it ought to reach the hearts of all honest people, and make the way plain before them. Men do many things to please themselves, their appetites, their love of popularity or of dominion, or to establish their own belief and see it prosper. Such people may pray, and read the Bible, give to the poor and do many other commendable things, but not having the love of God that would make them humble and obedient to God, their religion is vain, and God's true children are not to mingle with them in their worship, lest " they be partaker of their sins and plagues," but hold up the pure gospel and bid them measure to its standard.

If you love purity, you will love truth. God speaks the truth, and " the Devil is the father of lies." Then God's teachers and preachers must teach the truth, and we may expect the Devil's preachers and teachers to teach the opposite of truth—the false. Now, these false teachers do not come looking like wolves, bears, and tigers, ready to devour people; but they come looking as much as possible like God's true gospel workers, as the Bible says, " wolves in sheep's clothing;" and they come to deceive the people—make them think they are Christians when they are not; because they do not love God enough to find the truth and obey it.

You know in the garden of Eden when God told Adam and Eve a certain thing, the Devil told them the opposite, and so he is doing the same to-day. God tells us to love the truth and to keep his commandments: but the Devil says, " You cannot know what is truth; therefore it does not make any difference what you teach, believe, or do, so you are honest in it." But this is false, like all the rest of his doctrines; for every one who accepts the false loses very, very much that can never be regained after the final decision.

Remember, boys, *truth* is on the side of right, and no question is settled properly unless .it is settled right. Here is a poem that just suits our need, and very. clearly teaches a very important truth.

THE RIGHT WILL TRIUMPH.

However the battle is ended,
Though proudly the victor comes
With fluttering flags and prancing nags
And echoing roll of drums,

Still truth proclaims this motto
In letters of living light—
No question is ever settled
Until it is settled right.

Though the heel of strong oppression
May grind the weak in the dust,
And the voice of fame with one acclaim
May call him great and just,
Let those who applaud take warning
And keep this motto in sight—
No question is ever settled
Until it is settled right.

Let those who have failed take courage
Tho' the enemy seems to have won.
Tho' his ranks be strong, if he be in the wrong,
The battle is not yet done,
For, sure as the morning follows
The darkest hour of the night,
No question is ever settled
Until it is settled right.
—*Ella Wheeler Wilcox.*

The Christian having fought this great battle of truth against error is encouraged to "battle for truth," and though he keeps humble and meek, he remembers continually, "Greater is he that is in you than he that is in the world;" therefore he knows he shall gain the day. Very often the enemy sends out a scouting expedition with some slight suggestion against the word of God or some very finely expressed doubt or finely worded theory or beautiful teaching of men, covered over with misapplied scriptures; but when they are analyzed by the word of God as interpreted by the Holy Spirit of truth, they are discarded, and sent back to their owners. God provided for our need when he gave us the "Holy Ghost to lead us into all truth;" for "he shall take the things of Christ and reveal them unto you."

One of the most precious and forcible scriptures to my soul is this: "Eye hath not seen, nor ear heard, neither have entered into the heart of man, the things which God hath prepared for them that love him. But God hath revealed them unto us by his Spirit; for the Spirit searcheth all things, yea, the deep things of God." No matter how much false teaching we have received or how much of it surrounds us, if we love the truth and seek to know it, and study God's word, humbly relying upon the Spirit to lead us into the truth, he will do so; for that is his mission—yea, he will take of the deep things of God and reveal them unto us.

Many years ago, before I was converted, I had a religious belief that was very dear to me, and which I defended and upheld at every opportunity. At the same time I was not satisfied with my religious life, but measured myself by others, and thought: "Surely we are all on the same road, and as others seem to be satisfied I ought to be also." Sometimes I heard different teachings that made me doubtful of the security of my position, but it was carelessly put aside. After attending a meeting of this kind I began to see my spiritual need, and by making a more perfect surrender of myself to God I was converted, and my eyes opened to see the need of making more earnest inquiry of God concerning different teachings, and the Lord led me step by step "in a way I knew not," until I received the Holy Spirit as my guide and teacher. I realized that each individual must stand alone with God, and be responsible for himself. I could not depend on the judgment of others nor lean to my own understanding, but must have help from God to walk in the narrow way of truth; so every doctrine I had known was compared with the scriptures, and those that were false were discarded and the truth accepted. As I did this there was realized a deeper consecration to the service of God, and a deeper, richer blessing upon my soul. Looking backward, my soul rejoices in the victory and is strengthened to press forward.

Did you ever think how Christians walk step by step, by faith, in the light of truth? The scripture saith, "If we walk in the light, as he is in the light, * * * the blood of Jesus Christ his Son cleanseth us from all sin." God is light, and as we walk by faith day by day he gives us more light, and as we step out in that light more follows. So the heart is kept purged. If one failed to walk in the light, it would cause leanness of soul; or if he refused to walk therein, it would be rebellion, and that is the fruit of the flesh, and therefore he would be a sinner before God, and have to repent of it before he could enjoy God's approval. Very many dear souls stumble here and the enemy gains his desire—their eternal ruin. Therefore we are exhorted: "Walk while ye have the light, lest darkness come upon you."

This life of faith reaches every condition and circumstance; there is nothing too small or too great to take to the Lord and expect his direction. He is our wisdom; for his word says: "If any of you lack wisdom, let him ask of God, that giveth to all men liberally, and upbraideth not; and it shall be given him. But let him ask in faith, nothing wavering. For he that wavereth is like a wave of the sea driven with the wind and tossed. For let not that man think that he shall receive anything of the Lord." By keeping humble and looking to God for wisdom day by day, and walking in all the commandments of God blameless, we are kept in condition where we can look up to God in real assurance of faith for the things we desire for God's glory; for "if our heart condemn us not, then have we confidence toward God. And whatsoever we ask, we receive of him because we keep his commandments." It is such a precious privilege to be able to carry everything to God in humble, believing prayer, knowing that it is God's pleasure to do "exceeding abundantly above all that we ask or think."

Here is an incident in the life of a young man that we wish you to receive special benefit from. May it help you to remember two important things: that "God is a *prayer-hearing* and a *prayer-answering* God;" and that Christian mothers are praying for their sons and other mothers' sons; for love bears one another's burdens.

Dear Boys:

> We love the Lord, we love his cause,
> We love his ways, we love his laws.

And why do we thus

> Love God the Father, and God the Son?
> Because in us his *kingdom* is begun.

I am quite an old boy now, but was a little lad once, and was blessed with a kind, Christian mother, whose counsels were always right. Mother told me never to use tobacco, but in boyhood's forgetfulness I took a chew, and soon was "the *sickest mortal.*" Then I remembered my mother's instruction, and have never taken the second chew, for which I feel to praise God.

The war of the rebellion broke out when I was nineteen years old, and as my home was in Virginia, where we had to take sides, I naturally went into the Union army. I was always getting hurt in some way and had dyspepsia, and my friends said soldier life would kill me. Though I prayed not, I had all confidence in "mother's prayers;" and when severe danger threatened, I would always pray to God for help; and when danger was over I was reckless as ever. In battle men were shot down all around me but

I was not hurt—why? My mother's prayers warded off the bullets. On the 19th of December, 1863, I was captured by the Confederates. That was on the return of Gen. Arnill's raid on the Tennessee and Gordonsville R. R. at Salem (about which you can read in history). I was on detached service, in the Ambulance Corps. All were captured, and I was sent to Richmond, and onto Bell's Island, where I was starved to nothing but skin and bones, and thousands of men died under the cruel treatment. About the 1st of March, 1864, the Confederates began to take off squads of 100 men to send them to Andersonville prison. I conceived an idea to try the City Hospital, where I stayed ten days. My comrades carried me out of the stockade in a blanket and gave my disease chronic diarrhœa, and that set me free from the 100 I belonged to on the island, and three days after I left, my squad was sent to Andersonville, where it is very probable I should have died, had I gone.

We that did not die in the hospital were put out into an old tobacco-house, on the third floor, where there were dents caused by heavy machinery and these dents were full of water, it having been scrubbed just before we were put there. An older comrade asked, "Why did they put us on this wet floor." I answered, "That we might get our death with cold;" and he said, "It looks that way." There were 600 men on that floor, and about the 20th of March there came a Confederate officer and said, "There are four hundred here for parole. Now march down the steps in single file, so

I can count you." Please imagine the situation: two hundred had to be left, and nobody wanted to be of that number; so there was a rush made for the head of the stairs, and in that rush I found myself exactly behind the Confederate officer. I am perfectly satisfied that he could feel my heart beat against his back as I stood there perfectly still until he had counted 398, when he reached around and pulled me out and counted 399. Now he did not have to do that; there were men in the head of the stairs to fill the place; but he did it regardless of the beseeching faces in front.

My mother was on her death-bed at home praying continually that her beloved boy should be returned to her alive. She repeatedly asked God only to let her live to see my face, and then take her home to himself There is no doubt in my mind but God put it into my head to go to the City Hospital. Though I loved the men I was associated with in prison, when I thought of going to the hospital I gave them up willingly. Had I not gone when I did, I would no doubt have been sent to Andersonville and to a more horrible living death. Then God put it into the heart of the Confederate officer to pull me forward and count me in the four hundred parole. I got my discharge from the army January 29, 1865, and reached home February 1, and on the 7th my mother peacefully passed from earth to glory. I never forgot what she was to me, and I never could forget my mother's prayers, her self-denials, love, and counsel. They followed me until I gave my heart to God—

was saved and then sanctified wholly; thus made meet for the Master's use. I once wished for riches of this world, but I never gained them; and now I can see the hand of God in that; for through riches I would have lost my soul. But, glory to God! he has given me riches of grace, riches in faith, and in the belief and love of the gospel of my blessed Savior; and that is enough riches for me. I care not for the perishable things of earth.

My home is in heaven, I long to be there;
All will be happy, glorious, bright, and fair.
There will be no more sorrow, there will be no tears—
In that bright home far away.

Friends I shall see, who have gone on before
And landed safe on that beautiful shore;
I shall see Jesus, and that will be my joy—
In that bright home far away.

Now, dear boys, if you are blessed with kind Christian parents, always remember their counsels and obey their commands. The word of God says, "Honor thy father and mother, * * * that it may be well with thee, and thou mayest live long on the earth."—Eph. 6:2, 3. Thus you see long life is promised to those who honor their parents. Then we find other scriptures which it will be well for you to heed. Matt. 6:33: "But seek ye first the kingdom of God and his righteousness; and all these things shall be added unto you"—meaning all things needful. Thus it behooves us to seek the Lord in youth, that we may spend a long and useful life in this world, to God's glory.

Let us see to it that we will be enabled like Paul to exclaim: "For I am now ready to be offered, and the time of my departure is at hand. I have fought a good fight, I have finished my course, I have kept the faith: Henceforth there is laid up for me a crown of righteousness, which the Lord, the righteous Judge, shall give me at that day; and not to me only, but unto all them that love his appearing."—2 Tim., 4:6-8 This covers the whole ground of the Christian's experience. Paul's ministry was finished. He had done what he could—had done all that was required of him, had kept the faith, had not wavered nor doubted, but like Abraham "he believed God" and trusted him for everything. He cared not for the things of this world, but he had treasures in heaven, and he longed to be there with saints and with angels God's glory to share.

We love the souls of the boys and girls and would like to have them give their hearts, their lives, and their all into the keeping of our blessed Lord and Master, "who careth for all."

"Ask, and it shall be given you, brother;
He is the Lord who careth for all;
Come with your heart all broken and bleeding;
Come, he will hear and answer your call.

"Hurry and tell him, brother and sister;
Jesus, so tender, loving, and kind,
Waiting to comfort, bless, and deliver;
Hurry and tell him, peace you will find."

This is the way I came. I found it just as this verse states, and may you find this peace and keep it in your hearts till time shall be no more and a glorious eternity is a wonderful reality, and we may meet at the throne of God in heaven, is the humble prayer of your brother in Christ Jesus,

John F. Starcher.

Dear boys, you see the power of a mother's prayers and the influence of her life. Her darling boy (for the sight of whom she would linger in pain many days) has been saved and is prepared to meet her in glory, and we all feel like saying, "Praise the Lord!" for this great victory of a mother's prayers. But, oh, boys! I think of something even better than this that *you* may *do*. How many tears, heartaches, sighs, and sad and sorrowful hours would have been spared that mother if her son had turned to the Lord in the days of his youth! None but a *mother* can tell the sorrow our children cause us by grieving our very best Friend by disregarding his love and mercy and going on in sin year after year. O dear sons, gladden your mothers' hearts by giving yourselves *fully, freely* to the service of God *now*. Besides this you have the privilege of using the prayer of faith for the salvation of other precious souls, and thus winning them as stars for your crown of rejoicing, to cast at your dear Savior's feet when we shall sing the glad new song of redeeming love in the courts of glory.

There are several more great battles of faith and truth for the Christian, which we will put in different chapters. The next is the church subject. Will you please read all the scriptures you can find on the church?

THE CHURCH OF GOD.

PERHAPS some of you will think as you read this title, "Why, I never heard of that church!" but if you have read the scriptures you know something about it. For the good of some we will tell what will be interesting to you concerning it.

This church was built over 1800 years ago. It is the greatest church that ever existed; for it has Jesus as its founder, its ruler, its lawgiver, its priest, and its Savior. This church has withstood the lapse of time, all the powers of hell, and all the ignorance and willfulness of man. As it came from the hand of divinity, it is pure—" without spot or blemish or any such thing "—therefore all its members are saved people, who walk in the light of holy truth. Its doctrine is the gospel of Jesus Christ, and its extent is heaven and earth. These strong assertions we find are scriptural, which we desire to show by a few quotations. In Matt. 16:18 Jesus said: "Upon this rock I will build my church; and the gates of hell shall not prevail against it." The building was begun with the teaching of John, Jesus, and the apostles; and the church was fully set in order on the day of Pentecost, when the fullness of salvation was given by the baptism of the Holy Ghost, and the gifts of the Spirit bestowed severally as he willed, thus preparing each one to occupy his place and discharge the duties of his office. It was built between A. D. 32 (Matt. 16: 18) and A. D. 59 (1 Cor. 3:9; Eph. 1:23; 1 Cor. 12; 1 Pet. 2:5).

This church was prophesied of as a great temple of the Lord—" a habitation of God through the Spirit." God dwelt with his people in the wilderness in a tabernacle made after a certain God-given pattern, and this tabernacle was carried by them in all their journeyings until they reached the promised land of Canaan and had conquered their enemies. Then he made choice of a king to build a wonderful and magnificent temple, that he might have a suitable dwelling-place: but in this latter and better dispensation of gospel grace he dwells in the hearts of saved men, and they united by the Holy Spirit of God to form a most beautiful and precious temple which was prophesied of 519 years before Christ by the prophet Zechariah, in these words: " Thus speaketh the Lord of hosts, saying, Behold the man whose name is The Branch; and he shall grow up out of his place, and he shall build the temple of the Lord: * * * and he shall bear the glory, and shall sit and rule upon his throne;   *   *   *   and the counsel of peace shall be between them both.   *   *   *   And they that are far off shall come and build in the temple of the Lord, and ye shall know that the Lord of hosts hath sent me unto you. And this shall come to pass, if ye will diligently obey the voice of the Lord your God." Turning to Eph. 2:19-22 we see the fulfillment of this prophecy: "Now, therefore, ye are no more strangers and foreigners, but fellow citizens with the saints, and of the household of God; and are built upon the foundation of the apostles and prophets, Jesus Christ himself being the chief corner-stone. In whom all the building fitly framed together groweth unto an holy temple in the Lord: in whom ye also are builded together for an habitation of God through the Spirit."

What could be grander? Let us look at it carefully. Jesus takes his apostles and makes them foundation stones for his beautiful temple, and he himself becomes the chief corner-stone. Then he takes the rough stones from the quarry of sin, smooths them up by his redeeming grace, purifies them, and places them in the building as suits him; thus causing it to grow into a holy temple of the Lord. Each one being "filled with the Spirit," it makes his perfect dwelling-place, and our hearts are his throne upon which he sits to reign and rule. "The government is upon his shoulders," and he directs all into the holy way of truth and righteousness; therefore "of peace there is no end." Those who are far off in sin but "are made nigh by the blood of Christ," or those who live on down to the end of time shall be builded in; for God is able.

This church extends all over this world; for "in every nation he that feareth him [God], and worketh righteousness, is accepted with him," and Jesus says, " I am the door." No man can get into this church but by receiving Jesus as his Savior from sin. This is the door that *"no man* openeth and no man shutteth." Every Christian in this world belongs to this church, and every child of God who has gone through death's door into the realms of glory belongs to it; for " ye are come unto Mount Zion, and unto the city of the living God, the heavenly Jerusalem, and to an innumerable company of angels, to the general assembly and church of the first-born, which are written in heaven, and to God the Judge of all, and to the spirits of just men made perfect, and to Jesus." Thus we have found the church of God, and, as a city set upon a hill, it cannot be hid. It giveth light to all around, by preaching, teaching, and living the truth; for it is " the pillar and ground of the truth."

It is a very *visible* church; for it is composed of men, women, and children who have been saved and made peculiar by their godly lives.

Now, we want to show you that there is *only one Bible church.* " For as the body is one, and hath many members, and all the members of that one body, being many, are one body, so also is Christ. For by one Spirit are we all baptized into one body, whether we be Jews or Gentiles, whether we be bond or free; and have been all made to drink into one Spirit."—1 Cor. 12:12, 13. " Now ye are the body of Christ, and members in particular."—Ver. 27. Col. 1:18: " And he is the head of the body, the church." " Who now rejoice in my sufferings for you and fill up that which is behind of the afflictions of Christ in my flesh for his body's sake which is the church."—Ver. 24. Eph. 1:22, 23. " And hath put all things under his feet, and gave him to be the head over all things to the church, which is his body, the fullness of him that filleth all in all. Now we see the Bible recognizes but one body of Christians, which is the one church, and Jesus is the head over that one body. If we see a head, we expect to find only one body—it would be a great monstrosity that would have one head and a multitude of bodies. Although the world is filled with what are called " churches " and every one claims to be a " church of God " and puts Jesus as its head, we see it is a great mistake; for there is only one body for the one head, Jesus.

Now, boys, please try to understand this subject and get the Bible idea of the church. A great number of people of every nation, all believing in Jesus as their Savior, all filled with the Holy Spirit, all walking in the light of truth, all bound together by the cords of divine love and harmony, all under the control of one head, Jesus. Is that not beautiful? Do you not wish with me that all could see this spiritual church, and avoid the multitude of man-made organizations that consider themselves churches? We believe some of you do; for there is a great awakening on this subject, and many who are growing tired of this deception are looking for something better. The time is come when the bride (the church of God) is making herself ready for the coming of the Lord, and must appear in the beauty of purity and spiritual unity.

Let us see how this state of " many churches " arose. We find from the Bible that in the apostles' time there was but one true church, which continued for some time in its purity. There arose, about 270 A. D., a great religious power that persecuted and killed all the Christians it could find and spread its darkness and superstition throughout the world. Though error may for a time appear to conquer truth, she arises in renewed strength to victory. From the darkness of Catholicism came Martin Luther in the sixteenth century, teaching the gospel truth of salvation by faith; and the Bible, so long withheld from the people, again found its way into homes and hearts to shed its glorious rays of redeeming love in salvation of souls from the darkness of sin. This is called the Great Reformation, and was a wonderful time of victory for truth and righteousness. The great reformers, confused by the darkness of Catholicism, saw not the Bible church of God, but founded human organizations to carry on the gospel work. They retained much of the error of Catholicism, and in so doing ignorantly honored her, whom they desired to protest against, and for which they were called Protestants.

As different Bible truths were made clear to individuals they withdrew from the old organizations and founded new ones which they hoped to keep purer. But it would not be long until the new divisions would lose their spirituality and drift along in formalism, refusing to teach unpopular Bible truths and adopting new ideas and pleasing doctrines and beliefs, until again the more spiritual would come forth to form another " church." Thus has it rolled on, until our world is full of sects and divisions, each claiming to teach the pure gospel yet all differing and teaching in various ways just the opposite doctrines—showing clearly that truth does not abide within them. In the last few years the hearts and minds of the most devoted and spiritual people are turned toward unity. They see the evils of so many divisions, and are trying to find a way out of the difficulty. Others would like a grand union composed of all the sects, and are trying to find a ground for the union, but so far have failed to do so. Again, others see in a *"broadness* of *fellowship* between the divisions a grand advance toward brotherhood." Although man may think, plan, hope, and work, there is only one way out of the trouble, and that is the right way—God's way. We find that in the Bible, for we see how it was in the beginning, and as Jesus is the same and changes not, we know it ought to be the same to-day. Then the question comes, "What doth hinder?" and in the light of truth we must answer, "Nothing."

God's salvation will do as perfect a work now as ever; for it will purify, fill with the Holy Spirit, and unite the people of God, just as perfectly as in the apostles' time. Then the remedy is a full salvation that removes division and all willfulness and pride that would prevent souls from coming to the knowledge of the truth. The enemy has worked his false doctrines and the teachings of men in upon those who claim to serve God, until their eyes are blinded to the truth.

God never gave man the privilege of building or organizing churches, and so what they build withdraws honor from the one our Lord built. So, dear people, come back to God's church. Forsake the doctrines, teachings, and buildings of men, and come back to truth and Father's house. We know many precious souls are honest in believing it is right to belong to some sect, but if they will read all they can find in the Bible on divisions, false doctrines, false teachers, and the church of God, they will surely see differently if they come *willing* to see; for you know, boys, "No one is so blind as those who *will not see.*" Is any one thus willful about " his church?" then there is little hope of him seeing something better.

Eighteen years ago no one could hurt me worse nor make me more angry than to say a word against " my church." I even " shut my eyes " to things I knew were not right, and drifted along with the multitude. But after I was converted, and saw that " my church " did not teach purity of heart, I forsook her and entered another that did; and when in studying my Bible I saw " my new church " did not measure to the standard of the Bible church of 1 Cor. 12, I let it go also, and met with those who would worship God in the beauty of holiness. This was not done hastily or carelessly or without a tear or heartache, but I wept and prayed, and read and prayed, until I came to the point: "Let others do as they may, I must take the Holy Ghost and the word of God as my guide." It seemed I had to let go of every prop and stay—for I had unconsciously depended upon the judgment of preachers and friends—and lean alone upon God. How tremblingly and uncertainly I took hold of the great cables of truth and spiritual guidance! Surely God was very merciful to me in my human weakness and bore long with me, and I surely must do the same with others.

As I took my Bible to the secret closet and on my knees before God plead for direction, and claimed the promise "When he the Holy Ghost is come he shall lead you into the truth," he fulfilled it to me, and my eyes were opened to behold wondrous things out of God's law. I saw the lovely and pure temple of God, and that I had a place to fill in it to God's glory; and my soul was made happy in the love and wisdom of God. Now, dear boys, will you go and do likewise? Have you anything too good to yield to Jesus? or are you not willing to give up "your church" and take God's? May God help you all to take a stand for God's eternal truth and his holy temple, the one church of God.

ONLY ONE CHURCH.

Only one Church ? How can it be ?
Why here is one—yes, one, two, three
Upon this street, and four, five, six
Just there on that—so now we'll fix
Upon the number ten and five;
And if we look, we find they thrive.

Only one Church ! Yes, it is true,
And though it seems so strange and new,
This Church was built in century one,
By Jesus Christ—God's only Son—
And to his glory, honor, praise,
It now must last till end of days.

Only one Church ! The gates of hell
Cannot prevail; it's builded well
Upon the rock of apostles true,
And Jesus Christ the Corner, too:
The stones are smoothed and fitted in
Through grace and truth, that saves from sin.

Only one Church ! 'Tis grand and fair.
We wish you all would have a share
Of all its blessings and royal grace
That sanctifies and fills the place.
If all could see its holy worth,
They'd see no other on this earth.

Only one Church ! a body one:
The only head is Christ the Son,
Who moves each member at his will,
And helps them all their place to fill;
For in this temple of God and grace,
Each one may surely find a place

THE CHURCH OF GOD.

Only one Church ! A temple grand !
Upon the truth we all must stand,
And so we should inquire of God
And walk the way our Savior trod,
To see his works or find his will;
Then all his truth by us fulfill.

Only one Church ! His dwelling-place.
Why, now we see his holy grace
Could not conceive of anything
But union fair, or what would bring
The souls of men to higher thought,
To purer ways with virtues fraught.

Only one Church ! His ways above
The thoughts of man, and so in love
He built his house above the plane
Of strife and sects and " numbers " gain;
And so beneath his feet we place
All things that truth and love disgrace.

Only one Church ! We know the love
That binds our hearts is far above
All selfish zeal or sectish strife,
And honors God and gives a life
That seeks no way but what is right,
And trusts not flesh, but holy might.

Only one Church ! Our God is strong;
We know he's able to conquer wrong,
Bring his children from church of men
And lead them back to truth again—
Thus build them in *his* church so dear,
And place around the wall so clear.

Only one Church! Salvation's wall
Is strong and pure, and offers all
A fair retreat from worldly ways,
And grace and help for him who prays
And watches well; and keeps him pure
From all the ways that would allure.

Only one Church ! Oh, now I see !
There is but one will do for me—
The Bible church—it is so grand !
And though there's many o'er the land
That bear the name, 'tis falsely given,
And will not lead our souls to heaven.

Only one Church ! I join the strain,
And find it is a sweet refrain
To all who tarried so far from home,
But now forever have ceased to roam,
And think in word or sing in song,
Only one Church—the heav'nly throng

DIVINE HEALING.

One of the precious benefits of the church of God is divine healing of bodily affliction through faith in the promises of God. Perhaps some of our sons know all about it and have received the benefit through their own or others' prayers; but as many have not heard of this great blessing, or have not been where they could receive it from the hand of God, we feel it is quite necessary to dwell upon the subject for a little time, and give several testimonies. There is nothing that enlists human sympathy more than suffering. Whenever we see any one in distress and pain, or with a broken-down and disabled body as the effects of sin and evil practices, sadness fills our hearts. If we are thus touched with compassion, we know the great loving heart of God must be made *sad indeed* by the distress of his creatures.

Sickness and disease are brought upon us by disobeying the laws of health or are from the hand of the Devil, who seeks to destroy soul and body. In Job's case God permitted the Devil to try him, but would allow him to go just so far and no further; and while the Devil would have made it work for his destruction or to cause him trouble, God overruled it for Job's good. And so it may be every time, if people will only learn the lessons needful to them. The Psalmist says, "Before I was afflicted I went astray; but now have I kept thy word." Oftentimes sore affliction brings people where they become willing to seek God for salvation. In such cases God overrules the work of Satan for good. Others become more hardened by their distresses and trouble, but when health returns they gratefully acknowledge it as a good gift from God, and seek to serve him. In either case God is honored. There are some instances where the enemy gains the day by forcing dear ones to believe that God is delighted in their sufferings and distresses, and they hate him and refuse to yield to his service; and if they get well, they are found to give the glory to anything and everything but God. In such cases, by their own willfulness they turn from the great good they might receive.

God in his great love has provided a "sure cure" for all disease and affliction among those who are his children by faith. If you look back to his dealings with the children of Israel, you will see how kindly he dealt with them in healing them, or in protecting them from disease; and if you read the gospels, you will see how Jesus healed all manner of sickness and disease among the people, and sent out his disciples to "heal the sick," and the epistle of James gives this instruction to the children of God: " Is any among you afflicted ? let him pray. Is any merry ? let him sing psalms. Is any sick among you ? let him call for the elders of the church; and let them pray over him, anointing him with oil in the name of the Lord: and the prayer of faith shall save the sick, and the Lord shall raise him up; and if he have committed sins, they shall be forgiven him." In the commission to the disciples Jesus says to them, " These signs shall follow them that believe: In my name shall they cast out devils; they shall speak with new tongues; they shall take up serpents; and if they drink any deadly thing, it shall not hurt them; they shall lay hands on the sick, and they shall recover." While it is a popular belief that " the day of miracles is past," these few scriptures are strong against it, and have been relied upon by the sick and proved true by Christians on down to the present time. As God is bringing his children back to apostolic teaching and living there are multitudes of living testimonies to the willingness and power of God to heal all manner of sickness and disease.

There are many general promises that include healing. For instance, the Word says, " What things soever ye desire, when ye pray, believe that ye receive them, and ye shall have them." " If two of you shall agree as touching anything ye shall ask, it shall be done for you of my Father which is in heaven." "If ye shall ask anything in my name, I will do it." If a Christian is in trouble in any way, it is right for him to take it to the Lord in prayer and expect help from him. Sometimes people will apparently believe this, and yet when they come to God in sickness, instead of asking for healing they will ask for patience to endure their distress, and yet be taking all the medicine possible to cure them. This seems at least somewhat inconsistent. If one is in danger of death by drowning or by violence of men, no matter how wicked he may have been, he begins to call upon God for help; and if he is delivered from his danger, he considers it providential: but in sickness, while he may ask God to spare his life, he hesitates to ask for healing. This is a wrong position, and if all will study their Bibles, they will see how many precious promises would encourage us to look to God by faith for the removal of all disease.

When quite young a religious book fell into my hands and gave me a little knowledge of divine healing through the prayer of faith. Though not a Christian, I was led to believe that Christians ought to live so close to God as to have answers to prayer on all lines of human needs. Years after when I began to serve God, it seemed natural for me to trust for help in every time of need, and so sickness was taken to him in earnest prayer, and he many times healed and gave me strength for all motherhood's needs and trials. It has also been a great pleasure to take my children to God in all their sickness and find a present help and a Great Physician. Sometimes faith has been tried, but by persistently obeying and trusting the best I knew how the way of escape was found, and proved the help of the Lord is far above the earthly.

As we have thought of all our sons living under

different circumstances and conditions, the sick ones have come in for a good share of sympathy and love, and we feel very anxious to encourage them to seek the salvation of their souls, and then look to Jesus for their healing. There are many diseases peculiar to men that the family physician fails to reach, and though many patent medicines are sought as a relief they fail to reach the trouble, and so many are leading poor, miserable, aimless lives devoid of strength and manhood. Dear reader, there is help for all such needy ones at the foot of the cross and in the name of Jesus. It would be sad indeed to go on in suffering and weariness when God has given his word that he is able and willing to heal. So we hope you may all bring your diseases to the Lord, and let him set you free from their bondage. Think of the young men who bear in their faces and forms, and in their dispositions and manners, the marks of sexual evils and corruptions that bring awful diseases to prey upon the secret springs of life and vigor. If there is a class of people more needy than others, it is this one. Oh, how we Christian mothers do pray and trust that some precious boys or men of this needy class will press into the kingdom of God and find the help they need! We will give you several testimonies, of those who have found this help and proved its power to their great joy and eternal good, but before we do so there is another thought we wish to express, and then give a brother's experience as we remember it.

Sometimes young men and boys raised by religious

parents realize the truth of the gospel of Christ, and firmly believe that if they should get saved God would call them to preach the gospel, and, to avoid what seems to them an unpleasant duty, they refuse to heed the wooing voice of Jesus, and go on in sin. Sometimes disease fastens upon the poor body, and the enemy hurries the soul to its final doom. Oh, dear sons, if any of you who read these lines are standing in this position, let us entreat and prevail upon you to bravely take your place where God appoints; for in his order you will be prosperous and happy, and out of it you will never find the satisfaction you desire. If you all could know how much the Lord blesses and how wonderfully he prepares his workers for their field of labor, you would not be long in yielding to God. Years ago he so opened my eyes to see the need of gospel workers, and the sad condition of lost souls, that I would gladly have gone forth to herald the good news of salvation from sin; but not being free to do so, my prayer is going up to God that he may use me in some way to encourage others to yield gladly to the call, " Go ye into my vineyard." Never is my soul so blessed as when presenting the truth of God, with the precious anointing of the Spirit of God.

Now, boys, listen to this experience, and get all the good you can from it.

Brother B— when quite a boy was an earnest Christian, and soon heard the voice of God calling him, "Go preach my gospel." He listened and waited, then listened and drew back; and, although God assures us "his grace is sufficient," he refused to heed the voice, and went back into sin. He tried to enjoy himself, but soon consumption preyed upon his body, and in spite of poor health he married—one whom he thought would urge him forward in a life of gaiety, and thus he would escape the accusing voice of conscience. He kept at business until he fell from weakness, and was placed upon what all supposed would be his death-bed. Weaker and weaker he grew, until he could not turn his head; and yet he would not believe he was going to die. At last he overheard the doctor say to his mother, "Is he still alive?" This awakened him somewhat to his danger, and yet he smiled to think he knew more than the doctor thought —for he was able to hear. His hand lay upon the pillow before his eyes, and he thought he would test the matter in this way: If he could move his fingers, he would take it that he would get well; but if he could not, then he would believe he would die. He tried it, but could not move them. Then he thought, "I can still hear, see, and think. Then gradually his hearing left him, and his eyes began to dim, and his mind was becoming benumbed; and he said to himself, "Oh, this is death," and he saw the long eternity of despair and woe before him. Then he cried to God from the depths of his soul, "Oh, God save me! I'll preach your gospel." He knew nothing more, and lay unconscious several hours, and his friends waited to see the last breath drawn. He returned to consciousness, sat up, called for his clothes, and when his friends did not bring them (so startled were they) he arose from his bed, obtained them himself, dressed, and sat in the rocking-chair the rest of the day, took his meals as usual, and the next day went to his office, to the utter amazement of all who knew him, and when he told the doctor his experience, he replied, "If any one ought to preach the pure gospel, it is you." He gave himself to God and gospel work, and has been preaching for many years.

You see, dear boys, the power of God in bringing him back to life and health when he gave up his rebellion and looked to God for help. So may each of you receive all you need, whether for soul or body. We can glorify God better in health than in sickness. It needs a good, strong body for the Lord's active service in his vineyard. As he has made provision for it through the atonement of Christ, we can honor and please him by accepting it as a free gift from a loving Father's hands. There is no disease too great for his healing power; for he who is able to form the human body from earthly substance is able to repair it, no matter how little life or soundness there may be in it. Then another precious thought and blessed reality is this: There is nothing too small for his loving notice and kindly touch of healing power. Then may you all honor God by coming boldly to the throne of grace to find your "present help" in time of need. What God has done for others he is just as willing to do for you, if you come humbly and in simple faith. How sad it would be if the sons of Christian mothers, who have been prayed for in all their childhood sickness, and who have often received the healing touch from the Great Physician's hands, should in manhood's years and strength turn from this loving friend, and lean upon the arm of flesh in times of physical weakness and need.

Sometimes youthful lusts have laid the foundation for years of secret sorrow and pain, and various reasons have caused sickness, and restrained confidence from physicians, and the desire of the heart is to be restored to manhood's strength without the humiliation of a confession to any earthly friend or acquaintance. God, who knoweth all secrets, knows all about you, and stands ready to hear your soul's confession and forgive all wrong-doing and remove the effects from the body. Physicians agree in attributing much of the physical distress to social and sexual evils. Those who come to the Lord for help in sickness should remove all the cause thereof, as far as known, and be purged from every uncleanness and make strong decision to live in righteousness all the rest of life.

May the Lord bless these letters of testimony to the good of many young men and boys who are in physical distress and bound by disease. What a beautiful thing it is to see a youth entering manhood with a pure, strong body and active mind, unaffected by evil habits or disease! and how much more beautiful to see every ability and power engaged in the service of the Almighty! There is, however, a solemn grandeur and beauty in observing a poor sin-bound, disease-burdened, and destroyed manhood appealing unto the heavenly powers to obtain spiritual life, health, and strength to devote in humble service to that which was once rejected and despised. Surely he is wise who preserves his manhood and yields it gladly to the Lord's service, and truly he also is wise who, having through ignorance or willfulness "been brought low," seeks to regain the lost estate to glorify and honor the Giver. We greet you, dear boys and men, with love, honor, and highest esteem because of the noble and worthy battle you fight and win when you yield yourselves " just as I am" to the Lord of hosts, the mighty God of heaven and earth.

Dear Boys: Before I gave my heart to God and was saved from my sins, I had formed many bad habits, which proved to be snares laid for me by the enemy of souls, to enslave me to lusts and passions, and finally bring ruin and misery upon me for soul and body. As "the wages of sin is death," and "whatsoever a man soweth that shall he also reap," if we " sow to the flesh we will of the flesh reap corruption." I found it so, and proved that sin is deceitful; for while it promises pleasure, it in reality gives misery and woe. As Solomon has said concerning wine, "at last it biteth like a serpent and stingeth like an adder." I for one have been "reaping my wild oats" bitterly. While I lived in sin, following its pleasures and pursuits, I laid the foundation for disease, which preyed upon my body and corrupted my mind. As we indulge in carnal pleasures we surely "reap corruption." When God saved me I was as David says in Ps. 38 : 70. There was "no soundness in my flesh," but disease had fastened upon me, from which I had sought deliverance in various ways but had not found, until I learned to trust God for healing. I will tell you about it, as it may help some one.

At the age of sixteen I first comprehended what lust had done for me, and tried to free myself from its grasp; but it was too late. Through ignorance I had entered its snare through the influence of an old gray-headed man, who taught me the awful practice of self-abuse, or secret vice. I pray God may forgive him, and help me to sound an alarm to others; for we are surely to be pitied if we enter this evil through lack of instruction. Knowing how polluting, destroying, and degrading it is, I would use all possible means to prevent others from partaking of it, to their injury. It makes a young man fit for no society but that of those who are equally defiled, although they *need* the very best and purest companionship to lead them to reform.

After a young man has ruined his character, constitution, and health and is seeking deliverance, there are many traps and decoys to allure his confidence, and money, promising health, life, vigor, etc., through newspaper advertisements or quack doctors. I proved to my own satisfaction that they are mostly frauds, although recommended by missionaries or discovered on their mission tours, etc. Many of these are in league, and when one gets your name and address you are soon flooded with "important secret mail," from every direction, although the first guarantees a perfect cure—which proves them unreliable. This I learned in trying various remedies—was taking treatment from a specialist at the time the Lord healed me. I had many times asked the Lord, if there was a perfect remedy to cure me, that he would lead me to it. I had never heard divine healing preached at that time, but a brother came to our town preaching the full gospel of salvation and healing.

One night after the evening service and after retiring, the Holy Spirit asked me the question, "Do you want to be healed?" I said, "Yes, Lord." Then the question, "Will you preach the gospel?" was asked three times in succession, and I answered each time, "Yes, Lord." Then God began to fill me with his Spirit; the Holy Ghost permeating my whole being; it seemed like the disease was oozing out through the pores of the skin. I *knew* the Lord healed me, and to him be all the glory. Afterwards I believed the Lord would have me testify to healing, but I feared to because of the prejudice against healing from my friends. One evening I felt I must testify to it or I would lose it. So I asked the Lord for courage, and I testified that God had healed me, though I did not say what from, and again I felt the witness of the Spirit that the work was done, which strengthened my faith and gave greater boldness.

I have been afflicted several times since with other ailments, but Jesus has delivered me. Praise his name! "Many are the afflictions of the righteous, but the Lord delivereth him out of them all." I have found this great deliverance in the Lord, and, dear reader, you may have it too; for Jesus is able and willing to do the same for you. If you consecrate your life to him, search his word, believe his promises, and obey his precepts, you may know "that the mercy of the Lord is from everlasting to everlasting upon them that fear him," and " that remember his commandments to do them."

From one who loves you and wishes you well,

E. H.

Dear Boys: Although I was blessed with good religious parents who protected me from the companionship of evil associates, I was hardly more than five years old when I became guilty of practicing self-abuse. I do not know any way of my entering into it, only that it was *in me* to do it—an evil, lustful nature. Of course I did not know the terrible results that would follow in later years; so I kept it up almost incessantly, and the habit grew upon me.

When about the age of sixteen I began to learn the evil effects that were going to follow. So I began to retrace my footsteps, but the giant evil had such a hold on me then that it was the master of me; and, although I ceased the evil practice, its effects helped to bring on catarrh of the head, of the throat, and of the stomach, and began to spread into my lungs, which no doubt would soon have caused consumption. The disease which had fallen upon me through that evil practice continued to absorb the vitality of my mind. I spent four years in a high school, where this effect was very clearly manifest. At this time I put myself in a good doctor's hands for treatment, and continued it until I was saved, which was after my twenty-first birthday; but I kept getting worse all the time until I was saved. Shortly afterward the Lord healed me of all my diseases, in answer to prayer and obedience to the word of God, except the one which had obtained the mastery of me at the start. Sometimes I had such a loss of vitality that my mind was weakened until it was hard for me to battle against the enemy of my soul.

I often pondered in my mind whether it was the Lord's will to heal me of that sin-obtained one or not. Finally I decided to take it to the Lord, and as my soul began to sink deeper into God I had two of the brothers anoint me and pray for the healing of my body, and I was instantly healed, for which I give God all the glory. The Lord has also saved and sanctified my soul, by two works of grace, and has given me "the Spirit of love and of power and of a strong mind."

Your brother in Christ, H. R.

A PRAYERFUL MEDITATION.

O dear Lord, in love and pity
Help our souls to know thy grace:
May we see thy gracious favor
As we look upon thy face;
May we see the marks of suf'ring
On thy brow, in hands and side,
And remember they were given,
That in thee we might abide.

If thou lov'd us thus so dearly,
And in thee we ever dwell.
Sure it is that thou art willing
To our hearts thy love to tell—
By the bearing of our burdens,
By the healing of our pain.
By the witness of thy Spirit,
That thy suf'ring brought us gain.

By thy stripes is perfect healing,
In thy wounds are life and strength,
From thy pierced and wounded body
Flows the stream whose breadth and length
Covers earth with richest blessings,
And contains the healing balm -
For our sins and sore distresses,
That our sorrows thou shouldst calm.

Come we then with perfect freedom
To the fount of living power,
Lay we down our sins and sickness
And rejoice in thee each hour;
For thou art our Great Physician
And our souls' and bodies' health.
Thus we praise, and give thee honor,
And esteem our heav'nly wealth.

But, dear Lord, there are so many
Out of Christ, in sin and pain,
And they know not love and mercy,
Nor unite in glad refrain;
That we ask thee to endow us
With thy wisdom, love, and grace,
That we may so wisely teach them,
That they too may see thy face,

See thee, Lord, in all thy beauty,
Love, and power, and tenderness,
That their hearts may melt before thee
Feel it *all*, and never *less*—
That they too may give thee glory
And abide within thy love,
Safely housed from earthly sorrows,
Ready for thy home above.

TIME AND ETERNITY.

As these words meet our eyes the thought arises in our minds, "What is the difference between time and eternity?" Time is a measured portion of duration, and eternity is duration unmeasured by the flight of years. Time belongs to us now while the moments, hours, days, and years are fast passing into the past and bringing the future eternity nearer to us. Eternity is the long unmeasured future that lies before each of us, containing very much that is for our happiness or sorrow.

Time is the space given to man to prepare for eternity. To us as individuals it may be long or short, but whichever it is, it is always long enough to achieve the greatest possible results—even the obtaining of an eternity of life in the blissful abode of God. So time for each of us is fraught with grave responsibilities; and he who acknowledges the same is a wise man, but he who also uses every opportunity to bear and accomplish those responsibilities is far wiser. He who kindly and wisely ordereth all things for the good of man has ordained time to be one of the great factors to procure him the joys of enternal glory. We each appear upon the scene of time at the day of our birth, and leave it as death opens the door of eternity.

Time gives us each the opportunity to wisely choose the place of our abode for the long, endless, eternal future.

We see around us a multitude of individuals preparing a dwelling-place—a home—for themselves to occupy during the years of their natural lives. This is a wise effort and accomplishes much for the good of the people. Home is the dearest spot on earth to many hearts, because it is there the purest emotions and affections of hearts garner themselves for the purest earthly happiness. Few individuals are willing to be tossed about by the changing scenes of time all the days of life, and "die among strangers." Many hearts are made sad when the future holds no prospects of even a humble earthly home. How many times we hear in pathetic accents this expression: "My only earthly aspiration is just a small, comfortable home; were that obtained, it would be heaven and earth to me." This shows the inclination of the human mind and heart to provide for the present and future emergencies of time. But oh, how much wiser would it be to long after and provide for a beautiful home for the eternal future. So many are so actively engaged in preparing to live the earthly life in comfort and pleasure that they neglect to meet the requirement of time and prepare for eternity.

Our life—our day of time—is but a short period that shall determine the future eternal abode of the precious immortal soul. Two homes await our choice, and day by day our lives are determining, almost imperceptibly, which it shall be. If our hearts are clinging to earthly joys, worldly good, and selfish purposes and neglecting to accept of higher and purer things, then the decision is far below the heavenly and tends to land the soul in the eternal abode of the unbelieving and careless.

There are few in civilized countries who have not heard of heaven and hell; but to very many they are purely imaginary places, and each individual forms his own conception of them; and some are very doubtful of their existence, and treat everything pertaining to them with contempt. The Bible reader may form a more perfect conception of them from its teachings than the dreamer or worldly wise, and should endeavor to obtain a complete and true realization of them as God intended.

Heaven is a prepared place for a prepared people; it is a holy, lovely, and very desirable home intended for a "righteous nation." Jesus said, "I go to prepare a place for you; and if I go and prepare a place for you, I will come again and receive you unto myself, that where I am, there you may be also." When we remember that the Christian is to love the Lord with all his heart, soul, mind, and strength, then we can more clearly see that where he abides will be the most precious place to every faithful and loving disciple. As those who "know not God" do not enjoy his fellowship or the companionship of the children of God or the lovely and holy things of God, they would not enjoy heaven with all its glories. All through the word of truth heaven is held before the world as a very desirable and happy place; while hell is just the opposite, and all souls are faithfully warned to escape its sorrows and punishments.

Some of you may wonder why it should be necessary to punish the wicked by banishment from God's presence throughout eternity. There is a vast difference between good and evil, and just as great a difference between the results thereof. If one chooses evil instead of good, he also chooses the consequences thereof; and that is banishment from God, and companionship with those he has honored with his friendship and service—the wicked and the Devil. Those who are doubtful of these two places and the different characters that inhabit them should read their Bibles carefully, and pray God to reveal the truth to them. Many dear souls in their unsaved state have had a good look into the depths of hell, and have shrunk from its borders with real gratitude to God that their lives were lengthened to prepare for heaven. Others have considered these things a myth, and have boldly faced death as the "end of all," and yet have been made to testify to the agonies of hell as they passed over its border into its awful punishments. Sometimes dear people love to consider God so loving, kind, and merciful that he could not punish the evildoer; therefore they close their eyes and ears to the unpleasant reality, and drift down to the end of their time unprepared for eternity. They have forgotten that a holy God must uphold justice, and man as a free moral agent must have his choice.

O dear boys, do not yield to skeptical thoughts, but believe the truth and prepare to meet God when time shall end and eternity for you shall begin. Commence now to heed wisdom's voice and use your days and years of time so wisely and well that all that is good, true, and lovely may be yours for that endless eternity. As the soul yields to God and enjoys the spiritual blessings that attend the spiritual life of the soul and the grace of God, he often realizes the nearness of heaven and sees and feels its glorious reality. He is just as confident of its unspeakable glories as he is of his existence; for the very essence of heaven is in his soul. Sometimes, too, he is made sure of the existence of hell as he experiences its opposing, darkening, and hellish powers upon his soul in awful effort to lead him astray from God and truth. If he resists its influence, he is made doubly strong, and encouraged to a closer walk with God.

Time gives us each grand opportunities for the noblest work that can be imagined. When we see individuals giving their time and strength to the relief of the suffering, we can not but think, " That is a pure and good work," and that the individuals are surely moved by the noblest impulse of love and pity for the distressed. Often greatest difficulties and severest hardships are willingly endured to bring relief to the suffering. As we look upon the battle-fields strewn with dead and dying men, we see the gentle nurse searching out the needy ones and giving the last cup of water, bathing the fevered brow, sending the last message home, or raising the wounded and dying man's head to a mother's pillow while words of heavenly counsel and prayer bring the last look of peace and joy as the soul departs or yields the needed courage for the surgeon's knife. If this ministration of love and mercy is admirable and necessary, how much greater and more needful is that labor that encourages souls to prepare for the future and spend eternity *not* with the lost in eternal despair, but in heaven with the Lord of earth and glory. If it is a work of mercy to relieve the sufferings of the body for time, how much more merciful is that labor that shall save a soul from hell, from its eternal pangs and wretchedness!

Oh, dear boys! this is a strong reality, and should awaken each of you to your responsibility. Souls are needing help—are crying for the pure gospel and waiting for the help that you should give. God is laying his hand of love upon you, and saying, "Go work in my vineyard." He says we are "laborers together with him," and nothing can be so noble, grand, and worthy of desire as the privilege of winning souls to a life of holy service to God during the fleeting years of time, and an eternity of bliss in heaven. Jesus did the work God gave him to do, in yielding a sacrifice for the sins of the world. He earnestly and lovingly invited the people to come unto him for eternal life, and those who obey shall never see the eternal death of the soul in the painful realities of hell. If we have the love of God in our souls, it will constrain us to walk in the footsteps of Jesus in seeking to save the perishing.

If in the burning of a great building many people should be seen calling for help while supporting the unconscious (who make no effort for their escape, because they realize not their danger), and the multitude standing around made no effort to assist the poor inmates from the perilous position, we would agree in censuring them for their unmerciful conduct. This state of things, however, is seldom seen, for the heart of man is touched with sympathy, and in such cases earnest effort is made to bring the inmates the necessary assistance. All around us are precious souls who would like to be delivered from the power of Satan, and others who are unconscious of their great need. Surely we who name the name of Christ Jesus as our Savior should not be lacking in that love and sympathy that would do all possible to rescue them from their dangerous position. We can only do this wisely and well by seeking to know just what God would be pleased to have us do by his gracious assistance. We in our own wisdom and strength can accomplish nothing in this work, but if filled and led by the Holy Spirit of God, he will direct and accomplish his purposes.

While God would have an earnest and diligent people, and each has something to do for his glory and the good of souls, he makes choice of some to " preach the word;" and those thus called, if they keep humble, faithful, and true, shall win many precious souls to the Lord's service and be the instruments in his hands of preparing them for the blissful realities of an eternity of glory. Dear boys, you ought not to shrink from this grand and glorious work. God surely honors you when he entrusts it into your care, though he who teaches the gospel is servant of all who hear; for he is serving the truth of God unto them for their eternal benefit. Oh, that we might speak such words and live such lives as will lead precious souls to eternal peace and glory, and make them as stars in our crowns of rejoicing to cast at the feet of him who so loved us as to give his life a ransom for many!

"The field is the world," and it is white unto harvest; and the laborers are few, because many who claim to be sent of God are "seeking their own" instead of the things of God, and are scattering the sheep instead of bringing them to the one fold—the church of God. Thousands are going down to death without the knowledge of the truth, and heathen nations must hear the everlasting gospel of salvation before the end of time, which is rapidly nearing. Awake! *awake!* ye soldiers of the cross of Christ, and be as valiant to carry the glad news of *eternal freedom* to sin-bound souls as the nations are to fight for the freedom of the oppressed.

Time gives us the precious opportunity to live grandly and well while we pass our threescore years and ten in this world of sin, and prepare for the glorious realities of the heavenly eternity. To live grandly is to live in God's own good way, doing his will in all things—walking in the Spirit. The eternal life that gives us eternal existence with God must begin in the soul during the years of time. It comes unto us when we " believe on the Lord Jesus Christ to the saving of the soul," and continues as we yield unto God perfect obedience and live the life of faith. Then, dear boys, use well your gift of time, and make it yield you the choicest blessings of eternity.

Oh, that words could be stronger and express more forcibly the earnestness of mothers' hearts in their yearnings after their sons' eternal good. We ask not for any of you honor, riches, or fame; but that you may be so wise as to sit at the feet of the great King of glory and learn of him each day of time, that you may reap the fruit thereof in eternity. We are conscious of doing all we could to rightly direct your mind and hearts as we have dwelt upon these different subjects, and claim the promises of God that our labor shall not be in vain. We entreat each of you who shall receive good therefrom that you strive as earnestly to assist others and win them to the narrow way of truth and to an eternal home in heaven. Let the most wretched, the lowest in sin and folly, receive your sympathy and help as well as the proud and independent; for we all must stand before the Judge of all the earth to give account of our doings, " whether they be good or evil."

What can we say more to "our boys," our darling sons, to induce you to wisely use your gift of time? Soon death shall come to each of us, and to all who have faithfully spent time in preparing for eternity it will be a joyful entrance to purer scenes, to richer and deeper joys of eternity. Then may you so live your length of days that as death swings open the door of eternity your souls may forever bask in the glorious presence of him who hath power over death, and bids a joyous welcome to each blood-bought and fully redeemed soul. Shout aloud, ye ransomed throng, and enter joyfully your eternal abode, where there are joys forever more in the presence of the King of glory.

EXHORTATION FOR ETERNITY.

Now, dear boys! Our precious sons!
You surely are the favored ones,
Having the love and earnest prayer
Of mothers' hearts, their constant prayer,
Their counsel good, and hopeful cheer,
To guide you to a home so dear.

In your strength and youthful power,
Think of time as every hour
Brings you nearer its border line,
And to your Lord your hearts incline,
That you may grasp, in simple trust,
The words of God—the holy *must*.

For we *must* yield our hearts to him,
And serve him true when eyes are dim;
And we *must* guard each thought and act,
And live by faith in very fact,
Walk in the steps of holy love,
If we would reach the world above.

Now, dear boys, this is not hard;
For he who asks stands faithful guard,
To bear the burden, and give you grace
To run to heav'n, that holy place
Of which we read, and surely see,
As Jesus says, "Come, follow me."

This is no myth or simple tale,
Because his truth shall never fail,
And what he says *must* come to pass.
If you would not lament: "Alas!
Alas! my sorrows are doubly great!"
Then you *must* enter the narrow gate,

And "walk with God" in holy peace,
And find a sure and safe release
From fleshly ways and youthful lusts,
And take in freely the holy *musts*,
And thus prepare to end your days
In perfect love and holy ways.

Yes, time may end at any hour!
And so we pray for heavenly power
To guide our feet in wisdom's way,
That we may greet, without dismay,
The dying day and change of place,
That gives the saved so great a grace.

For heaven is true a lovely home,
To draw our feet—we need not roam,
But walk in ways of truth and love,
Guided by the "Holy Dove,"
Then live forever in perfect peace,
Where joys and praise shall never cease.

Then come, dear sons, and join the throng
Who praise the Lord in holy song,
And love to think of how with thee
In joy and bliss we'll ever be
In heavenly home so glorious fair—
Oh, meet us, boys, forever there!

www.ingramcontent.com/pod-product-compliance
Lightning Source LLC
Chambersburg PA
CBHW022146300426
44115CB00006B/361